WOMEN AND DEPRESSION

Risk Factors and Treatment Issues

Final Report of the
American Psychological Association's
National Task Force on
Women and Depression

Edited by

Ellen McGrath

Gwendolyn Puryear Keita

Bonnie R. Strickland

Nancy Felipe Russo

American Psychological Association
Washington, DC

AAX5440

Published by
American Psychological Association
1200 Seventeenth Street, NW
Washington, DC 20036

First printing: November 1990
Second printing: May 1991

Copies may be ordered from
APA Order Department
P.O. Box 2710
Hyattsville, MD 20784

Cover designed by Thorina Rose, Alexandria, VA
Typeset by Electronic Publishing Services, Baltimore, MD
Printed by BookCrafters, Chelsea, MI
Technical editing and production coordinated by Susan Bedford

Library of Congress Cataloging-in-Publication Data

Women and depression: risk factors and treatment issues: final
  report of the American Psychological Association Task Force on Women
  and Depression/edited by Ellen McGrath . . . [et al.].
      p. cm.
  Includes bibliographical references.
  ISBN 1-55798-104-3
  1. Depression, Mental. 2. Women—Mental health. 3. Depression,
Mental—Risk factors.   I. McGrath, Ellen. II. American
Psychological Association. Task Force on Women.
  [DNLM: 1. Depression—epidemiology. 2. Depression—therapy.
3. Risk Factors. 4. Women—psychology. WM 171 W8723]
RC537.R67 1990
616.85′27′0082—dc20
DNLM/DLC
for Library of Congress   90-14448
                                                                   CIP

Printed in the United States of America on acid-free paper.

Contents

Contributors

Women and Depression Task Force Members

Ellen McGrath, PhD Independent practice of psychotherapy, Brooklyn Heights, New York; Adjunct Associate Professor, New York University; Associate Clinical Professor of Psychiatry and Human Behavior, University of California Irvine Medical School.

Deborah E. Belle, EdD Assistant Professor of Psychology; William T. Grant Foundation, Faculty Scholar in the Mental Health of Children, Boston University.

Karen Blaker, PhD, RN Media Psychologist formerly of "Ask Dr. Blaker," New York, New York.

Laura Brown, PhD, ABPP Independent private practice of psychotherapy and forensic psychology; Associate Professor of Psychology, University of Washington, Seattle, Washington.

Lillian Comas-Diaz, PhD Independent practice of psychotherapy, Washington, DC; Executive Director, Transcultural Mental Health Institute.

Jean A. Hamilton, MD Associate Professor of Psychiatry at University of Texas at "Southwestern" at Dallas, Texas. Former Director of the Institute for Research on Women's Health.

Michelle Harrison, MD Independent private practice specializing in premenstrual syndrome (PMS), Cambridge, Massachusetts.

Robert Hirschfeld, MD Chief, Anxiety and Affective Disorders Research Branch, National Institute of Mental Health, Rockville, Maryland.

Gwendolyn Puryear Keita, PhD Staff Liaison, Women and Depression Task Force; Assistant Executive Director and Director of Women's Programs, Public Interest Directorate, American Psychological Association, Washington, D.C.

Joyce B. Lazar, MA Chief, Prevention Research Branch, and Former Director of Depression/Awareness Recognition and Treatment Program (D/ART), National Institute of Mental Health, Rockville, Maryland.

Jan Lerbinger, MS Research Associate, McLean Hospital, Belmont, Massachusetts.

Vivian Parker Makosky, PhD Former Director, Education and Public Affairs Office, American Psychological Association, Washington, D.C.

Carol Nadelson, MD Past President, American Psychiatric Association; Vice Chair, Department of Psychiatry, New England Medical Center, Boston, Massachusetts.

Robin Post, PhD Independent private practice of psychotherapy; Associate Clinical Professor, Department of Psychiatry, University of Colorado Health Sciences Center, Denver, Colorado.

Alice Rubenstein, EdD   Independent private practice of psychotherapy, Monroe Psychotherapy & Consultation Center, Pittsford, New York.

Nancy Felipe Russo, PhD   Director, Women's Studies Department, Arizona State University, Tempe, Arizona; Chair, National Coalition of Women's Mental Health.

Caitlin Ryan, MSW   AIDS Policy Center, Intergovernmental Health Policy Project, George Washington University, Washington, D.C.; Former Project Director, Lesbian Health Survey.

Maggie Scarf   Author of *Body, Mind & Behavior, Unfinished Business*, and *Intimate Partners*, New Haven, Connecticut.

Bonnie R. Strickland, PhD, ABPP   Professor of Psychology, University of Massachusetts, Amherst, Massachusetts; Past President of the American Psychological Association, 1987.

Marilyn Weiss   Past President, National Depressive and Manic–Depressive Association, Hyland Park, Illinois.

Theoretical Consultants

Elaine A. Blechman, PhD   Director, Behavior Therapy Program, Albert Einstein College of Medicine, Department of Psychiatry, Bronx, New York.

Rosalind Dymond Cartwright, PhD   Professor and Chair, Department of Psychology and Social Sciences and Director, Sleep Disorder Service, St. Lukes Medical Center, Chicago, Illinois.

Diane L. Chambless, PhD   Associate Professor of Psychology and Director, Agoraphobia and Anxiety Program, American University, Washington, D.C.

Gary Emery, PhD   Director, Los Angeles Center for Cognitive Therapy, Los Angeles, California.

Iris Goldstein Fodor, PhD   Professor of School Psychology, Educational Psychology Department, New York University; Co-Chair, Women's Studies Commission, New York University, New York, New York.

Carla Golden, PhD   Associate Professor of Psychology, Ithaca College, Ithaca, New York.

Lissy F. Jarvik, PhD, MD   Chief, Psychogeriatric Unit, West Los Angeles Veterans Administration Medical Center, Brentwood Division, Los Angeles, California.

Margaret Jensvold, MD   Director, Institute for Research on Women's Health; Independent private practice of psychiatry, Washington, D.C.

Gerald Klerman, MD   Associate Chair for Research, Department of Psychiatry, Payne Whitney Clinic, Cornell University Medical College, New York, New York.

Camille Lloyd, PhD   Director of Student Counseling, University of Texas Health Science Center, Houston, Texas.

Susan Mikesell, PhD, RN Independent private practice of psychotherapy, Washington, D.C.

Susan Nolen-Hoeksema, PhD Assistant professor of psychology, Stanford University, Stanford, California.

Martin Seligman, PhD Professor of Psychology, Department of Psychology, University of Pennsylvania, Philadelphia, Pennsylvania.

Julia Sherman, PhD Independent practice of psychotherapy, Madison, Wisconsin.

Myrna Weissman, PhD Chief, Division of Clinical–Genetic Epidemiology; College of Physicians and Surgeons, Columbia University, New York, New York.

Advisory Committee

Nancy Domenici Mental Health Activist, Washington, D.C.

Suzanne Dworak-Peck, ACSW Past President of the National Association of Social Workers, Silver Spring, Maryland.

T. George Harris Founder and Editor of *Psychology Today*, New York, New York.

The Honorable Patricia Schroeder United States House of Representatives.

Margretta M. Styles, EdD, RN, FAAN Past President of the American Nurses Association, Inc., Kansas City, Missouri.

Preface

As President of the American Psychological Association (APA) in 1987, I had the opportunity to propose various initiatives around issues and problems facing psychology. For many years, I had had special interest in women's health. I was also part of the National Institute of Mental Health's (NIMH) major initiative, Depression/Awareness, Recognition, and Treatment (D/ART). I knew that depression is one of this nation's most serious and prevalent mental disorders, afflicting some 20% of our population at some time in their lives and that women are twice as likely as men to suffer from depression. I was also aware that psychologists, who have been in the forefront of research on and treatment of "the depressions," have considerable understanding and expertise that could be organized, integrated, and shared.

The Board of Directors of APA approved my proposal for a Task Force on Women and Depression. With the strong support of Leonard Goodstein, then Chief Executive Officer of APA (and the current Chief Executive Officer, Raymond Fowler), the Public Interest Directorate, under the very able leadership of James Jones, agreed to provide staff. I began to work closely with Gwendolyn Puryear Keita, Director of the Women's Programs Office, who would serve as the organizing strength of this endeavor.

In considering who might chair the Task Force, I knew that I wanted to find someone who not only was an expert in the area of women and depression, but could bring energy and organization to what I thought would be a complex and formidable venture and could be a superb spokesperson for women's mental health issues. Ellen McGrath seemed to be the ideal choice. For many years, she had been in independent practice with a major focus on work with women, especially depressed women. Dr. McGrath had also been active in the Division of Psychotherapy and in APA governance. She agreed to chair the Task Force and we began to identify psychologists and others who were well recognized experts in the areas of depression research and treatment and who could bring specific expertise as well as balance to the group. We found that we had a wide array of talent from whom to choose and that individuals were uniformly and enthusiastically willing to become involved.

Because the phenomenon of depression and its implications for women are so complex and because we wanted to include representatives of groups that had not been well served in the past, we appointed a large interdisciplinary Task Force. This included representatives from the other health professions, as well as a student and a consumer of mental health services. The core mental health disciplines were represented via an Advisory Group that also included major public figures. To ensure that the Task Force had access to the most up-to-date information on the research, risk factors, and treatment of depression, we also developed a list of theoretical consultants, who gave presentations in their areas of expertise to the Task Force and/or responded to written material.

The Task Force met on three occasions with considerable excitement and good spirit about the task at hand. We were dismayed to learn of the prevalence of depression among women and the horrendous emotional toll of the disorder. On the other hand, we were pleased to learn of women's strengths in meeting adversity and gratified to know of the progress that has been made in understanding depression. We became aware of extraordinary breakthroughs in our understanding of the risk factors, maintenance, and treatment of depression. We learned of new focused and short-term psychosocial treatments of depression and became cognizant of the new medications that are available. While the Task Force tried to cover the spectrum of depression, especially focusing on women who have not been well served in the past, we quickly found that because of the magnitude of the task, we would not be able to be as comprehensive as we would have liked. We realize that much remains to be done but we are proud of these beginning efforts.

I am particularly grateful to the large number of people who made this endeavor possible. Members of the Task Force and the Theoretical Consultants gave generously of their time and energy. The overworked APA staff were always available and helpful. And so many women and men, when they heard of the Task Force, volunteered to help in whatever way they could—by sharing their experiences, by pointing us to material we might have overlooked, and by expressing their support and appreciation for our efforts. We do hope this report will benefit them and serve to alert the public about the mental health needs of women. We also trust that the findings will be useful to researchers and clinicians who have an interest in depression.

Bonnie R. Strickland, PhD, ABPP
Professor of Psychology
University of Massachusetts
Amherst, Massachusetts

Introduction

In 1987 Bonnie R. Strickland, then President of the American Psychological Association, formed an APA National Task Force on Women and Depression. The purpose of the Task Force was to idenfity the risk factors for and treatment needs of women with depression. This task was to be accomplished by summarizing existing research and synthesizing current theory on women and depression. The Task Force was organized in recognition of the fact that depression was and is one of the most serious mental health problems of the eighties and nineties. Women's risk for depression exceeds that of men by two to one. This is one of the most consistent findings in the research literature and occurs throughout many different countries and ethnic groups. The main exception is the rate of bipolar illness, where men and women are approximately equal in reported incidence rates.

There are currently at least 7 million women in the United States with a diagnosable depression. Most will go untreated, although there are new treatment technologies which can reduce depressive symptoms for 80–90% of patients in 12 to 14 weeks. Since depression is often a progressive illness, lack of treatment and lack of attention to the specific needs of depressed women are tragic, unnecessary losses.

The reasons for women's risk for depression must be understood if this mental health problem is to be conquered. Advancing this understanding and serving as a catalyst for needed research in risk factors and treatment approaches for women were primary goals of the Task Force. For this reason, the Task Force was composed of a combination of research and academic members, as well as a number of mental health professionals directly engaged in the treatment of depression. The Task Force was multidisciplinary, representing depression experts in psychology, psychiatry, social work, psychiatric nursing, consumer advocacy groups, and public interest and government agency groups. Task Force members met periodically from 1987 to 1989. This report is a summary of the findings of the American Psychological Association Task Force on Women and Depression.

The report is divided into three major parts, covering risk factors, treatment issues, and depression in specific female populations. In Section I, the Task Force identified at least six areas as possible contributors to women's greater risk for depression, examining the literature with respect to reproductive events, personality and other psychological factors, family roles and intimate relationships, work roles, victimization, and poverty. Section II discusses diagnostic and treatment issues for depressed women. A chart is provided to present an overview of the treatment research on women and depression; updated information on antidepressants, including gender differences, are described; and specifics of interpersonal therapy, feminist therapy, and cognitive–behavioral therapy are discussed in some detail. Section III describes the needs, experiences, and treatment issues of specific subgroups of women at risk for depression, such as ethnic minority women, adolescents, professional women, lesbians, older women, substance abusers, women with eating disorders, poor women, and physically abused women.

Current theory, research on risk factors, treatment research, and treatment techniques with depressed women yield a mixed picture of painful realities and practical hope. Painful realities include the finding that depression can be persistent. In one study, 51% of those with major depression had high levels of symptoms 9 years later. The ongoing NIMH Collaborative Study of the Psychobiology of Depression found that after 6 months, 19% of the previously recovered are depressed again and 24% have new symptoms. Depression is heterogeneous. It is not a continuum from the "blues" to major depression and, eventually, suicide. Rather, depression varies in kind and in the contribution of different risk factors. Joyce Lazar, member of the Task Force and Chief of Prevention Research at NIMH, commenting on these statistics, noted that depression is like arthritis—a chronic problem that varies in kind and causality, and that often recurs but from which an individual can get major relief.

The Task Force underscored the need to maintain the distinction between an isolated *symptom* of depression and a persistent set of symptoms, or *syndrome*, since different correlates may be associated with different depressive syndromes. As you will see, given available research and reporting practices, the Task Force had difficulty adhering to this distinction. However, in most instances, an attempt was made to specify whether the study addressed depressive symptoms, major (unipolar) or bipolar depression, dysthymia, or other subtypes of depression.

The Task Force focused considerable effort on the causes of these conditions for women. Highlights of the findings from the section of the report on risk factors include the following:

- Women are at higher risk for depression due to a number of social, economic, biological, and emotional factors. Consequently, we need to study women's depression from a *biopsychosocial* perspective.
- Women's depression is related to certain cognitive and personality styles, that is, avoidant, passive, dependent behavior patterns; pessimistic, negative cognitive styles; and focusing too much on depressed feelings instead of action and mastery strategies.
- The rate of sexual and physical abuse of females is much higher than previously suspected and is a major factor in women's depression. One study estimated that 37% of women have a significant experience of physical or sexual abuse before the age of 21. Several Task Force members felt these figures were an underestimate and the real numbers may be as high as 50%. More research is strongly needed in the area of violence against women and consequent depression. Depressive symptoms may be long-standing effects of posttraumatic stress syndrome for many women.
- Marriage confers a greater protective advantage on men than on women. In unhappy marriages, women are three times as likely as men to be depressed than married men and single women. Mothers of young children are highly vulnerable to depression; the more children in the house, the more depression is reported.
- Poverty is a "pathway to depression." Seventy-five percent of the U.S. poverty population (annual income of $5,776 or less) are women and children. Minority women, elderly women, chemically dependent women, lesbians, and professional women are also high risk groups for depression and need special attention and support.

The Task Force was encouraged when it turned to the treatment possibilities for depressed women. Diagnosis has become relatively more refined, antidepressant medication has increasingly matured, and there are several shorter term therapies which seem particularly well suited for reducing women's depression. Highlights from the Task Force report on treatment issues include the following:

- Careful diagnosis is critical in the treatment of depression. Diagnostic assessment for women, in particular, should include taking a history of sexual and physical violence, an exploration of prescription drug utilization, past and current medical conditions, and a reproductive life history to see how menstruation, birth control, pregnancy, childbirth, abortion, and menopause may have contributed to the woman's depression.

- Although there is little research available on longer term psychodynamic psychotherapies, making it difficult to assess their effectiveness in treating depression, the Task Force was enthusiastic about results of efficacy research on interpersonal therapy and cognitive–behavioral therapy and about the sociocultural perspective of feminist therapy. Interpersonal therapy may be especially helpful for women due to its emphasis on relationships and the development of better relationship skills as a core source of empowering women. Cognitive–behavioral therapy offers management techniques which fit recommendations from some of the latest depression research such as the value of distraction, mastery, and action strategies in alleviating depressive symptoms in women. For example, understanding and identifying cognitive distortions and negative thinking and developing behavioral skills to move more quickly into action and problem-solving modalities may help women counteract earlier conditioning toward passivity and helplessness. Feminist therapy attends to issues of power and powerlessness, encourages egalitarian relationships (including that with the therapist), explores sources of depression that are societal as well as individual (e.g., sexism), and emphasizes empowerment of clients.

- Antidepressants are effective and even necessary in treating certain kinds of depressions. The drugs, however, may work differently for women than for men.

- Depression in women is misdiagnosed at least 30–50% of the time. Approximately 70% of the prescriptions for antidepressants are given to women, often with improper diagnosis and monitoring. Prescription drug misuse is a very real danger for women.

- Antidepressants and the structured therapies have about the same success rate for depressed women with less severe depressive disorders. The dropout rate for antidepressants is high (up to 67%), however. We need to know if there is a danger that antidepressants may encourage dependency, passivity, and a victim psychology in women, which could reinforce depression over time.

These conclusions are supported by existing research, theory, and/or clinical practice. Please keep in mind, however, that this report is not an exhaustive survey of the literature related to women and the depressions. For example, the sections on eating disorders and some of the biological correlates of depression are only briefly reviewed, as are the needs of several of the special populations. The public policy implications of this report are extremely important, but need to be better developed elsewhere.

Countless volunteer hours were donated by the leaders of the various Task Force teams (Nancy Russo, Jean Hamilton, Laura Brown, Robin Post, Alice Rubenstein, Joyce Lazar, and Karen Blaker). Each Task Force member and theoretical consultant also make a significant contribution to some section of the report. Gwendolyn Puryear Keita, Director of the Women's Programs Office, was heroic in her efforts to keep this project on track and see it to completion at a time of financial and organizational transition in the American Psychological Association.

How can readers help? Readers of the report can help by sharing the report with their colleagues from any of the health and mental health disciplines; integrating information on women and depression into their courses; encouraging practitioners to obtain continuing education about women's lives, particularly with regard to the areas identified in the report; giving the report to policy makers at national, state, and local levels, and so forth.

The Women and Depression Task Force addressed the nature of depressions among women. However, NIMH's Depression/Awareness, Recognition, and Treatment Project is a broader effort addressing depression research, treatment, and training issues for women and men. For more information about D/ART, write: D/ART, Public Inquiries, Room 15C-05, National Institute of Mental Health, 5600 Fishers Lane, Rockville, MD 20857.

Initial findings of the Task Force have already been presented at a number of international, national, and regional professional conferences; reported in over 50 newspaper stories and numerous magazine articles; and presented on a number of national radio and TV shows, including *The Today Show, Good Morning America, The Oprah Winfrey Show*, the *ABC Home Show*, and *Everyday with Joan Lunden*. A "Women and Depression Press Kit" has been developed and distributed and public lectures have been given on the subject of women and depression. This was all part of a Task Force commitment to reach the public as well as mental health professionals with this important information about women and depression and support the need for further research regarding the specific risk factors and treatment needs of depressed women. Hopefully, our efforts will be successful and help reduce women's pain and suffering from depression.

Ellen McGrath, PhD, Chair
APA National Task Force on Women and Depression

I

Women and Depression: Risk Factors and Research Issues

This section summarizes the Task Force's review of the literature on depression, focusing on factors that contribute to women's higher risk for depression. Issues related to definitions of depression and its subtypes, as well as conceptual and methodological limitations of current research approaches, are discussed. The need to study women's depression from a *biopsychosocial* perspective is underscored. Because space and time limitations prohibited a comprehensive review of the literature, the Task Force identified six areas for special attention: reproductive events, personality and other psychological factors, family roles and intimate relationships, work roles, victimization, and poverty. Significant research findings in these areas are summarized, and recommendations for future research and public policy are offered.

Gender Differences in Depression Rates

Women are at higher risk for most types of depression, whether one looks at case records or community surveys (Goldman & Ravid, 1980; Nolen-Hoeksema, 1987; Strickland, 1989; Weissman & Klerman, 1977, 1985; Weissman, Leaf, Holzer, Meyers, & Tischler, 1984). This is one of the most consistent findings in the literature (cf. Nolen-Hoeksema, 1987, 1990). The difference holds for White, Black, and Hispanic women (Russo, Amaro, & Winter, 1987; Russo & Sobel, 1981) and persists when income level, education, and occupation are controlled (Ensel, 1982; Radloff, 1975). In addition to the United States, gender differences in depression have been reported in Denmark, Scotland, England, Wales, Canada, Nigeria, Kenya, Iceland, Israel, Australia, and New Zealand (Nolen-Hoeksema, 1987, 1990; Weissman & Klerman, 1977). Gender differences in help seeking or in willingness to report symptoms do not adequately explain women's excess in depression (Nolen-Hoeksema, 1987, 1990; Weissman & Klerman, 1977, 1985).

Although female-to-male ratios for prevalence of unipolar depression vary from one study to another, the ratio averages close to 2:1. Nolen-Hoeksema (1987) conducted an extensive review of research on unipolar depression. Considering only "strong studies" (those using standardized assessment procedures or diagnostic systems to identify depression and using samples of 50 or more participants), she found mean female-to-male ratios of 1.95:1 in studies of treated cases of depression conducted in the United States and 2.39:1 in studies conducted outside of the United States. Both

1

men and women experience depression, and some of the same risk factors predict depression in both men and women, including genetic, biochemical, and hormonal factors (Engeland & Hostetter, 1983; Gershon, 1983; Gershon, Berrettini, Nurnberger, & Godin, 1986); presence of parental psychopathology; personality; stress and negative life events; and more severe life strains associated with poverty, physical illness, family relationships, home and work circumstances, and loss (e.g., Allen, 1976; Billings, Cronkite, & Moos, 1983; Hamilton, 1988; Hammen et al., 1987; Klerman & Weissman, 1985a, 1985b; Nolen-Hoeksema, 1987, 1990; Strickland, 1988). The focus of the Task Force, however, was to identify factors that might help explain the higher risk for depression in women. Sometimes the factors explored were unique to women (e.g., menstruation and pregnancy). Sometimes such factors contributed to depression in both sexes (e.g., violence and poverty), but were more likely to be experienced (or to be experienced more severely) by women.

There is some evidence for a genetic component in depression (Allen, 1976; Klerman & Weissman, 1985a), and some theories have postulated sex-linked components of depression (e.g., Cloninger, Christiansen, Reich, & Gottesman, 1978; Perris, 1966; Winokur & Tanna, 1969). However, such theories have not received consistent support in the research literature (Merikangas, Weissman, & Pauls, 1985; Nolen-Hoeksema, 1987), and the Task Force found no reason to pursue them. Instead, the Task Force focused on areas of research involving the characteristics, roles, and circumstances of women that might, indeed, generate an understanding of why women's depression rates are higher than those of men.

Definition and Measurement of Depression and Its Subtypes

In examining the research relating to gender differences in depression, the Task Force underscored the need to maintain the distinction between an isolated *symptom* of depression and a persistent set of symptoms, or *syndrome*. This is important because different correlates or precursors may be associated with different depressive syndromes (Hamilton, 1988). Certain syndromes are defined as disorders.

The common belief that depression varies along a single continuum from ordinary "blues" to major depression may be incorrect, because depressions may differ in kind as well as degree. Depression is heterogeneous. Various subtypes of depressive disorder have been recognized in the diagnostic system of the American Psychiatric Association, including major (unipolar), bipolar, dysthymia, adjustment disorder with depressed mood, and organic mood disorder. More controversial disorders recognized in the *Diagnostic and Statistical Manual of Mental Disorders* (*Third Edition-Revised*) (*DSM-III-R*; American Psychiatric Association, 1987) are schizoaffective disorder and the proposed category of late luteal phase dysphoric disorder.

Table 1 lists the most relevant diagnostic categories and their essential features as they appear in the *DSM-III-R* (American Psychiatric Association, 1987). The *DSM-III-R* also recognizes other features, such as seasonal patterns, recurrent major depression, melancholic or chronic types of major depression, and mood disorders with psychotic features.

Table 1
Depression-Related Diagnoses Recognized in *DSM-III-R*

Major category/diagnostic subtype	Page numbers in *DSM-III-R*
Organic mood syndrome (293.83)—A prominent and persistent depressed mood resembling a major depressive episode that is due to a specific organic factor (e.g., hormone- or drug-induced depression).	111–112
Schizoaffective disorder (295.70)—At some time in the disturbance there is either a major depressive or manic syndrome concurrent with symptoms that meet certain criteria of schizophrenia.	208–210
Mood disorders	213–214
Bipolar disorders[a]—The essential feature is the presence of one or more manic or hypomanic episodes (usually with a history of major depressive episodes).	214–218
Bipolar disorder (296.XX)—One or more manic episodes.	225–226
Cyclothymia (301.13)—Numerous hypomanic episodes and numerous periods with depressive symptoms.	226–228
Bipolar disorder NOS—Residual category that includes disorders with hypomanic and full major depressive episodes, sometimes referred to as bipolar, II.	
Depressive disorders[b]—The essential feature is the presence of one or more periods of depression (syndrome) *without* a history of either manic or hypomanic episodes.	218–224
Major depression[c] (296.XX)—One or more major depressive episodes; can be specified as recurrent.	228–230
Dysthymia (300.40)—A history of depressed mood more days than not for at least 2 years, which did not begin with a major depressive episode.	230–233
Depressive disorder NOS (311.00)	223
Adjustment disorders—A maladaptive reaction to an identifiable psychosocial stressor.	329–330
Adjustment disorder with depressed mood (309.00)—An "incomplete depressive syndrome" that develops in response to a psychosocial stressor; predominant symptoms include depressed mood, tearfulness, and feelings of hopelessness.	331
Personality disorders	
Dependent personality disorder (301.60)—Frequently complicated by depressive disorders.	354
Codes for conditions not attributable to a mental disorder	359–362
Uncomplicated bereavement (V62.82)—Normal reaction to the loss of a loved one. Can include a "full depressive syndrome."	361–362
Late luteal phase dysphoric disorder—A proposed diagnostic category needing further study, coded as "300.90 unspecified mental disorder (late luteal phase dysphoric disorder)."	367–369
Decision tree for differential diagnosis of mood disturbances	380–381

Note. DSM-III-R = Diagnostic and Statistical Manual of Mental Disorders (Third Edition-Revised) (American Psychiatric Association, 1987); NOS = not otherwise specified. Numbers in parentheses are code numbers.
[a]For bipolar and bipolar NOS, a further specification is "seasonal pattern."
[b]For a current bipolar disorder or major depression, the episode can be subclassed as psychotic features. For recurrent major depression and depressive disorder NOS, a further specification is "seasonal pattern."
[c]A current major depressive episode can be specified as "melancholic" or "chronic" type.

Of most concern here is the fact that gender differences have been substantiated for some subtypes, whereas there is less agreement about others (Nolen-Hoeksema, 1987, 1990). Women's greater risk for major depression (Boyd & Weissman, 1981; Nolen-Hoeksema, 1987; O'Connell & Mayo, 1988; Weissman & Klerman, 1985) and for dysthymia (Weissman, Meyers, et al., 1986) is well documented, whereas there is no evidence for major gender differences in rates for bipolar disorder.

Changes in diagnostic categories over time cloud comparisons of research conducted at different time periods. It becomes important to use past research as a guide, but to stimulate new inquiry if gender differences in depression in the current social context are to be fully understood. Although the *DSM-III-R* is a basic reference in diagnosing depression, and *DSM* diagnoses are the basis for a substantial amount of research, there is controversy over the appropriateness of some diagnoses that are included (e.g., late luteal phase dysphoric disorder) as well as the methods used to develop them. This lack of consensus about definitions of depression-related diagnostic categories (e.g., see Gallant & Hamilton, 1988) provides a fruitful area for research.

Some investigators have suggested that additional categories will delineate meaningful subtypes of depressive syndromes not currently recognized in the *DSM-III-R*. Hamilton, Lloyd, Alagna, Phillips, and Pinkel (1984) reviewed the literature on some novel subtypes of depression for possible gender differences. Women's rates were higher than men's for atypical depression (characterized by hypersomnia, hyperphagia, and increased libido; Klein, Gittelman, Quitkin, & Rifkin, 1980; Quitkin, Stewart, McGrath, & Liebowitz, 1988), rapid-cycling bipolar illness (defined as having four or more affective episodes a year; Parry, 1989), and seasonal affective disorder (marked by changes in symptoms in response to seasonal changes such as decreased sunlight; Jacobsen, Wehr, Sack, James, & Rosenthal, 1987).

Subtypes are not mutually exclusive, and their overlap may have complex implications for the course of recovery and relapse. For example, the Collaborative Study on the Psychobiology of Depression identified the phenomenon of double depression, whereby a major depression was found to be superimposed on a dysthymic disorder (Keller, Lavori, Endicott, Corywell, & Klerman, 1983). The presence of double depression was found to have implications for recovery of major depression. Whereas 78% of patients diagnosed with a major depressive disorder (but with no preexisting chronic depression) recovered from that disorder after 2 years, 97% of such patients who were also diagnosed as having a dysthymic disorder (i.e., were diagnosed with a double depression) recovered from that major depression. However, among the patients with double depression, only 39% recovered from both depressions, and 58% continued to suffer chronic dysthymia. Chronic dysthymia after recovery from major depression predicted a pernicious course, with an elevated probability of relapse into a major depression. It was reported that gender did not directly affect recovery rates, but the interaction of gender with other important variables, such as marital status, income, acuteness of onset, and severity was not reported. Although this research is of considerable interest, the findings were not replicated in a less severely depressed population that did not include patients with bipolar disorder (Gonzales, Lewinsohn, & Clarke, 1985). Research has suggested that the largest gender differences in depression are found for less severe symptoms, with gender differences markedly reduced when symptom severity is controlled (Clark, Aneshensel, Frerichs, & Morgan, 1981; Craig & Van Natta, 1979).

Researchers often use summary scales to conduct research on depression. A variety of scales have been developed that ascertain the presence of depressive symptoms such as crying, feelings of unhappiness, and eating and sleep disorders. As Newmann pointed out (1984), gender differences found in research using summary scales may be misleading, because these scales do not separate milder forms of distress, such as sadness, from a more severe depressive syndrome. Russo (1988) provided a summary of the scales and their limitations.

Although subclinical depressive symptoms measured by summary scales correlate with clinical depression, whether they signal a vulnerability to clinical depression is unclear. Such symptomatology also correlates with low self-esteem and stressful life events—which themselves may be precursors to the onset of clinical depression. One study found that preclinical depressive symptoms had no increased risk for subsequent clinical depression over and above that explained by the low self-esteem and stressful life events and difficulties that were correlated with those symptoms (Brown, Bifulco, Harris, & Bridge, 1986).

High levels of such symptoms are estimated to affect 20–25% of community samples (Kaplan, Roberts, Camacho, & Coyne, 1987). It has been estimated that approximately half of those who score high on self-report measures of depression are clinically impaired (Link & Dohrenwend, 1980), and it has been reported that 51% of those with high levels of symptoms at one point in time reported high levels of symptoms 9 years later (Kaplan et al., 1987). There is some evidence of continuity between depressive symptoms and the syndromes of clinical depression (Akiskal, 1987; Weissman, Meyers, et al., 1986). Thus, depressive symptomatology often does not reflect a minor or transitory state, and interest in more severe forms of clinical depression should not result in a lack of research and therapeutic attention to milder versions. Whether sadness, depressed mood, or other depressive symptoms are risk factors for onset of a major depression or not, they themselves reflect considerable suffering.

Conceptual and Methodological Issues in Understanding Gender Differences in Depression

The range of theories that attempt to explain women's depression spans biological, psychological, social, and cultural variables (Herman, 1983; Klerman & Weissman, 1985a, 1985b; Nolen-Hoeksema, 1987, 1990). No one theory or set of theories fully explains gender differences in depression. While there is substantial research on the diagnosis, treatment, and recovery of depression per se, the state of the art of depression research is such that little is understood about the etiology of women's depression as it might differ from that of men. Consequently, the Task Force focused on research that might elucidate differential risk factors for depression in women, as a first step toward identifying possible causal mechanisms. Excellent summaries of risk factors are available for unipolar (major) depression (Klerman & Weissman, 1985a, 1985b; Nolen-Hoeksema, 1987, 1990) and for suicide, which has been linked with depression (Roy, 1985). The Epidemiological Catchment Area (ECA) study is the best source of systematic information on dysthymia (Weissman, Leaf, Bruce, & Florio, 1988). Little is known about the epidemiology of adjustment disorder with mixed mood.

The Task Force underscored the importance of examining gender differences in risk factors as they differentially relate to the onset, maintenance (chronicity), severity, and relapse of subtypes of depression over the lifecycle, and of testing for mediating, moderating, and direct effects (Baron & Kenny, 1986). Even if direct effects of gender are not apparent, important interaction effects may be operating. For example, in research on use of mental health facilities, gender differences in the relation of marital status to depression are found to differ depending on race and ethnicity (Russo & Sobel, 1981; Russo et al., 1987). Also, Kessler and Neighbors (1986) suggested that effects of race and social class on mental health appear to be interactive, rather than additive, with race differences in psychological distress more pronounced among individuals with low incomes. Although not discussed by those authors, inspection of their table of findings suggests an interaction between race and income on depressed mood that is twice as strong for women as it is for men.

Some of the most interesting research on long-term outcome of major depression identifies marriage and lower income (gender-related variables), as predictors of chronic outcome—yet a report of that research did not analyze the data for gender differences (Keller et al., 1983). Research on depression that does not specify the gender of the sample or analyze for gender differences can result in misleading findings and inappropriate conclusions.

Age interacts with other variables, particularly income and health status, to compound difficulties in diagnosing and treating depression in women. For example, Haug and Folmar (1986) reported that compared with elderly men, elderly women were more likely to have lower incomes and to perceive their incomes as less adequate. They were also more likely to live alone, lack a spouse, and exhibit emotional, cognitive, and health impairments.

It has been assumed that aging is associated with higher risk for depression, but as Newmann (1988) has pointed out, methodological problems and inconsistencies make it difficult to draw firm conclusions from current research. She identified critical methodological issues in research on depression and aging, including the need to separate effects of correlates such as increased probability of illness, infirmity, or disability. Physical changes in aging such as sleep difficulty, lowered interest in sex, loss of appetite, and constipation are more likely to be reported by older women than older men, increasing the chance of a misdiagnosis of depression (Berry, Storandt, & Coyne, 1984). Himmelfarb (1984) suggested that health status and health locus of control are critical mediators in the relation between aging and depression for women. Cohort effects compound methodological difficulties in depression research, and not only with regard to aging. There is some evidence that the sociodemographic characteristics of depressed populations may be changing. The prevalence of depression has increased in younger adults, with the onset of depression occurring at younger ages (Klerman & Weissman, 1985a). This change appears to be due to an increase in the percentage of men experiencing depression rather than a decrease in the percentage of women becoming depressed. This change in the ratio of men to women has also been reported by Murphy, Simons, Wetzel, and Lustman (1984) and Hagnell, Lanke, Rorsman, and Ojesjo (1982).

Suicide statistics are also changing. Suicide rates among young adults have increased. Although young men continue to outnumber young women in completed suicides, the use of violent—and potentially more lethal—methods has increased among younger women (Holden, 1986). As summarized by Hamilton (1986), several gender-related risk factors for suicide have been reported for adolescents and young adults. For example, sexual abuse—which is more frequently experienced by young women than by young men (Koss, 1990)—has been associated with suicide attempts and completions (Josef, 1986). Rosenthal (1986), however, reported a relation between chronic sexual abuse and lethality of suicide attempts, rather than attempts per se.

In summary, research on the relation between gender and depression requires complex conceptual and methodological approaches that recognize the relation may depend on subtype of depression; vary with subgroups of women of differing race/ethnicity, socioeconomic status, marital status, age, and health status; and change over time.

Needed: A Biopsychosocial Context for Interpreting Research on Depression

The Task Force identified the need to develop ways of thinking about women's depression in a *biopsychosocial* context. Understanding the complexities of women's higher risk for depression requires understanding the interaction of women's biology with their environment. It requires clear definitions of depression and of the biological, psychological, and social variables used to predict it. Most of all, it requires understanding the social construction of women's biology, a biology that all too often becomes equated with genetics. As Hamilton (1984) has stated, both greater conceptual clarity and a more integrated look at psychobiology, *in context and across the life cycle*, are required if the relation between gender and the various depressions is to be understood (cf. Hamilton & Conrad, 1987; Hamilton, Lloyd, et al., 1984). The recurrence of major depression reinforces the need for longitudinal research on both onset and relapse over the life cycle. Unfortunately, the efforts of the Task Force have been constrained by existing research approaches and findings.

A complete analysis of gender differences in depression in a biopsychosocial context would include the effects of biological factors such as physical illness, disability, medications, REM sleep dysfunction, and pelvic pain (Cartwright, 1988; Hamilton, 1988; Nadelson, Notman, & Ellis, 1983; Turner & Noh, 1988). Because of limitations, however, the Task Force focused on selected reproductive-related events, personality and other psychological characteristics, social roles, and life circumstances that appeared to offer the most likely opportunities for explaining and predicting women's increased risk for depression. Highlights of research in these areas are summarized in the following sections.

Reproductive-Related Events and Depression

Reproductive-related events—including menstruation, pregnancy, childbirth, infertility, abortion, and menopause—are unique experiences for women and have been hypothesized to be related to women's depression, although they alone do not explain the overall gender difference in depression rates (Hamilton, 1984; Weissman & Klerman, 1977). Understanding the impact of reproductive events requires examining the interaction of biological, psychological, and social factors in more sophisticated paradigms than those that currently dominate the literature.

There is mixed evidence regarding the influence of fluctuations in female hormones and other biochemicals on mood and on the frequency of occurrence of depression in women (Nolen-Hoeksema, 1987, 1990). Nonetheless, understanding how endocrinology contributes to reproductive-related depression (and depression in general) is clearly important. Gonadal and adrenal steroids affect neurotransmitters, which play a role in regulating mood and behavior, and neuroendocrine physiology. Biochemical manifestations of depression in general are receiving increasing research attention (Gold, Goodwin, & Chrousos, 1988a, 1988b), as is the manner in which such manifestations relate to reproductive events (Hamilton, 1984). To advance, research must investigate neuroendocrinological effects in both genders. Moreover, theoretical models based on biological changes must account for stability in mood and behavior that occurs despite substantial changes in hormones and neurotransmitters. Researchers must recognize that neuroendocrine response is altered by the social context, and they cannot afford to ignore social roles, status, and other sociocultural variables (Hamilton, 1984).

A major aim of the Task Force is to encourage depression research, particularly in the area of reproductive-related events, that is based on more sophisticated biopsychosocial perspectives. It is important to recognize that the biological changes associated with reproductive-related events play critical roles in defining social statuses and roles for *both* genders. Mood and behavior changes correlated with reproductive events may also occur for both women and men (Hamilton, 1984; Wexler, Mason, & Giller, 1989). Careful examination of risk factors for both genders from diverse and sophisticated perspectives that consider reciprocal relation among variables may help us to understand the etiology of gender-related differences in depression.

A life cycle perspective appears to be one of the keys to understanding depression in women. Hamilton, Parry, and Blumenthal (1988a) have identified possible predictive relations between a lifetime history of major affective disorder and reactions to reproductive-related events, such as premenstrual dysphoria and postpartum depression, as well as correlations among reactions to such events. For example, severe premenstrual mood changes have been associated with a lifetime history of major depression (Endicott, Halbreich, Schact, & Nee, 1981; Hamilton et al., 1985). More recent data (McMillan & Pihl, 1987; Rubinow & Schmidt, 1989; Trunnell, Turner, & Keye, 1988), however, suggest that premenstrual dysphoria may be somewhat independent of other affective disorders.

One study reported that 10–40% of women having an affective disorder also experienced an episode of affective disorder during the postpartum period (Bratfos & Haug, 1966). Other research has found premenstrual mood changes correlated with severe postpartum "blues" (Brockington & Kumar, 1982; Hamilton, 1984). High levels of prenatal depression have been correlated with increased depressive symptomatology at 6 weeks postpartum (Buesching, Glasser, & Frate, 1986), and postpartum depression has been found to exacerbate premenstrual mood swings (Dalton, 1977).

There is a need for longitudinal research and better clinical history taking with regard to mood and behavior changes around reproductive events to advance understanding of their relation to depressive symptomatology. Advances in reproductive-related research will require more consensus on methodological approaches, including definitions and assessment techniques for reproductive-related mood and behavior changes and the timing of such measurements. Although much needs to be learned, the literature is sufficient to emphasize the importance of taking a reproductive life history in evaluations of depressive patients (Hamilton, 1984; Hamilton et al., 1988a; Parry, 1989). The discussion that follows highlights research on selected reproductive-related events—menstruation, pregnancy and childbirth, infertility, abortion, and menopause—and their relation to depression in women.

Menstruation

For some women, mood and behavior changes appear to be linked to the menstrual cycle (Logue & Moos, 1985). In their review of the literature, Hamilton et al. (1988a) report that 20–80% of women report mild to minimal mood or somatic changes premenstrually; an estimated 5% of women experience severe premenstrual symptoms. Common premenstrual symptoms include depressed mood; irritability; hostility; anxiety; changes in sleep, appetite, energy, and libido; and somatic symptoms. Many of these symptoms are found in clinical depression, but the symptoms of clinical depression are much more severe than are typical premenstrual symptoms.

The onset of menstruation occurs typically in the late preteen or early teenage years, and premenstrual symptoms also typically begin in adolescence. Gender differences in depression also appear to emerge in adolescence, at about 14–15 years of age (Kandel & Davies, 1982; Nolen-Hoeksema, 1990; Rutter, 1986). In the past, few researchers have examined factors contributing to negative affect in adolescent girls. Recent research, however, suggests that emerging gender role conflicts, increasing devaluation of the female gender role, and fear of success may contribute to an increase in female adolescent depression (Brooks-Gunn & Warren, 1989; Gilligan, Lyons, & Hammer, 1989). These factors are discussed in a later section of this report.

Premenstrual symptoms appear to have their highest prevalence in the late 20s and early 30s. Some studies (Craig, 1953; Dalton, 1964; Morton, 1950) have indicated that monthly symptoms also may occur after cessation of ovarian functioning.

The reasons for age-related variations in symptom frequency and continuation of symptoms after cessation of the menses are unclear. Research is complicated by the possibility that a cyclic mood disorder may exist independently of the menstrual cycle. Cycles of affective symptoms and menstruation may overlap and then dissociate.

Menstrual cycle research is extremely difficult and complex (Koeske, 1981). Defining the limits of normal cycling and of affective symptoms involves complex analyses of physiological markers such as hormone levels and correlation of physiological markers with mood. In some cases, researchers have relied on retrospective reporting of symptoms, but this technique is suspect. In one study (Hamilton et al., 1985), only 20–50% of women who retrospectively reported premenstrual complaints were actually observed to have such complaints when daily reports were kept. In addition, ascertaining the effects of psychosocial factors, including beliefs and expectations about menstruation, is vital.

Pregnancy and Childbirth

Hamilton et al. (1988a) pointed out that pregnancy is associated with a low incidence of psychiatric disorders, and mood changes occurring in pregnancy most often occur in women who are predisposed to affective disorders. The relative lack of psychiatric disorders during pregnancy, despite elevated levels of steroid hormones, contrasts with the changes in symptoms that sometimes occur with cyclic hormonal elevations.

Hamilton et al. (1988a, 1988b) suggested that cyclic affective changes that occur premenstrually and in the postpartum period may have more similarities with each other than with noncyclic or nonrecurrent affective changes (e.g., changes occurring with use of oral contraceptives or with menopause). They suggested that the difference between these affective changes may reflect adaptations in gonadal steroid receptor functioning. Unfortunately, little research has been conducted on gonadal steroids such as androgen, which are found in both men and women. In fact, as noted by Hamilton, most research has concentrated on steroids of primarily ovarian origin, such as estrogen (Hamilton, 1984). Moreover, little comparative research has been designed to ascertain if there are clinical correlates specific to biological changes at childbirth.

Many women experience some form of negative affect after childbirth. Between 50% and 80% of women experience the "baby blues," a mild postpartum dysphoria. This typically occurs about the 3rd or 4th day after delivery and lasts from 1 to 14 days. Some women experience more severe forms of postpartum distress that may resemble several major categories of psychiatric disorder, including mania, delirium, organic syndromes, and schizophrenia. However, the most common syndrome of severe postpartum illness is depression. Severe postpartum depression is distinguished from the more common "baby blues" by the severity and frequency of symptoms, timing of the course of the disorder, and epidemiology. Its onset may occur from 6 weeks to 4 months after delivery, and it may last from 6 months to a year. Prenatal depression may predict postpartum depression (Hamilton et al., 1988a). In addition, Whiffen (1988) used a prospective design to study 115 women giving birth to their first child; 16% were diagnosed as depressed at 8 weeks postpartum. Predictors of postpartum depression included prepartum life stress, depressed mood during pregnancy, early postpartum anxiety, cognitive impairment, optimistic expectations for infants, and low marital adjustment.

Pregnancy occurs in a social context that includes women's attitudes and feelings about being pregnant. Unwanted pregnancy, whether it is terminated in childbirth or abortion, may lead to an exacerbation of problems for women with histories of psychiatric disorders (Adler & Dolcini, 1986).

Simplistic biological explanations of disorders correlated with reproductive events are clearly inadequate to fully explain the gender difference in depression. Research suggests that psychological distress, including bipolar and psychotic illness, increases for men around the pregnancy and delivery time of their partners (Freeman, 1951; Hamilton, 1984; Towne & Afterman, 1955).

Understanding the correlates and sequelae of pregnancy and childbirth requires that researchers not limit their explanations to the physiological aspects of childbirth. It requires an examination of the context in which pregnancies occur, including women's mental health histories, and women's attitudes toward being pregnant. Psychosocial models that attempt to understand the relation between life stressors and depression discussed later in this report might be fruitfully applied to understanding the relation between childbirth and depression.

Infertility

In 1985, 13% of 40-year-old women in the United States were childless, compared with 9% in 1975. Although some of these women may not have wished to have children, it is probable that some were unintentionally childless because of impairments in fertility (National Center for Health Statistics, 1989). For some women who wish to have children and find that they either have great difficulty becoming, or are unable to become, pregnant, infertility can be a crisis that leads to depressive symptoms (Daniluk, Leader, & Taylor, 1985). Research on the relation of infertility to depression has included clinical impressions and numerous anecdotal reports that have limited usefulness, although such information can be helpful in describing the depth of psychological pain and sense of hopelessness associated with infertility. As reported by Mazon (1984), clinical observations have shown that infertility patients may report feeling damaged, defective, or "bad." This sense of "badness" may extend to negative assessments of the person's overall desirability, physical attractiveness, or performance. Infertility patients may report high levels of guilt, which can sometimes be focused on past events such as having had an abortion, particularly under illegal circumstances when there was a greater risk of subsequent infertility (Mazon, 1984; Noble, 1987).

Depression in fertile women has been shown to increase when their partners are diagnosed as being infertile (Connolly, Edelmann, & Cooke, 1987). Attempts to achieve pregnancy may be associated with intense mood swings, anxiety, irritability, emotional liability, and depressive symptoms (Daniluk et al., 1985; Mazor, 1987). Another crisis may arise when a couple is faced with having to decide when to quit trying to achieve pregnancy (Noble, 1987).

In a study of 200 infertile couples seeking assistance at a fertility clinic, 40% of the women reported that infertility was the most upsetting experience of their lives (Freeman, O'Neil, & Lance, 1985). Using the Schedule for Affective Disorders and Schizophrenia to assess depressive symptoms in a fertility clinic population, Bell (1981) found that almost 50% of the women exhibited some symptoms of depression, with 40% demonstrating mild to moderate symptoms and 7% severe symptoms. Paulson, Harman, Salerno, and Asman (1988) used the Institute for Personality and Ability Testing Depression Scale and a clinical interview to evaluate 150 women undergoing infertility treatment, with a control group of 50 women. Of the 27 women who sought psychological counseling, 14% exhibited moderate symptoms of depression.

There is a body of research related to infertility that sometimes includes information on depression, but focused psychological research related to depression and infertility is needed as well. Both partners may experience depression, and it is unclear whether or not depression related to infertility contributes to the gender difference in depression rates. In any case, research on the relation of infertility to depression can benefit from a biopsychosocial perspective, one that controls for history of psychological distress and depression in both partners; examines the fertility-related values, beliefs, and behaviors of significant others as well as the couples themselves; explores the depressive effects of medical interventions, including hormonal treatments; and includes infertile couples who do not seek help from infertility clinics.

Abortion

Nearly one out of three pregnancies in the United States is terminated by abortion (Russo, 1986). Although there is a myth that severe guilt and depression often result from abortion, this is not substantiated in the scientific literature dealing with emotional responses after a legal abortion (Adler et al., in press). The predominant response to such an abortion experience is relief. Feelings of depression, regret, and guilt may also be experienced after the procedure, but they are typically mild and transitory, and do not affect general functioning (Adler, 1975a, 1975b; Adler & Dolcini, 1986; Belsey, Greer, Lai, Lewis, & Beard, 1977; David, Rasmussen, & Hoist, 1981; Ewing & Rouse, 1973; Freeman, 1978; Marecek, 1986; Shusterman, 1979; Smith, 1973). Studies assessing psychological functioning before and after a legal abortion experience report that distress is highest prior to the procedure, drops immediately afterward (Cohen & Roth, 1984; Moseley, Follingstad, Harley, & Heckel, 1981), and continues to drop for several weeks (Fingerer, 1973; Freeman, 1977; Major, Mueller, & Hildebrant, 1985).

Abortion's relative risk of mental disorder compared with other reproductive-related events has not been fully ascertained. Athanasiou, Oppel, Michelson, Unger, and Yager (1973) compared women who experienced early abortion, late abortion, or term delivery. Those authors concluded that compared with term births, abortion was a "benign procedure . . . , psychologically and physically" (p. 231). After reviewing the literature and developing a portrait of the relative risks of abortion, childbirth (with and without adoption), miscarriage, single motherhood, and other medical procedures, Wilmoth and Adelstein (1988) concluded that abortion held no more risks for depression than did other significant life events, including childbirth. They also underscored the inadequacy of research knowledge about the psychological sequelae of the variety of outcomes of pregnancy.

The positive psychological effects of abortion have not been fully assessed, although they might have implications for understanding women's lack of depression after abortion despite the stress of an unwanted pregnancy. Freeman (1977) found that after an abortion women reported feeling more self-directed and instrumental, reflecting a personality change in the women's sense of autonomy and efficacy. It should be noted that such characteristics are associated with positive mental health for women (Bassoff & Glass, 1982; Whitely, 1985).

Although abortion itself does not appear to be a significant risk factor for depression, that does not mean that some women might be more at risk than others for negative consequences of an abortion experience. Psychological response to abortion varies, depending on the woman's mental health history, the reason for the abortion, the developmental stage of the woman (particularly in adolescence), the stage of pregnancy in which the abortion takes place (correlated with the reason for the abortion, the type of abortion procedure, and the developmental stage of the woman), and social support for the woman's decision (Adler & Dolcini, 1986; Adler et al., in press). Schwartz

(1986) identified 32 systematic and scientifically sound studies on the psychological consequences of abortion. Psychiatric problems were rare, 1–2% in most studies in which preexisting history was controlled. However, previous psychiatric history and pressure to have an abortion (against own judgment or religious beliefs) were found to be risk factors for serious psychiatric responses that did occur. Coping expectancies are also related to psychological adjustment after abortion. Major et al. (1985) found that women who expected to cope well with their abortion were significantly less depressed, had more positive moods, anticipated fewer negative consequences, and reported fewer physical complaints both immediately after the abortion and at a 3-week follow-up.

No scientific evidence was found to support efforts to define women's responses after abortion as a clinical disease meriting a new diagnostic category labeled post-abortion syndrome (Speckhard, 1987). Although unwanted pregnancy and its resolution are a potential source of stress, abortion may or may not compound, relieve, or other-wise affect that stress. Because the psychological impact of abortion is affected by coping expectancies, it is irresponsible to promote a diagnostic category so lacking in scientific evidence. Further, given the effects of social support for the woman's decision, expressions of social disapproval, including attacks on abortion clinics and harassment of women seeking abortions, would be expected to produce negative effects correlated with the abortion experience.

Menopause

Menopause is defined as the cessation of menstrual bleeding and is a result of the cessation of production of ovarian hormones. Women are defined as postmenopausal if they have not had menstrual bleeding for 1 year (World Health Organization Scientific Group, 1981). It usually occurs naturally at approximately age 50 or can be caused artificially through irradiation or surgical removal of the ovaries. Menopausal symptoms parallel those of depression, including sleep disturbance, fatigue, irritability, and other mood changes.

There is some evidence that depressive symptoms are at their highest in a woman's 20s and in her 40s and 50s (Neugarten & Kraines, 1965), although this is not reflected in mental health service use statistics (Belle, 1982a). The degree to which depressive symptoms in the 40s and 50s are related to hormonal changes in menopause or earlier health status is not clear. Depression may be a precursor rather than a consequence of menopausal difficulties. Longitudinal research has found that depressed women were twice as likely to report menopausal symptoms, such as hot flashes, and were more likely to seek medical help for menopausal symptoms compared with other women (McKinlay, McKinlay, & Brambilla, 1987a). There is an increase in consultations for emotional problems in perimenopausal (1–2 years before cessation of menstruation) and early postmenopausal (1–2 years after such cessation) women. Women of this age group historically have received more prescriptions for psychotropic drugs than women of other ages and men of similar ages (Skegg, Doll, & Parry, 1977).

Most information on menopausal women comes from women who seek treatment, helping to create a stereotype of the menopausal woman who has a variety of diffuse symptomatology and who seeks health care. However, in their longitudinal research using a community sample, McKinlay et al. (1987a) found that for most women menopause was not associated with either physical or mental health problems, and that most of the variance in the health status of menopausal women can be explained by previous health status and help-seeking behavior. That research also found that the most marked increases in depression with menopause were associated with the multiple sources of social stress (e.g., adolescent children, ailing husbands, and aging parents) rather than biological factors. Further, when several health-related variables were present, their effect on depression was multiplicative rather than additive (McKinlay, McKinlay, & Brambilla, 1987b).

As Hamilton et al. (1988b) have observed, gender-comparative research is needed to clarify age-related trends in affective disorders that may occur differentially in men and women. Such trends may be related to developmental changes in social roles and life circumstances rather than to menopausal hormonal changes. Bungay, Vessey, and McPherson (1980) conducted such research. They reported gender differences at age 50 in some symptoms related to depression, but not others. After controlling for some age-related life events, such as children leaving home, they found gender differences in difficulty making decisions, loss of confidence, night sweats (related to sleep difficulty), anxiety, forgetfulness, difficulty in concentration, tiredness, and feelings of worthlessness. No gender differences in difficulty sleeping, loss of interest in sexual relations, or loss of appetite were observed.

Research on menopausal effects must differentiate the effects of normal menopause and the cessation of menstruation following surgical hysterectomy with oophorectomy. By age 50, nearly 30% of U.S. women have undergone surgical menopause instead of experiencing the natural cessation of ovarian function. McKinlay et al. (1987b) have found that depression is correlated with surgical menopause, although the effects appear to be short-lived. McKinlay et al. reported that most of women's self-perceptions of health status and concomitant use of health services in menopause were associated with the occurrence of surgical menopause. McKinley et al. (1987a) did not find depression to be associated with natural changes from pre- to postmenopause, and reported the most marked increases in depression in women with stress from multiple sources.

Similarly, in their review of the literature, Nadelson et al. (1983) concluded that women experiencing the most distress at menopause were women who had relied on their childbearing and child-rearing roles for status and self-esteem. In fact, psychosocial variables at menopause were more clearly associated with depression than actual endocrine changes. Social class affected the expression of symptoms, with middle and upper class women more likely than lower class women to find menopause liberating because of increased opportunities resulting from cessation of childbearing.

Finally, the role of hormone replacement therapy continues to be problematic. Although some patients with treatment-resistant depressions may show improved well-being from estrogen therapy, existing evidence does not justify the routine use of estrogens for treating postmenopausal women for depressive symptoms (Hamilton et al., 1988b). Moreover, in women with a history of depressive disorders, the initiation of hormone replacement therapy should be monitored closely because estrogen may play a role in triggering rapid-cycling moods in women (Oppenheim, 1984).

The Relation of Personality Traits and Other Psychological Factors to Depression in Women

As Klerman and Hirschfeld (1988) pointed out, "The role of personality in relation to depression has received considerable attention in the literature . . . and may serve as a model for general relations between personality and psychopathology" (p. 43). The relation among gender-related personality traits, personality types, and personality disorders to depression has yet to be fully examined. This section of the report reviews research related to personality traits and other psychological factors as they relate to gender differences in depression in five ways:

- as possible contributors to vulnerability to depression,
- as possible sources of protection from depression,
- as possible precursors to depression,
- as possible mediators of the response to depression, and
- as possible consequences of depression.

Contributors to Vulnerability

As Newmann has pointed out (1987), research hypotheses that assume a special vulnerability of women to depression have received considerable attention in the literature. It has been suggested that female gender role socialization produces a variety of maladaptive characteristics or styles of defining and coping with life stresses that increase the risk of developing or maintaining a depressive syndrome in response to stress (Abramson & Andrews, 1982; Kessler, 1979; Kessler & McLeod, 1984; Kessler, McLeod, & Wethington, 1985; Nolen-Hoeksema, 1987; Radloff & Rae, 1981).

Low self-esteem is clearly an important factor in depression, although theoretical explanations for its role in depression vary (e.g., Abramson, Metalsky, & Alloy, 1989; Abramson, Seligman, & Teasdale, 1978; Beck, 1967; 1987). Brown and Harris (1978) suggested a model that includes both "vulnerability" factors and provoking agents, arguing that the presence of a vulnerability factor does not in itself increase the risk for depression in the absence of a provoking agent. In their model, low self-esteem establishes a propensity for depression (Brown et al., 1986), with social variables interacting to increase risk (e.g., loss of mother by death or separation before the age of 11; the presence of three or more children age 14 or under at home; lack of paid employment; and lack of an intimate, confiding relationship with a husband or boyfriend). Moreover, the psychological mechanisms for translating the social variables into psychological vulnerability are not clearly articulated.

Although this research is widely cited, and parts of the model have received some support (Brown & Prudo, 1981; Campbell, Cope, & Teasdale, 1983), the specific risk factors Brown and Harris proposed have not been consistently replicated and there is a question as to whether risk factors act independently or have synergistic effects (Tennant, 1985). In addition, the research did not include male participants and factors, and agents that might contribute to the excess in women's depression cannot be identified.

Researchers have also attempted to explain depression in women by suggesting that women's orientation toward others contributes to higher risk. However, reviews of a substantial body of research (Bassoff & Glass, 1982; Thomas & Reznioff, 1984; Whitely, 1985) have found no consistent relation between depressive symptomatology and the trait of expressiveness (i.e., orientation toward and concern for others) as measured by the Personal Attributes Scale (Spence, Helmreich, & Stapp, 1975). Unfortunately, most of this research was conducted on college populations and dealt with symptomatology rather than clinical depression.

Instead of internal psychological factors, it may be that the external reality of women's dependence on others and the external expectations that women respond to the needs of others (with concomitant rewards and punishments for their actions) are the key factors in understanding the association between women's relationships and depression. For example, interpersonal sensitivity is an interactive process, more related to the status of the individuals involved than to gender (Snodgrass, 1985). It may also be that without a provoking agent (Brown & Harris, 1978), such as a relationship loss, the trait of expressiveness will not correlate with depression.

Explanatory style as a vulnerability factor. Abramson et al. (1978) suggested that the habitual way that people explain negative events might be a risk factor for depression. They suggest that people who have a "pessimistic explanatory style," that is, who typically explain negative events as caused by stable, global, and internal factors, should suffer longer lasting and more general symptoms of depression than people who explain such events in the opposite way.

More than two hundred published studies have since examined the role of explanatory style in depression. In a meta-analysis of 104 studies involving 15,000 normal and clinically depressed subjects, Sweeney, Anderson, and Bailey (1986) found the predicted relation to be consistent and of moderate effect size. Is a pessimistic explanatory style a precursor or correlate of depression? Peterson and Seligman (1984) have provided an impressive review of both longitudinal and experimental studies that have found that groups matched for depression at Time 1, but differing in explanatory style at Time 1, have more depression at Time 2 if they start with a more pessimistic style (see also Alloy, Peterson, Abramson, & Seligman, 1984; Brewin, 1985; Firth & Brewin, 1982; Metalsky, Abramson, Seligman, Semmel, & Peterson, 1982; Nolen-Hoeksema, Girgus, & Seligman, 1986; Peterson, Luborsky, & Seligman, 1983).

Less perceived life control has been found to be associated with increased depressive symptomatology in women (Warren & McEachren, 1983), and if women receive more "learned helplessness training" than men, they may be more likely to develop pessimistic explanatory styles. Whether this does in fact occur and is an important factor in explaining gender differences in depression has yet to be determined. Future research should explore the relation of gender and gender roles to the various components of explanatory style, and include explanation of both negative and positive life events of relevance to women's social roles and life events (e.g., wife, mother, and worker roles; events in workplace vs. home; and rape and other forms of violence).

In 1989, Abramson et al. revised the 1978 theory of helplessness and depression. They offered a theory of hopelessness depression that deemphasized causal attributions and focused on the expectation of hopelessness as a proximal cause for what they considered a new subtype: hopelessness depression. In this model, both helplessness expectancies (i.e., the expectations that outcomes are not controllable) and negative outcome expectancies (i.e., not being able to attain highly valued outcomes or to avoid aversive outcomes) combine to create the condition of hopelessness that leads to depression in response to negative life events. Although explanatory style plays a contributory role in this revised model, it is seen as operating only in the presence of negative life events.

The interaction of psychological factors with negative life events must be understood if the role of gender in depression is to be understood. These researchers did not address gender issues, and indeed this new model has yet to be adequately tested. Nonetheless, it has promise for informing our understanding of gender differences in depression.

Contributors to Protection From Depression

Stress is ubiquitous in women's lives—from poverty (Belle, 1988, 1990; Belle, Dill, Longfellow, & Makosky, 1988) and violence (Koss, 1988, 1990), to name just two sources considered by the Task Force. Newmann (1986) examined the extent to which gender differences in depression might reflect women's higher levels of stress versus a psychological vulnerability to depression. She reported that women were indeed more likely to experience stressors such as spousal absence, social isolation, financial difficulties, and health problems. However, given similar life circumstances, women were no more vulnerable to developing depressive syndrome than were men. Young married women were, however, more likely to report higher levels of sadness than their male or never married female peers.

How does this expression of sadness relate to risk for the development of depression? The answer is unclear. Specifying the criteria for distinguishing between women's normal expression of feelings (which may reflect social norms as well as personality) and clinical depressive reactions is seen as a necessary foundation for answering that question.

In discussing her finding that women are more likely than men to report feelings of sadness that are not related to depressive syndrome, Newmann (1984) pointed out, "The capacity to experience and express feelings of sadness in the face of loss or disappointment is generally viewed as a mark of mental health and may be an effective deterrent to the development of more severe symptomatology" (p. 137). This deterrence might come directly, from the protective effect of catharsis, or indirectly, through more effective engagement of social support, which in turn may have protective effects. Longitudinal research suggests that social support and depression either act concurrently to mutually influence each other or are influenced by a third variable (McKinlay et al., 1987b).

The answer to the question "Why aren't more women severely depressed?" may be that women's willingness to report sadness—thus elevating their scores on depression measures—prevents the development and/or maintenance of a more severe clinical depression. The Task Force encourages a more balanced approach to research on women and depression, one that would focus on the interaction of life stressors with women's strengths as well as their vulnerabilities, and simultaneously consider onset and recovery.

Instrumentality and competence as protectors. The past decade has witnessed substantial research on the relation between mental health and the gender-related traits of instrumentality (a "masculine" trait that reflects a sense of agency or mastery), and expressiveness (a "feminine" trait that reflects a sense of communion, or concern with others). In general, for the populations studied (more than 80% of which were college students), the positive association that was found between mental health measures and androgyny (the presence of both masculine and feminine traits) was primarily due to instrumentality (Bassoff & Glass, 1982; Whiteley, 1985).

Most measures of mental health used in this research emphasized anxiety, affective, and somatoform disorders, and it may be that by definition such disorders, including depression, reflect a lack of positive traits traditionally considered "masculine," insofar as masculinity is equated with mastery, autonomy, efficacy, and competence.

Current measures of masculinity, such as the Bem Sex Role Inventory and the Personal Attributes Questionnaire (PAQ) are biased towards positive traits, such as competence and mastery. As PAQ developer Janet Spence has pointed out, this has distorted the concepts of masculinity and femininity. The Task Force agrees with the recommendation (Russo, 1988) that researchers cease to equate masculinity and femininity with these limited operational definitions and begin to consistently refer to gender-related traits by their appropriate names (in this instance, instrumentality and expressiveness). Research that examines the relation among instrumentality, self-esteem, and depression is needed, because these factors are highly correlated (Whitley, 1983).

Another approach to understanding the relation of traditionally "masculine" characteristics to depression is found in the behavioral model of Blechman (1981). She examined the role of competence in depression. Blechman defined as competent those people who receive high levels of favorable interpersonal and achievement consequences. In her competence model, a problem-solving repertoire and situational freedom are necessary and sufficient conditions for competence, which is required for mental health. Depression is the logical emotional consequence of incompetence. She presented evidence that women are more likely than men to attain lower levels of favorable achievement consequences. Women are also more likely to be viewed by others as being less skillful than men regardless of women's actions and skill levels (Etaugh & Brown, 1975).

Future research could benefit from a biopsychosocial perspective, as illustrated by Cartwright's (1988) work on gender differences in depression as revealed by biological markers of REM sleep. In her current research (Cartwright, 1989), she is comparing the nature and rates of depression among women undergoing marital separation and divorce, examining differences in response between traditionally feminine women who invest in the wife role and more androgynous women who have multiple roles. Although her sample consisted of "normal" volunteers (who were therefore unmedicated and not in treatment), more of the traditional women appeared to be clinically depressed, in terms of both psychological tests and sleep patterns. Early results suggested that nondepressed men and women were strongly identified with characteristics of both gender roles, which is consistent with the aforementioned instrumentality literature. Regardless of the final outcome of this particular study, the paradigm of simultaneously looking at biological, psychological, and social variables in both genders is a model for other researchers to follow.

Mediators/Moderators of Depression

Gender-related personality traits such as instrumentality may modify depression, affecting such things as the symptoms that are expressed and the disorder's course. Full understanding of gender differences in depression may not be possible if they are studied in isolation from other diagnoses for which there are also gender differences. It has been hypothesized that disorders such as depression and alcohol and drug abuse reflect a similar underlying pathology that becomes expressed differently for men and women.

Horowitz and White (1987) asked, "Do males with 'feminine' identities develop internalized styles of disorder while females with 'masculine' identities develop pathologies that involve acting out?" They studied the relation of instrumentality and expressiveness to styles of pathology—distress, delinquency, alcohol problems, and drug problems. For both men and women, expressiveness was not found to be an important predictor for any of the pathological styles studied. In contrast, for both men and women, instrumentality was negatively correlated with both distress and alcohol and drug problems (although the effect was weaker for the latter problems). These correlations increased over the course of adolescence. Few female subjects were involved in the delinquent activities studied (property crime, petty theft, and violent crime), the results were not consistent, and the correlations were weak. However, the few adolescents still involved in delinquent activities at age 21 were male subjects who were most *strongly* instrumental.

Instrumentality may interact with explanatory style to mediate women's response to stressful life events in ways that cycle into depression. For example, in one study (Baucom & Danker-Brown, 1984), for high-instrumentality women, success facilitated performance on subsequent tasks; failure did not affect it. For low-instrumentality women, failure impaired subsequent task performance, but success did not. High-instrumentality women were more likely than low-instrumentality women to use mechanisms to enhance their egos in response to outcomes—they attributed success to ability and effort, and failure to task difficulty.

In his review of the literature, Brewin (1985) concluded there is empirical evidence that explanatory style affects the processes of coping and recovery from depression. Depressed men and women both appeared more likely to use emotion-focused responses and less likely to use problem-solving coping responses in response to stressful life events (Billings et al., 1983).

Nolen-Hoeksema (1987) proposed a response style theory to explain gender differences in depression. She suggested that in response to dysphoria, men engage in physical activities (i.e., have an active response set) to distract them from their mood. Women, in contrast, are less active and ruminate about the causes of their mood and the implications of their depressive episodes. A ruminative response set, as compared with an active response set, may amplify depressive episodes by (a) interfering with instrumental behavior, thereby increasing failure and feelings of helplessness; (b) increasing chances that an individual will consider depressive explanations for his or her depression; and (c) increasing the accessibility of negative memories. Thus, according to Nolen-Hoeksema, the gender differences in depression may be due to women's ruminative styles, which amplify and prolong their depressive episodes, in contrast to men's active response styles, which dampen their depressive episodes. Further, men may be less likely than women to recall depressive symptomatology (Angst & Dobler-Nikola, 1983).

Further research is needed on the relation among gender differences in response to dysphoric mood, expression of symptomatology, and course of the disorder. We need to know more about the importance and impact of relationships among attributions to events, attributions to symptoms, and actual coping strategies for subtypes of depressive disorders. Evaluation of depression awareness programs is also needed to ensure that they direct women into appropriate treatment rather than simply increase rumination about symptoms.

Precursors of Depression

"Feminine personality" can be conceptualized as a mild manifestation of clinical depression. The traditional theoretical focus in work to identify preclinical manifestations of depression has been on genetics, character, and temperament. The idea has been that feminine personality traits are milder manifestations of depressive disorders. Both feminine personality traits and depressive disorders are considered to have the same genetic foundation (Hirschfeld, 1986; Klerman & Hirschfeld, 1988). Research on the diagnosis of "dependent personality disorder" and its relation to depression reflects this perspective.

Some psychoanalysts have proposed that there is a "depressive personality," characterized by dependency, obsessionality, low self-esteem, and narcissism, that is a predisposition to clinical depression (Arieti & Bemporad, 1978). As noted by Klerman and Hirschfeld (1988), whether chronic depression is a reflection of major depression, a depressive personality, or a dysthymic temperament is unclear. Personality disorders and depressive diagnoses are highly correlated—one study reports that 40% of depressed patients have an Axis II personality disorder diagnosis (Shea et al., 1987). The presence of a personality disorder in depressed patients has been found to be associated with earlier onset, more prior episodes of depression, more suicidal potential and history, and poorer response to pharmacological treatments (Hamilton & Jensvold, 1989).

Misdiagnoses may account for some of the overlap. Several researchers have noted the similarity in diagnostic criteria between the *DMS-III* (American Psychiatric Association, 1980) and *DMS-III-R* (American Psychiatric Association, 1987) Axis I (affective disorder) and Axis II (borderline, antisocial, avoidant, and dependent personality disorders) as evidence that patients diagnosed as borderline may have unrecognized bipolar or atypical depression.

Research on victimization has also raised questions about possible misdiagnosis of borderline personality disorder in women. Bryer, Nelson, Miller, and Krol (1987) found that childhood physical and sexual abuse was associated with a high proportion of borderline personality diagnoses, along with suicidal symptoms. Several authors have argued for initially diagnosing abused patients as having posttraumatic stress disorder (PTSD) rather than a personality disorder or psychosis (Gelinas, 1983; van der Kolk, 1988; van der Kolk, Herman, & Perry, 1987). As is made clear in the PTSD diagnosis (American Psychiatric Association, 1987), many of the symptoms of PTSD and depression overlap (e.g., depressed mood, sleep and appetite disturbance, social withdrawal, lowered self-esteem, and psychomotor retardation or agitation). Research that clarifies the relations among personality diagnoses, depression, and other disorders with overlapping symptoms is clearly needed. The lack of conceptual and diagnostic clarity compounds the difficulty of understanding the role of gender in the etiology, diagnosis, and treatment of such disorders.

Research that explores the relation of gender-related personality traits to each diagnostic category is also needed. How dysthymia is ultimately categorized—as an Axis I clinical symptom diagnosis, as dysthymic temperament, as dysthymic personality disorder, or as depressive personality disorder—may depend on how well the relation of gender to the behaviors involved in the diagnosis is understood.

Personality and Psychological Factors as a Consequence of Depression

Does depression influence women's personality, changing their perception of themselves and their style of interacting with others? Depressive state can affect personality trait scores: The reliability and validity of personality measures of neuroticism, dependence, and introversion have all been found to be affected by depressive state (Hirschfeld, 1986; Hirschfeld, Klerman, Clayton, & Keller, 1983). Because these traits are stereotypically considered "feminine" qualities, it is likely that other gender-related personality dimensions would be affected as well. Eaves and Rush (1984), for example, have suggested that attributional biases may be a consequence of long-term depression, but more research is needed before there is confidence in this proposition (Brewin, 1985; Hamilton & Abramson, 1983).

Flett, Vredenburg, and Pliner (1985) pointed out that experiences related to depression could change one's perception of one's instrumentality. Their longitudinal study, which examined changes in PAQ and Beck Depression Inventory (BDI) scores after a period of 3 months, suggested that depressive symptomatology preceded a reduction in instrumentality scores. The sample was limited to Canadian 1st-year undergraduates, however. Further, even if the correlation is replicated, one still cannot distinguish whether depression influences instrumentality or if another factor, such as self-esteem or self-concept, affects both.

As noted earlier, gender-related differences in depression begin to appear in adolescence (Kandel & Davies, 1982; Nolen-Hoeksema, 1990; Russo, 1986). Gender-related personality traits change developmentally (Abrahams, Feldman, & Nash, 1978; Cunningham & Antill, 1984; Flett et al., 1985; Feldman, Birigen, & Nash, 1981; Horowitz & White, 1987; Puglisi, 1983). Because adolescence and young adulthood are major formative periods in the development of adult gender role identities, and because it is also the time when onset of depression is implicated, adolescence is an important developmental period to examine. Comparative research on the relation between depression and personality formation—over the life cycle in general, but particularly during adolescence and young adulthood—is needed if gender differences in depression are to be fully understood.

Women's Roles and Status in Relation to Depression

It is often thought that interpersonal roles and relationships are particularly important to women and that "caring" is women's particular province (Chodorow, 1974; Gilligan, 1977; Miller, 1976). Bernard (1971) has argued that "stroking" is the quintessential female function, one that permeates every role a woman performs. In this supportive function, as outlined by Bernard, a woman shows solidarity, raises the status of others, gives help, rewards, agrees, concurs, complies, understands, and passively accepts. Whether these behaviors reflect internal psychological characteristics or pervasive gender role expectancies and norms continues to be debated. In any case, women have been found to provide nurturance and emotional support to others more frequently than do men. Women are named disproportionately as counselors and companions by both men and women (Fisher, 1982), and as confidants and sources of affirmation and understanding by their own school-aged children (Belle & Longfellow, 1984), adolescents (Kandel & Lesser, 1982; Kon & Losenkov, 1978; Youniss & Smollar, 1985), and spouses (Campbell, Converse, & Rodgers, 1976; Lowenthal & Haven, 1968; Warren, 1975). Women also tend to remain more involved in the tribulations of their adult children (Loewenstein, 1984) and to provide much of the care for elderly relatives (Brody & Schoonover, 1986). In many communities, the instrumental and emotional assistance shared among female kin, friends, and neighbors, particularly around child rearing, is crucial in ensuring day-to-day survival and maintaining family solidarity (Belle, 1982b; Cohler & Lieberman, 1980; McAdoo, 1980; Stack, 1974; Young & Willmott, 1957). Other researchers have argued that women are more supportive friends than are men (Caldwell & Peplau, 1982; Wheeler, Reis, & Nezlek, 1983).

Women generally do derive substantial satisfaction from their marriages, children, and friendships, and research finds that participation in such interpersonal roles and relationships is positively related to mental health. Women who have the most complete role configurations (i.e., wife, parent, and worker) experience fewer depressive symptoms than those who do not participate in marriage, parenthood, or employment (Kandel, Davies, & Raveis, 1985).

Roles as Contributors to Depression

Although relationships can bring great satisfaction to women, problems and strains in such relationships constitute a greater risk factor for depression than problems or strains in other realms of life (Kandel et al., 1985). Women's role obligations to care for, support, and "stroke" others can also heighten women's risk for stress and depression (Belle, 1982a). In family gender roles such as wife and mother, and in community roles such as neighbor and friend, women are expected to respond to the pain and the needs of others, whether or not their own needs for support and validation are met. Research often shows that involvement in social relationships is less protective for women than for men, or that particular social involvements are actually associated with negative outcomes for certain groups of women.

Given women's overrepresentation among informal support providers and confidants, it is hardly surprising that women suffer more than men from the "contagion of stress" that is felt when disturbing life events afflict those to whom we are close.

Dohrenwend (1976) found, for instance, that when men and women were asked to list recent events that had occurred to themselves, family members, and other people important to them, a higher proportion of the events women reported had happened to family members or friends rather than to the respondents themselves. Eckenrode and Gore (1981) reported that women whose relatives and friends experienced stressful life events such as burglaries and illnesses found these events personally stressful and reflected this vicarious stress in their own poor health. Wethington, McLeod, and Kessler (1987) showed that although men are distressed by events that happen to their children and spouses, women are distressed not only by these events but also by events which occur to other members of the social network. Women's greater "range of caring" thus exposed them to a greater risk of depression.

Similarly, Cohler and Lieberman (1980) discovered that among the middle-aged and elderly ethnic men and women they studied, the women who were more involved with relatives and friends experienced more psychological distress than their less involved peers, whereas network involvement among the men was either unrelated to mental health or showed small positive associations with morale. The authors related this finding to the social norms of the ethnic communities from which the respondents were drawn, social norms that mandated that women care for the needs of others.

Cohler and Lieberman (1980) argued that caring for the needs of others in midlife competed with women's own agendas for psychological development. Studies of medical students and dental students have shown similarly that among female students, social relationships were positively associated with depressive symptoms, while negative associations were found for the male students (Foorman & Lloyd, 1986; Goldstein, 1980). This suggested that in demanding training environments social ties may be detrimental for women because they compete with the academic and occupational agendas.

Family Roles and Intimate Relationships

Within marriage, husbands more often than wives report being understood and affirmed by their spouses (Campbell et al., 1976; Vanfossen, 1981) and husbands are much more likely than wives to rely solely on the spouse as confidant (Veroff, Douvan, & Kulka, 1981). Women appear to be more vulnerable than men to problems persisting within marriages, problems that are then associated with symptoms of depression and anxiety (Perlin & Lieberman, 1979). It has been reported that unhappily married women experience more depressive symptoms than either happily married or unmarried women (Aneshensel, 1986). Jack (1987) found the clinically depressed married women she interviewed to be frustrated in their attempts to "fit their relational capacities and needs into the roles of 'wife' and 'good woman' " (p. 164). These women also reported being "isolated and lonely within relationships of inequality and emotional distance" (p. 165).

As reported by Weissman (1987), the ECA data on marital status and risk of depression paralleled the findings of these studies, showing that marriage conferred a greater protective advantage on men than on women. An unhappy marriage, however, constituted a grave risk to a woman's mental health. The ECA data showed the gender-related difference in 6-month prevalence rates for major depression was more pronounced for married than for separated/divorced or single men and women. In unhappy marriages, women were three times as likely as men to be depressed, and almost half of all women in unhappy marriages were depressed. In happy marriages the incidence of depression was much lower, but women were almost five times as likely as men in such marriages to experience depression (Weissman, 1987).

Whether homemakers or employed wives, women with young children experience high levels of stress (Thoits, 1986). Women's risk of depressive symptoms and demoralization has been found in several studies to be higher among mothers of younger children and to increase with the number of children living at home (Brown, Ni Brolchain, & Harris, 1975; Perlin & Johnson, 1977; Radloff, 1975). Responsibility for adolescent children can also be stressful (McBride, 1987).

Women have been found to experience more change than men in the transition to parenthood (Beisky, Lang, & Huston, 1986; Cowan et al., 1985) and the asymmetrical nature of family roles is probably most apparent in households including young children. Fisher (1982) found that women, especially mothers of young children, were much more likely than others to report too many demands from members of their households. He also found that having children restricted the social involvements of mothers more than those of fathers, limiting women's friendships, social activities, and social supports. The relation of depression to such demands and involvements has yet to be ascertained.

In addition to the stress associated with child rearing, increasing numbers of women have primary responsibility for caring for aging parents. The stress of caring for an aging parent, either while still raising children or after the children have left home, is also likely to increase the risk of depression (Jarvik & Small, 1988; National Institute of Mental Health, 1987; Russo, 1988). Dychtwald (1989) reported that 80% of older Americans are estimated to receive care from their families and that the average American woman will spend more years caring for parents than children. The average age of female caregivers is 57, with more than one third being 65 or over.

Although much previous research and theorizing has emphasized the threat to women's mental health from loss of attachment bonds, recent work reviewed below suggests that women are at higher risk for depression when they experience persistent strains in their ongoing relationships. Future research needs to attend to these persistent strains and to elucidate further how women's interpersonal roles and relationships affect their mental health. It is clear that the stresses associated with gender roles and the nature of marriage, the presence and dependence of children, and the need to provide care for older adults constitute risk factors that substantially contribute to gender differences in depression. There are additional gender-related sources of stress—from work roles and other life circumstances and events—that further compound women's risk for depression.

Employment Roles

Whether women are employed by choice, necessity, or a combination of both, such work plays an important role in their lives. Occupational status and prestige are important predictors of mental health for both men and women, and reports of a gender difference in depression are more likely to be found in studies with samples that have larger differences in male and female employment rates (Golding, 1988).

Research on the effects of employment has been biased toward focusing on job-related variables for men and home and family variables for women (Amaro, Russo, & Johnson, 1987). Thus little is known about how the characteristics of women's employment settings might relate to risk for depression, even though it has been shown that women's satisfaction with multiple roles of worker and mother is affected by job-related variables: job performance, job progress, job duties, and reason for working (McHenry, Hamdorf, Waithers, & Murray, 1985). Psychological distress has also been associated with job stress, perceived support and cooperation from peers and co-workers, and lack of discrimination (Amaro et al., 1987; Aneshensel, 1986). Issues related to sexual harassment, a widespread and pernicious form of discrimination in the workplace (Hamilton, 1989), are discussed in the section on victimization.

Working wives. Findings from research on the effects of wives' employment on mental health have been mixed. In some studies, employed wives have been found to be less distressed than housewives (Gove & Geerken, 1977; Kessler & McRae, 1982). In others, no significant differences between these two groups have been found (Perlin, 1975; Radloff, 1975; Roberts & O'Keefe, 1981).

This inconsistency may be partially explained by differences in response of husbands to wives' employment. Kessler and McRae (1982) found that when husbands helped with child care, employment was associated with improved mental health, but employment did not affect the mental health of women whose husbands did not help them with child care. Similarly, Ross, Mirowsky, and Huber (1983) reported that if employment was consistent with the values and preferences of both husband and wife and the husband shared in child care, employment improved the mental health of wives.

Ross and Mirowsky (1988) specifically examined the relation of wives' employment, motherhood status, and access to child care on depression levels. They found that for wives not employed outside of the home, children increased depression levels. Mothers who had no difficulty arranging child care and who had husbands who shared child care had very low depression levels, comparable to the low levels of husbands and employed women with no children. In contrast, employed mothers with sole responsibility for child care and difficulties arranging for it had extremely high depression levels. Having children and access to child care had no effect on husbands.

Thus, it is clear that the relation between women's work outside of the home and depression is complex. Future research is needed on the effects of women's roles and relationships in their families as well as their families' links to other institutions (such as child-care providers).

Economics and education. Research on married couples has linked perceived economic hardship to depression for both men and women, but the relation is complex, involving educational level, occupation, income, and numerous other variables. Ross and Huber (1985) found that for men, economic factors were highly correlated with depression; although such factors were also correlated with depression for women, education level and children were important as well. Although education was relevant to depression for men insofar as it was associated with increased earnings, education was important in its own right for women.

Professional status. Although lower income is a risk factor for depression for both women and men (Belle, 1990), higher earnings associated with professional achievement do not mean invulnerability to depression. Depression and suicide are highly correlated (Robins, Murphy, Wilkinson, Gassner, & Kayes, 1959), and elevated suicide rates may signal elevated rates of affective disorder. Nolen-Hoeksema (1990), in fact, reported depression to be associated with approximately 80% of all suicides.

Research on suicide in professional women—chemists, nurses, physicians, medical students, pharmacists, and psychologists—suggests a higher risk for suicide over women in the general population (Craig & Pitts, 1968; Li, 1969; Mausner & Steppacher, 1973; Pitts, Schuller, Rich, & Pitts, 1979; Powell, 1958; Walrath, Li, Hoar, Mead, & Fraumeni, 1985). An elevated risk for suicide was not found for teachers (Blachly, Osterud, & Josslin, 1963) or student nurses (Theodore, Berger, & Palmer, 1956), however.

In trying to understand the differences in risk across occupational groups, the fact that the elevated risk for suicide is greatest for women in professions that have been traditionally male dominated is noteworthy (Lloyd, 1988). Also, in contrast to the situation in the general population, in which suicide rates are much higher for men and women, professional women commit suicide at rates that are either generally comparable to or greater than the suicide rates among their male peers (Mausner & Steppacher, 1973). It is important to recognize that in the professional groups studied, women have more access to lethal methods of attempting suicide than women in the general population, and women in general have a higher rate of suicide attempts than men. Further, there may be cohort effects that cloud interpretation of findings (Carlson & Miller, 1981; Solomon, Ostrov, Offer, Howard, & Schwartz, 1983). One must also keep in mind that suicide has been linked to alcoholism and drug addiction (Robins et al., 1959; Roy, 1985).

Few studies have attempted to assess depressive symptoms or depressive disorders among professional women. The only study to use structured interviews with practicing professional women (Weiner et al., 1979) reported higher rates of depressive symptomatology for women physicians (51%) and Ph.D. psychologists (37%) than would be expected for the general population (25%) (Weissman & Meyers, 1978). In contrast, the one study of women in a traditional occupation (nursing) that reported a significant gender difference found that it was the *male* nurses who had significantly higher levels of depressive symptomatology compared with female nurses (Firth, McKeown, McIntee, & Britton, 1987).

For physicians, the trend toward more depression among women compared with male peers is also found in training. Four studies using standardized self-rating depression scales have reported higher rates of depressive symptoms for female medical students compared with their male peers—differences that appear to widen with years in school (Lloyd & Gartrell, 1981, 1984; Salt, Nadelson, & Notman, 1984; Vitallano et al., in press).

Using *DSM-III* (American Psychiatric Association, 1980) criteria to assess major depressive disorders in medical students, Zoccolillo, Murphy, and Wetzel (1986) found a prevalence rate of 16% for women and 7% for men—a gender difference comparable to that in the general population. However, the lifetime prevalence rate for major depression in these students was 15%—three times greater than that of age-matched controls in the general population. Lloyd (1988) reviewed this research in more detail.

Although the pattern of findings is suggestive, the lack of research on various occupational groups makes conclusions difficult. The few studies that do exist focus on female medical students, residents, and physicians. More research is needed to ascertain the extent and correlates of depression in diverse groups of professional women. Literature addressing special issues for professional women (Heins, 1985; Lloyd, 1983; Nadelson & Notman, 1972) raises several etiological possibilities, including factors associated with gender discrimination, identity formation, achievement–affiliation conflicts, and conflict between the professional roles and those of wife and mother. As Lloyd (1988) has pointed out, explanations of gender differences in depression may require a concept of relative rather than absolute social and economic disadvantage and a consideration of multiple etiological factors. Some of the recent theorizing that has related social comparison and negative self-evaluation to depression, although not specifically applied to gender differences at present, might be helpful in this regard (Swallow & Kulper, 1988).

The Interaction Among Work and Family Roles

Aneshensel's research (1986) provides some perspective on the complex relation among the variety of roles women may fulfill. She examined the joint effects of strain from marital and employment roles on women's experience of depression. Aneshensel found that although the effects of stress in those roles were additive and not synergistic, the effects differed depending on marital and employment status. Where there was a combination of low marital strain and low employment strain, employed wives had the lowest rates of depression. Using this lowest rate as a comparison base of 1.00, Aneshensel ranked the other groups in order from least depressed to most depressed:

1. employed wives with a combination of low marital strain and low employment strain (1.00);
2. employed wives with low marital strain but high employment strain (1.37);
3. unmarried women with low employment strain (1.64);
4. nonemployed wives with low marital strain (2.08);
5. employed unmarried women with high employment strain (2.25);
6. employed wives with high marital strain and low employment strain (2.63);
7. nonmarried, nonemployed women (3.41);
8. employed wives with high marital strain and high employment strain (3.60); and
9. nonemployed wives with high marital strain (5.47).

These findings indicate that employed wives with marital problems, even if they had job strain, were at lower risk for depression than wives who did not work. Whether nonmarried women had lower risk for depression than wives depended on the wives' marital strain. And even if wives had marriages with low strain, if they were also not employed, they had a higher risk of depression than employed nonmarried women who had low employment strain. Thus, knowing marital and occupational status was not sufficient to predict risk—and the difference in effects for the various groups reached more than 5 to 1.

It is clear that knowing only whether a woman is married or single, is employed or unemployed, or has children or does not, or even knowing more than one of these facts, is not sufficient information upon which to predict risk for depression (Aneshensel, 1986; Ross et al., 1983; Ross & Mirowsky, 1988). More sophisticated approaches are needed to advance knowledge about the aspects of roles that increase or decrease such risk. Future research must study more systematically the relation between depression and women's education and work roles and statuses, using models that simultaneously examine the relation among job and family variables. It is important for research to move beyond a focus on the *occupancy* of particular marital or work roles and statuses to actual assessment of the *quality* of those roles and statuses.

Research should employ models that simultaneously examine numerous variables, including stressor and protective aspects of roles and circumstances related to marital role conflicts and sources of support, degree and nature of responsibility for immediate and extended family care and significant others, expectations of partners concerning work and family life, characteristics of work settings and work roles that provide protection from depression, personal expectations and aspirations for achievement, educational and economic resources of women and their family members, and relationships among friends and co-workers.

Victimization and Poverty as Factors Affecting Depression in Women

Specific life events and circumstances are correlated with depression in both genders, but are more likely to be experienced by women. For example, individuals who have less education, low income, low socioeconomic status, and are unemployed are at higher risk for depression (Golding, 1988). Women are disproportionately found in these categories compared with men. Thus, gender may operate in an indirect manner, through channeling women into social and environmental contexts that themselves are risk factors for depression. The Task Force focused on two critical, but neglected areas for understanding women's depression: victimization and poverty.

Victimization

Victimization in interpersonal relationships is a significant risk factor in the development of depressive symptomatology in women. What is presented clinically as depressed mood may be long-standing posttraumatic responses to experiences of intimate violence and victimization, for example, childhood sexual or physical abuse, marital or acquaintance rape, woman battering, sexual harassment in the workplace, or sexual abuse by a therapist or health care provider. The contribution of these factors to rates of depressive symptomatology in women has been neglected, partially because victimization histories in most psychiatric patients tend to be ignored or conceptualized as the source of a disordered personality rather than as depressive symptomatology (Bryer et al., 1987). The long-term psychological sequelae of victimization are just beginning to be explored, and typically depression is not among the priorities of such research.

In examining effects of victimization, the Task Force focused on traumata that occur in the context of interpersonal relationships, rather than those resulting from accidents or natural disasters. This emphasis on interpersonal relationships as the locus of victimization reflects women's experiences of trauma and focuses attention on the importance of examining the impact of relationships on women's mental health. A large percentage of such traumata will have occurred repetitively and have been inflicted by a person known to, and often intimate with, the victim (e.g., family members, friends, co-workers, or trusted health care providers). These are experiences in which responses to trauma may have become overlearned and accommodations to surviving victimization internalized into basic characterological structures. For example, victim-ization experiences have been found among persons diagnosed with borderline per-sonality disorder (Bryer et al., 1987; van der Kolk et al., 1987).

Prevalence of victimization of women. Base rates for victimization experiences are higher for women than for men. Survey research in nonclinical populations has found rates of childhood sexual assault ranging from 21.7% (Bagley & Ramsey, 1986) to 37% (Russell, 1986) among women, with significantly lower rates being seen among men. These figures may be an underrepresentation of the extent of physical and/or sexual abuse of women (Koss, 1990). Battering by an intimate partner may occur in the lives of as many as 25% (Steinmetz, Strauss, & Gelles, 1980) to 50% (Walker, 1984) of women; again, rates of battering of men are significantly lower. Estimates of marital and acquaintance rape suggest that 12–14% of all women have suffered these forms of assault (Finkelhor & Yilo, 1985).

Another form of victimization frequently experienced by women is sexual harass-ment on the job. At least one survey (New York Public Interest Group, 1981) indicated that as many as 71% of all working women may experience sexual harassment. Because sexually harassed women often lose jobs and suffer other losses and life changes as a result of such victimization (Institute for Research on Women's Health, 1988), the high frequency of such events should be considered as a possible precursor for depressive episodes in women.

The overall prevalence of victimization of women is difficult to ascertain. Violence against women is likely to be underestimated. Moreover, national crime statistics are not designed to accurately assess the true extent of acts of interpersonal violence (Koss, 1988).

Physical effects of victimization in relation to depression. Certain kinds of vic-timization experiences can produce physiological changes that may lead to depressive symptoms. Victims of battering and rape may have minor or moderate head injuries that are likely to go undetected because of the failure of the victim to seek medical care, or because of a lack of overt sign of neurological distress. Such head injuries can lead to persistent depressed affect and other changes in cognition, motivation, and behavior that mirror the symptoms of depression (Kwentus, Hart, Peck, & Kornstein, 1985). The exact incidence and prevalence of head injuries in this population have never been studied. However, it is reasonable to suggest that some depressive symptoms seen in the survivors of violent assault may be due to physiological changes to the brain resulting from closed-head trauma. Recent findings on the neurological concom-itants of PTSD (Kolb, 1988; van der Kolk, 1988) suggest another possible biological link between victimization and depression.

Psychological effects of victimization and their relation to depression. Research inquiring directly into possible links between interpersonal victimization and depression in women is just beginning. Victimization literature is beginning to generate data on depression, however. Victims of interpersonal violence share many of the symptoms of persons with a primary diagnosis of depression: hopelessness, helplessness, negative self-esteem, a restricted range of affects, high levels of self-criticism, self-defeating interpersonal strategies, and difficulties in forming and retaining intimate relationships. At least one researcher (Walker, 1979, 1984) has postulated a psychological response pattern to the experience of interpersonal victimization that relies on Seligman's (1975) learned helplessness model.

When victims of interpersonal violence are studied, high rates of depression are commonly found. In a study of 60 battered women, Hilberman and Munson (1977–1978) found that depressive illness was the most frequent diagnostic category. Ellis, Atkeson, and Calhoun (1982) reported that their sample of raped women had higher scores on the BDI than did a matched sample of women who had not been raped, with 19% of the rape survivors being severely depressed and another 26% being moderately depressed. In a series of structured interviews with adult survivors of incest and rape, Roth and Leibowitz (1988) found that the most recurrent themes in these women's self-descriptions were helplessness, rage, and self-blame, suggesting higher rates of depression in that group.

In one study (Bagley & Ramsey, 1986) directly measuring depression in women who had histories of victimization, women who had a history of being sexually abused as children had significantly higher depression scores on the Center for Epidemiologic Studies Depression Scale (CES-D) and manifested lower self-esteem on other questionnaires. The Bagley and Ramsey research is of particular significance because they employed the CES-D, an instrument that is commonly used in epidemiological studies that have reported higher rates of depression among women than among men.

In another study of global psychological functioning in a group of women who had been sexually abused as children, Murphy et al. (1988) used the Symptom Checklist-90-Revised and other measures, and found that the women who had been abused had elevated rates of depression compared with a control group of women who had not been abused. Finally, in two recently published studies, Gidycz and Koss (1989) and Jehu (1989) reported that high rates of depression were found in both adolescent and adult women who had experienced childhood sexual abuse.

Carmen, Reiker, and Mills (1984) conducted a chart review of 188 male and female psychiatric inpatients and found that histories of interpersonal victimization were mentioned in the charts of 43% (65 women and 15 men) of the patients, with the records of another 7% of the patients showing indications of abuse. (The 65 female subjects who had been abused comprised 53% of all the female patients whose records were examined; the male subjects who had been abused represented 23% of the male patients. It is worth noting that 72 of the abused patients—or 90% of those abused—had been abused by family members).

Jacobson and Richardson (1987) conducted in-depth structured interviews with 100 psychiatric inpatients (50 men and 50 women) and found that 81 of them reported histories of at least one of the following four kinds of assault (violence): physical assault as a child (including child abuse and abuse by peers), physical assault as an adult, sexual assault as a child, and sexual assault as an adult. Of the 81 patients who had reported assault in their histories, 40 (49%) had experienced more than 20 episodes of abuse, 49 (60%) had experienced two or more kinds of assault, and 18 (22%) has experienced either three or all four kinds of assault. The rates for women were higher than those generally reported in the female population, which are typically reported as about 20–50%, depending on the nature of the assault. Jacobson and Richardson noted that their rates may be higher than those found by Carmen et al. (1984) because of their use of face-to-face interviews and the focused nature of the questions they asked. They also pointed out that it is not yet common practice for victimization histories to be taken as part of standard psychiatric or psychological diagnostic or intake procedure.

Sorenson and Golding (1990) examined the relation of criminal victimization to depression and suicidality (self-report of suicide ideation or attempt) in the general population. They extended previous analyses of 2,700 adults from the Los Angeles Epidemiological Catchment Area (ECA) survey and found that being a crime victim was associated with increased suicidality and depression. Those who were mugged, sexually assaulted, or who experienced multiple victimization were at greatest risk for depression and those who were mugged were at greatest risk for suicidality.

In one study of women undergoing outpatient therapy for bulimia (Root & Fallon, 1988), rates of victimization histories were roughly double that of the general population. Root and Fallon also noted that the women in their sample tended to present with subclinical depressive symptoms that in some cases rose to clinical levels as bingeing and purging behavior diminished. A similar high rate of victimization has been found among chemically dependent women (Murphy, Coleman, Hoon, & Scott, 1980). Other data have shown high rates of victimization among persons diagnosed with borderline personality disorder (Bryer et al., 1987; van der Kolk et al., 1987).

The long-term psychological sequelae of victimization are just beginning to be explored, but depression is not among the outcomes typically examined. There is a need for much careful and systematic research that would explore the covariance of histories of victimization with depressive symptoms and other contextual variables such as race, class, age cohort, response to the victimization experience from the interpersonal environment, whether the victimization was a single occurrence or repetitive, and relationship of the victim to the victimizer.

There is an urgent need for careful and systematic exploration of the relation between victimization and depression in women across various populations. When working with depressed women, mental health professionals should begin to inquire into histories of interpersonal violence. Specialists in interpersonal victimization need to attend more carefully to the emergence of possible depressive symptoms among their subject populations and to become more familiar with the formal diagnoses of various depressive subtypes. Theorists also should consider the possible link between victimization and depression and develop models to guide integrative research.

Understanding factors related to victimization and the role they play in depression is a vital part of developing treatment methods, in addition to being of particular importance to the development and implementation of programs of prevention and early intervention. In their study of women who had been sexually abused as children, Murphy et al. (1988) found that the type and severity of psychiatric symptoms varied according to age at molestation and length of time over which molestation occurred. Tsai, Feldman-Summers, and Edgar (1979) found similar relation between age at the end of molestation and self-reports of distress. This suggests that early interventions and/or interventions that focus on certain age groups might be effective in reducing the impact of certain types of victimization, thus preventing the development of depressive symptoms later in life.

Such information is also vital to the development of public policy initiatives that are intended to reduce rates of various forms of interpersonal violence. Understanding the nature, frequency, and signs of victimization among age groups, as well as the short- and long-term effects of victimization, is important to designing programs specific enough to address prevention needs of the populations they must serve (Koop, 1987).

There is also a need to know whether treatment for depressed women with histories of victimization would be more effective if victimization issues were addressed more directly. Brown (1987) and Reiker and Carman (1986) have suggested that the absence of focused interventions and the failure to address the impact of interpersonal victimization on psychological functioning may lead to a failure in psychotherapy and inappropriate reliance on pharmacological treatment. Research inquiring into the differential effectiveness of such treatment modalities might improve the quality of services being offered to women with depressive symptoms.

Finally, the neurobiological effects of interpersonal violence as they contribute to the development and maintenance of depressive symptoms, syndromes, and disorders require study. This is unexplored territory in the area of interpersonal violence, because most current data on the links between trauma and biology are derived from male combat veterans.

Poverty

High levels of depressive symptoms are particularly common among individuals with economic problems (Belle, 1982b; Brown et al., 1975; Makosky, 1982) and those of lower socioeconomic status (Hirschfeld & Cross, 1982). Although women, particularly low-income women, are subject to stressful life events (Makosky, 1982), people of low socioeconomic status exhibit an elevation in symptom scores not explained by differences in life events scores (e.g., Dohrenwend, 1973; Radloff, 1975).

Poverty is among the life circumstances that have been found to be related to depressive symptomology (Brown et al., 1975; Goldman & Ravid, 1980; Henderson et al., 1978; Henderson, Duncan-Jones, Byrne, Scott, & Adcock, 1978; Perlin & Johnson, 1977). A longitudinal study that assessed depressive symptoms in the community found that inadequate income was associated with an elevated risk of depressive symptoms over the 9-year period of the study (Kaplan et al., 1987). These authors also reported that among specific life stressors included in their study, the factors most strongly associated with an increased risk of high levels of depressive symptoms were job loss and "money problems," even controlling for income.

Another study, using the BDI, reported low income as a risk factor for depression in Mormon women (Spendlove, West, & Stanish, 1984). At the same time, a retrospective community study in Calgary, Canada, found that "social class" was not associated with the onset of depression in the 12 months prior to the interview (Castello, 1982). Kaplan et al. (1987) suggested that the consequences of inadequate income over time include high levels of personal uncertainty, anomie, social isolation, and high frequency of negative events and that these factors constitute the pathway by which inadequate income exerts its impact on depressive status. This interpretation is consistent with the path model presented by Belle et al. (1988), which states that demographic factors such as income are related to depression indirectly via their effects on stressors and supports, which in turn are also related to depression indirectly via their effects on subjective stress level; it is the stress level that most directly predicts depression.

The ECA study has used the newly developed Diagnostic Interview Schedule, which is based on the diagnostic categories of the *DSM-III*, in a multisite longitudinal study that provides the opportunity to examine the relation between income and dysthymic disorder, as well as between income and major depression. The major study examining the relation between income and dysthymic disorder was conducted by Weissman et al. (1988). This study provided the first published community survey on rates of dysthymia as defined by the *DSM-III*. The authors reported that the incidence of dysthymia was higher among women compared with men (up to age 65) and among young persons with low income.

The ECA study did not find significant socioeconomic correlates of major depression (Weissman, 1987). At the same time, ECA data summed across all five research sites provided evidence that the estimated relative risk of major depression for the lowest socioeconomic status (SES) group compared with the highest SES group was 1.79 (Holzer et al., 1986). This relation between depression and SES included the finding that the second-lowest SES group showed the highest prevalence. Among women, the highest rates for depression were experienced by those 18–29 years old in the lowest SES quartile and those 30–44 years old in the second-lowest quartile.

One study in Sweden compared middle-aged women with a major depressive episode with age-matched controls who had no history of major depression and found that husband's income and the family income were lower in the depressed group even when adjusted for age and marital status (Hallstrom & Persson, 1984). In another study, 70 recovered nonbipolar depressed women patients were compared with never mentally ill controls, matched for age, sex, and marital status (Hirschfeld, Klerman, Clayton, Keller, & Andreasen, 1984). Although income per se was not discussed, Hirschfeld et al. reported that the formerly depressed women were significantly lower in social class and education level and were less likely than control women to be employed full time. Research is needed to further clarify the relation between poverty and different types of depression. Models that examine both direct and indirect affects are essential.

Diagnostic Bias and Its Effects on Diagnosing Depression in Women

The *DSM* is widely used by mental health professionals both to develop research protocols and as a diagnostic reference. The publication of the third edition of the *DSM* (American Psychiatric Association, 1980) and of its later revision, *DMS-III-R* (American Psychiatric Association, 1987), was received with acclaim. Indeed, as noted by Loring and Powell (1988) about the original third edition, these new editions were improvements over earlier versions in that they presented detailed operational definitions of each diagnostic category and each definition had been developed and tested for reliability during field trials (albeit, the field trials frequently employed somewhat limited subject populations). However, as the *DSM-III* and *DMS-III-R* came into wider use, a number of issues were raised and continue to generate discussion and controversy.

The Need for Reliability and Precision

Winokur, Zimmerman, and Cadoret (1988) have described the lack of reliability of diagnoses and difficulty in obtaining diagnostic precision even when clinicians are careful and compulsive about following criteria set out in the *DSM*. Of particular interest is evidence that there may be systematic bias in the structure of diagnostic categories that results in an increased probability of misdiagnosis of depression in women. Russo (1984) suggested that interaction effects of age, gender, and race on most frequently diagnosed types of disorder can reflect the paradoxical effects of gender role stereotyping. As has already been noted in this report, for disorders such as depression that are congruent with gender role stereotypes, prevalence rates for women are markedly higher than for men. For disorders that are incongruent with society's idealized view of femininity and the "good" woman (e.g., alcoholism is not congruent with the idealized view), women's needs have been neglected and may go untreated or misdiagnosed.

Research on Bias and Diagnosis

Lopez (1990) presented evidence that clinicians' beliefs about diagnostic base rates influence their diagnostic judgments. Thus, clinicians' knowledge of the widely publicized gender-related differences in depression rates may increase the probability that a female patient will be diagnosed as experiencing a form of depression even if the diagnostic information fits a different diagnostic category. In diagnosing psychological conditions in men, gender role stereotyping of diagnoses may lead to failure to diagnose depression.

In an important analogue study, Loring and Powell (1988) examined the effect of the gender and race of a patient on diagnosis when clear-cut diagnostic criteria were presented. The result of this study were most interesting. Loring and Powell asked 290 psychiatrists to use *DSM-III* criteria to make clinical judgments with regard to the symptomatology demonstrated in two case studies that reflected actual cases receiving psychiatric treatment for undifferentiated schizophrenia with a dependent personality disorder. Indeed, that diagnosis was the modal response—38% of the psychiatrists applied it to the case. When the patient was described as a White man or when no gender or race information was provided, 56% of the psychiatrists chose undifferentiated schizophrenia as the diagnosis. However, when the patient was identified as either a Black woman, a White woman, or a Black man, the proportion of psychiatrists who diagnosed undifferentiated schizophrenia ranged from 21% to 23%.

Clearly, gender and race interacted with diagnosis in complex ways in the Loring and Powell (1988) study, but the most interesting point here is that biases related to gender and race were evident when the responses of psychiatrists who did not use the diagnosis of undifferentiated schizophrenic disorder were analyzed. Regardless of their own race, male psychiatrists were biased toward giving a diagnosis of recurrent depressive order to female patients, whether the patient was identified as Black (diagnosed as depressed by 40–43% of the male respondents) or White (diagnosed as depressed by 50–53% of the male respondents). In addition, male psychiatrists were more likely to use the Axis II category of histrionic personality disorder when diagnosing White female patients, even though the cases used in the research provided little evidence for such a diagnosis. In contrast, regardless of their own race, female psychiatrists were more likely to diagnose White female patients as having a brief reactive psychosis (50% of the respondents used this diagnosis) and did not show any bias toward a particular diagnosis for Black female patients.

The results of this study are of concern to scientists who rely on clinical judgments in their research, as well as to other individuals, including practitioners, who are concerned about proper treatment. And, specifically, there is concern because psychotropic drugs used to treat depressive disorders are not the same as those used to treat undifferentiated schizophrenic disorder.

Analogue methodology has been criticized as a means of studying clinical judgment. However, Loring and Powell (1988) took considerable pains to address the potential problems of analogue methodology in their research. And, as Lopez (1990) points out, the analogue method has been successful in detecting extent and types of bias if used in a theoretical context and in a sophisticated manner. This method has an important role to play in expanding knowledge about the processes of clinical judgment.

Similarly, Lopez (1990) pointed out that because diagnosis relies on judgment, research on gender bias in information processing and decision making may be helpful in pointing to where and how stereotypes might operate in the variety of clinical judgments that go into diagnosis. He argued for a more sophisticated conceptualization of bias in clinical judgment, one that focuses on general cognitive processes that lead to judgment error and that includes attributions of presenting problems, beliefs about base rates for disorders, and memory. He provided an excellent review of how patient variables (including gender, race, and class) contribute to a variety of types of bias in such judgments, including inappropriately perceiving patients as more disturbed or as requiring more treatment (overpathologizing), inappropriately judging symptomatology as normative for members of a group (minimizing), inappropriately applying a diagnosis as a function of group membership (overdiagnosing), and inappropriately avoiding application of a diagnosis as a function of group membership (underdiagnosing). These types of biases might be correlated in practice (particularly overpathologizing and overdiagnosing), but they are conceptually distinct.

A case in point. Concern has been expressed about the possible impact of stereotyping found in the proposed late luteal phase dysphoric disorder published in the appendix to *DMS-III-R* (American Psychiatric Association, 1987). The label chosen for the diagnosis suggests a biological causality that has yet to be scientifically established, creating assumptions that may direct and distort future research on menstrual cycle effects in stereotyped ways (Gallant & Hamilton, 1988; Hamilton & Gallant, in press). Further, if clinicians' beliefs in base rates contribute to misdiagnosis, what effect will a gender-specific diagnostic label have on the diagnostic process? Assuming that scientific research validates the need for a new diagnosis, a gender-neutral label, such as cyclic dysphoric disorder, would be more appropriate.

Clearly, more research is needed to determine the validity of *DMS-III-R* categories and their application, particularly with regard to their contribution to identifying higher rate for depression in women. And, a full exploration of how gender bias might affect both the development of diagnostic criteria and clinical judgment in their application has yet to be made. Research that examines the effects of gender bias and stereotyping at all phases of the treatment process is necessary before drawing conclusions about the contributions of gender bias in diagnosis and treatment to gender-related differences in the occurrence of depression in women.

Recommendations for Research

The Task Force identified numerous areas in need of research if gender differences in depression are to be understood. Research that focuses on methodological as well as theoretical issues is needed. The following specific recommendations are divided into methodological issues, which cut across content areas in depression research, and six general content areas: reproductive events, psychological variables, interpersonal roles and relationships at home and work, victimization, poverty, and diagnosis.

Methodological Issues

A fundamental requirement for understanding women's depression is the advancement of research methodology. The Task Force recommends the following:

1. Basic research needs to be conducted that focuses on refining conceptualization and measurement of variables related to psychological traits, social roles, and life circumstances, as well as depressive-related symptoms, syndromes, and disorders over the life cycle.
2. Researchers need to focus on explaining *gender differentials* in depression rates, rather than explaining levels of depression in women (which may or may not reflect factors unique to women). This requires gender-comparative research.
3. Researchers need a biopsychosocial perspective that recognizes the social construction of women's biology and provides greater conceptual clarity and a more integrated look at causes of gender differentials in depression over the life cycle.
4. Predictors for gender differentials in depressive subtypes relating to course, severity, relapse, recurrence and chronicity as well as onset, need to be identified.
5. Gender differentials in co-occurrence of diagnoses of depressive subtypes as well as related disorders need to be examined.
6. Interaction effects of variables associated with age, race/ethnicity, physical disability, sexual orientation, and marital status need to be examined, even if direct effects of gender are not apparent, before drawing conclusions about the lack of any gender effects.

7. Attention must be paid to the methodological issues that cloud understanding of the relation between women's aging and depression.

Reproductive Events

The Task Force underscored the need for more research knowledge about the psychological consequences of reproductive-related events, particularly with regard to outcomes of pregnancy. It recommends

1. research that simultaneously examines the interaction of biological, psychological, and social factors affecting mental health outcomes of reproductive-related events, including fertility and infertility, for both sexes;
2. longitudinal research and better clinical history taking with regard to mood and behavior changes around reproductive events, with particular attention to interrelation among histories of affective disorders and responses to reproductive-related events over the life cycle;
3. investigation of endocrinological effects related to reproductive events in both genders, with particular attention to gonadal and adrenal steroids;
4. research that explores relations among neuroendocrinological variables and social roles and statuses;
5. gender-comparative research that clarifies age-related trends in depression that may occur differentially in men and women and that may be unrelated hormonal changes; and
6. increasing clarification of the interaction of biological psychological, and social factors, including race/ethnicity and social class, affecting depression in women in menopause.

Psychological Variables

The Task Force underscored that advances in understanding relations among gender-related psychological variables (including personality traits and personality types), and social roles and life circumstances will depend on basic research that clarifies these concepts. The National Institute of Mental Health should take the lead in promoting such basic research. The Task Force also recommends

1. evaluating the reformulated learned helplessness/hopelessness model's usefulness for explaining depression in clinical settings and better establishing a case for differential impact on onset of depression in women;
2. better specifying the criteria for distinguishing between normal expression of feelings and clinical depressive symptoms and exploring how the ability to express feelings might contribute to women's ability to avoid depression;
3. conducting research that separates effects of preclinical depressive symptoms, psychological characteristics such as low self-esteem, and stressful life events on the development and course of clinical depression;
4. examining the relative contributions to depression of personality traits that orient women toward interpersonal relationships, for example, expressiveness versus the actual realities and qualities of those relationships;

5. examining the psychological factors related to mastery, instrumentality, and personal control as they relate to risk for and recovery from depression;
6. exploring the relation of gender-related personality traits to each diagnostic category, particularly with regard to categories related to dysthymia;
7. creating paradigms that separate the reciprocal interaction of personality traits and styles and depression over the life cycle; and
8. paying special attention to relation among events in the formation period of adolescence and risk for depression over the life cycle.

Interpersonal Roles and Relationships at Home and Work

The Task Force recommends
1. research that simultaneously examines how relationships among work- and family-related variables both increase and reduce risk for depression in women of diverse education, class, and race/ethnicity;
2. identification of the positive and negative contributions of types of social support both at home and at work for men and women as they relate to depression; and
3. expansion and clarification of the concept of "vicarious stress" and how it relates to women's excess in depression.

Victimization

The relation between types of victimization and depression needs to be explored, with attention to the adequacy of diagnostic definitions. There is a particular need for research on types of events that give rise to PTSD symptoms for women, because there continues to be disagreement about the nature of stressors that result in PTSD. The Task Force underscored the importance of understanding the contribution of victimization to the onset, course, and recovery of depression, recommending that
1. effects of interpersonal violence, particularly as it relates to disorders related to depression, be given the top priority in mental health research that looks at mental health effects of crime and violence;
2. research be conducted that explores the extent and impact of head injuries and their relation to depression among victims of interpersonal violence;
3. the covariance of victimization histories, depressive symptoms, and other contextual variables including race/ethnicity, class, age cohort, social support around the victimization experience, number and type of victimizing experiences, and relationship of victim to victimizer be ascertained; and
4. the neurobiological effects of interpersonal violence, including sleep disorder, as they contribute to the development and maintenance of depression be assessed.

Poverty

The Task Force observed that poverty is a global concept, operationalized as income, and that specific factors associated with poverty that contribute to depression need to be elucidated. It also recommends

1. testing models that consider both direct and indirect effect of low income on stress that results in depression; and
2. conducting research on poverty as it predisposes or exposed women to other risk factors such as health problems, victimization, and feelings of powerlessness.

Diagnosis

The Task Force underscored the needs for research on the validity of the conceptualization and application the *DSM-III-R* categories as they relate to depression, recommending

1. increased attention to factors influencing clinical judgment in the diagnosis of depression in men and women; and
2. research on how stereotypes vary by gender, race/ethnicity, and marital status, how those stereotypes relate to diagnostic categories, and how their relation affects clinical judgment.

Primary Prevention

The Task Force stressed the importance of public policy and primary prevention in efforts to reduce the incidence and severity of depression in women. It recommends developing coalitions among organizations of mental health researchers, practitioners, and consumer advocates to promote public policies that will reduce women's risk for depression as a strategy for primary prevention.

II ——————————————————————————

Treatment for
Women With Depression

The Task Force examined the following questions regarding treatments for depressed women: Which treatments are effective? How and why are they effective? For which groups of women are specific treatments effective? What are the differences, if any, between the treatment needs of depressed women and those of depressed men? To determine which treatments are effective, the Task Force reviewed outcome studies in psychotherapy, phototherapy, and pharmacotherapy research on women and depression.

The systematic study of the efficacy of different treatments for depression is a relatively recent and underdeveloped field (Rehm, 1989). Diagnostic differentiation and detailed criteria for major depressions, dysthymia, and bipolar states were not clearly established until 1980 with the publication of the *Diagnostic and Statistical Manual of Mental Disorders (Third Edition)* (*DSM-III*; American Psychiatric Association, 1980). Prior to the establishment of this consensus definition in *DSM-III*, it would have been difficult to adequately research the unique needs of any depressed population. However, since 1980 and the establishment of clearer diagnostic criteria, few outcome studies have compared treatment responses of men and women or have addressed treatment efficacy for women.

This section of the Task Force report begins with a brief overview of theories about and treatment approaches to depression, followed by discussions of the diagnostic, methodological, and role/gender issues relevant to the treatment of depressed women. Then studies using psychotherapy, phototherapy, pharmacotherapy, and combination psychotherapy/pharmacotherapy approaches to the treatment of depression are reviewed. This section concludes with specific recommendations relevant to women and depression based on the review of treatment research.

Overview: Theories and Treatments of Depression

The dominant theories of depression are psychological, behavioral, sociological, existential, and biological. Psychological models focus on negative thinking or devaluation of oneself, the role of hopelessness and negative expectations, loss of self-esteem derived from a sense of helplessness or lack of control in attaining one's desires, object loss derived from separation or disruption of an attachment, and aggressive impulses turned against the self. Behavioral theorists focus on the acquisition of depression-related behaviors such as competence and learned helplessness. Sociological theorists focus on role deprivation and conflict, as well as lack of control over one's outcomes.

Existential theory focuses on a loss of meaning and purpose to one's existence. The biological theorists believe the roots of depression to be found in a genetically vulnerable nervous system, depletion of biogenic amines, and hyperarousal. Most researchers, however, while limiting their studies to a specific area, consider depression to be a complex interaction of many factors.

Psychotherapy, phototherapy, pharmacotherapy, and electroconvulsive therapy are used, singly or in combination, in treatment of various depressions. The choice of treatment depends on the nature and severity of the depressive symptoms. Psychotherapeutic approaches include a range of psychodynamic, psychoanalytic, behavioral, supportive, cognitive, feminist, family, and group therapies. Phototherapy is used in treatment of those individuals having seasonal affective disorder, a cyclic illness characterized by recurrent episodes of fall/winter depression alternating with periods of spring/summer euthymia (normal mood) or hypomania (mild elation and behavioral activation). Pharmacotherapy for major depression involves prescribing drugs specific to the needs of the depressed individual, and taking into consideration past and current psychiatric and medical history. The drugs most commonly used are the tricyclics, monoamine oxidase inhibitors, and lithium. Electroconvulsive therapy has been found to be effective in severe depression that are life threatening for those not responding to psychotherapy and medications.

Diagnostic Considerations in Assessing the Needs of Depressed Women

As with all psychotherapy patients, but particularly depressed women, assessment becomes the first and most critical phase of treatment. Formal assessment is typically conducted within the first few sessions of psychotherapy, although ongoing assessment should occur during each meeting with a patient as new material emerges and responses to treatment can be observed. Although the general rules of thorough assessment should be followed in working with depressed women, the Task Force suggests that certain issues need to be taken into careful consideration when working with this population. These include (a) gender issues in assessment and (b) consideration of risk factors specific to women in the development of depressive symptoms.

Gender Issues in Assessment

Gender issues are not typically addressed in psychological assessment. Although gender is a ubiquitous phenomenon whose effects are present in all aspects of human identity and interpersonal functioning, standard approaches to assessment tend to take gender for granted and to assume the normalcy of the status quo. Although this inattention to gender issues can hamper a thorough assessment process with any patient (Brown, 1986, 1990), it can lead to even more problems when the patient is a depressed woman. As this report documents, a number of factors in women's lives that are intimately linked to gender roles can play a part in increasing women's risk for depressive symptoms.

Gender role analysis (Brown, 1986, 1990) (Table 2) is a useful strategy for making gender salient to the assessment process. Gender role analysis requires the assessor

Table 2
Proposed Outline for Integrating Gender Issues Into Assessment

Preassessment

Clinician familiarizes herself/himself with scholarship and research on gender and its relation to clinical judgments of mental health
  Examines literature on interaction of gender with race, class, age, age cohort, culture, and other demographic variables
  Examines literature on gender and personality development, with special attention to those theories not promoting androcentric norms
  Becomes knowledgeable about experiences that occur at higher base rates in one gender than in the other and the impact of those experiences on the entire gender

Clinician examines her/his own conscious and nonconscious biases and expectations regarding gender
  Seeks supervision and consultation from colleagues who are attentive to subtle aspects of gender in the countertransference
  Explores costs and benefits of compliance with, as well as change from, preexisting beliefs, stereotypes, and perceptions of others regarding own gendered behaviors

In the assessment process

Actively inquires into the meaning of gender membership for the client
  In the client's family and culture of raising
  In the client's current social and cultural environment
  Regarding changes in the meaning of gender over lifespan

Attends to the presence and meaning of gender role compliance or noncompliance in the client
  Assesses what rewards and penalties have been for compliance or noncompliance, both historically and currently

Attends to the client's response to the assessor's gender and own response to client's gender
  Notices how issues of perceived attractiveness of one party to the other have an impact on the interchange and the assessor's opinions of the client

Develops hypotheses about the gendered aspects of the interaction between the client and the assessor

Inquires into the presence of gendered high and low base rate phenomena

Checks the diagnosis arrived at to guard against inappropriate imposition of gender-stereotyped values regarding healthy functioning

Note. From *Professional Psychology: Research and Practice, 21,* p. 14. Copyright by the American Psychological Association. Reprinted by permission.

to observe and interpret symptoms and other behaviors in the patient through the lens of a heightened awareness of culturally determined norms and roles for each gender. A gender-aware assessor is knowledgeable about such factors as gender base rates of risk factors and knows that certain normative behaviors expressed by each gender can and are often misinterpreted as evidence of pathology. Gender role analysis in assessment also assists the clinician in examining her or his own preexisting stereotypes and biases related to gender that might skew the validity of a diagnostic impression with a depressed women.

For example, in assessing the type, severity, and appropriate interventions in a given woman's depression, a gender role analysis approach would lead to such questions as Which of these symptoms are primarily exaggerations of this woman's feminine gender role? Which symptoms are inconsistent with her gender role? Has this woman had experiences of interpersonal victimization? If so, could some of these symptoms be manifestations of posttraumatic stress syndrome (PTSD)? Gender role analysis would suggest that out-of-role symptoms may be indicative of different types or severity of depression than those that are role normative.

Gender role analysis also requires assessors to take into account their own gender biases regarding patient behavior. For example, are we assessing a patient as more or less disturbed because of our expectations of what a "healthy woman" should be? Since the data show us that clinicians still perceive mentally healthy women as more like a depressed person (Rosencrantz, Delorey, & Broverman, 1985), it will be only by giving careful attention to nonconscious gender preconceptions that our assessment of depressed women will be free from the effects of such bias.

Consideration of Risk Factors

Once an awareness of gender issues has been established, a careful assessment of a depressed woman goes beyond the basics of establishing the symptom pattern and conducting a mental status examination to determine the presence or absence of risk factors in the woman's history. Also essential is the development of a complete picture of the social and interpersonal context in which such experiences have occurred. Sesan (1988) has pointed out that the most common example of bias in the treatment of women is the failure to adequately assess such risk factors and contextual variables. A necessary minimum strategy for a context-relevant assessment would include gathering information about the factors listed in Table 3.

Care should be taken to view the current presenting symptoms within the context of the depressed woman's history and experiences. In differentiating between types of depressive diagnoses, care must be taken to rule out hypotheses that are weakly supported by the overall picture. This can especially be the case when attempting to ascertain whether specific symptoms are primarily those of a depressive disorder or are manifestations of the emergency state of posttraumatic working through. Because diagnostic decisions often guide the choice of treatment approach, a complete and contextual assessment will be more powerful than a simple elicitation of symptoms.

To aid in assessing more precisely the correct DSM-III-R diagnosis for an individual, clinicians may find it helpful to employ one of several diagnostic interview schedules. These findings can then be integrated with a gender-role analysis to arrive at a complete and contextual diagnosis. There are presently four major standardized diagnostic interview schedules available in the English language (see Rabkin & Klein, 1987, for a more complete review). They are (a) the Present State Examination, (b) the Schedule for Affective Disorder and Schizophrenia, (c) the Diagnostic Interview Schedule, and (d) the Structured Clinical Interview for *DMS-III-R* (SCID; Spitzer, Williams, Gibbon, & First, 1990). The SCID was specifically designed to generate

Table 3
Factors Included in a Context-Relevant Assessment

I. Current risk
   A. Abuse and/or exploitation
   B. Social support system
   C. Educational, employment, and financial status
   D. Membership in oppressed/marginalized groups
   E. Use/abuse of mood-altering substances
   F. Health status, including reproductive events

II. Historical risk
   A. Family history of depression and other mental illness, including alcoholism
   B. Developmental history
   C. History of abuse, exploitation, and/or trauma, including possible repressed memories
   D. History of use/abuse of mood-altering substances
   E. Health history, including reproductive history
   F. Prior psychiatric history, including treatment experiences

III. Contextual
   A. Race, class, sexual orientation, cultural/religious background, and current status
   B. Educational and occupational experiences
   C. Nature and presence of social support networks
   D. Personal values and philosophies
   E. Personality variables, coping styles, and expectancies related to instrumentality, mastery, and competence

---

DMS-III-R diagnoses. It assists the clinically trained mental health professional to make Axis I and selected Axis II diagnoses, and also covers Axes IV and V.

Methodological Problems With Current Psychological Research for Depressed Women

A number of methodological problems are inherent in applied research involving clinical populations. Patients in general are free to exercise choices to terminate their involvement in a research project prematurely or to participate in additional treatment outside the study. Similarly, they may choose not to comply fully with medication or other treatment regimes. Specific methodological problems may include heterogeneous and unclear diagnosis, high dropout rates, patients seeking alternative treatment, difficulties with medication, brevity of follow-up studies, and demand characteristics of the study.

Heterogeneous and Unclear Diagnoses

Given the heterogeneity of depressive disorders and the relatively recent refinement in depressive diagnosis (*DSM-III*; American Psychiatric Association, 1980), the diagnosis of patients is sometimes mixed or unclear. This is especially true in studies that rely primarily on scores from self-report measures, such as the Beck Depression Inventory (BDI; Beck, Ward, Mendelson, Mock, & Erbaugh, 1961; Hayman & Cope, 1980; Padfield, 1976). Differential treatment responses have been reported for patients who are chronically depressed (Weissman, Klerman, Prussof, Sholomskas & Padkin, 1981), severely depressed (Rounsaville, Klerman, Weissman, & Chevron, 1985), and endogenously depressed (Conte, Plutchik, Wild, & Karasu, 1986).

High Dropout Rates

In many studies, early termination of treatment is a significant problem. Most researchers report dropout rates between 15% and 35% (Weissman et al., 1981; Wilson, 1982). Patients may decide not to participate in the designated treatment program, terminate therapy prematurely, or fail to participate in treatment follow-up evaluations. Patients who are assigned to tricyclic antidepressant (TCA) treatment are most likely to terminate prematurely because they are unwilling to take antidepressant medication or find the side effects intolerable. Weissman et al. (1979) reported a 67% dropout rate for patients in TCA-alone treatment. Those patients who drop out are more likely to be noncompliant, have negative expectations about treatment, or feel they are not benefiting from the treatment. When potential negative responders are eliminated from statistical comparisons, outcome results are likely to overrepresent treatment success.

Patients Seeking Additional Treatment Outside the Study

A proportion of patients, especially those who are on waiting lists for treatment, who have minimal-contact conditions, or who are asked to participate in follow-up periods are likely to seek alternative treatment (Hayman & Cope, 1980; Wilson, 1982). Weissman et al. (1981) reported that treatment was not controlled during the follow-up period of their study and patients apparently sought a variety of treatments. Approximately 40% entered therapy and 50% received TCAs. Outcome results are likely to be contaminated by these nonprogrammatic treatments. During follow-up periods, patients in continuing unscheduled therapy may continue to improve to a greater extent than those who have terminated (La Pointe & Rimm, 1980). Simultaneous ongoing therapy has been found to reduce the effectiveness of a treatment program (Steinmetz, Lewinsohn, & Antonuccio, 1983).

Difficulties With Antidepressant Medication

Some patients may be differentially responsive to one medication over another. Yet many studies use only one medication, most commonly the TCAs, imipramine and amitiptyline. Many studies also use a standard dose of TCAs (150 mg per day in several studies), which may not be optimal for all individuals (Friedman, 1975). If TCAs are not prescribed at an optimal level they may be ineffective. If it is then concluded that pharmacotherapy is less effective than psychotherapy, the reported results may be partly a consequence of suboptimal dosage or a mismatch of type of medication with patient (Murphy et al., 1984). In addition, lack of attention to gender differences in response to medication may also reduce effectiveness.

Brevity of Follow-Up Studies

In most studies, the follow-up period ranges from 1 month to 1 year (Comas-Diaz, 1981; Hersen, Bellack, Hemmelhoch, & Thase, 1984; Weissman et al., 1981). Because depression recurs in many patients more than a year after treatment has lapsed (Weissman, Kasl, & Klerman, 1976), studies with a brief follow-up period of less than a year may overrepresent the success of treatment.

Demand Characteristics of the Study

Treatment responses that rely primarily or exclusively on self-report measures (Hayman & Cope, 1980; Padfield, 1976; Wilson, 1982) may be influenced by demand characteristics of the study. Patients may want to show appreciation to their therapists or comply with their perception of the therapists' wishes. Using ratings by clinicians who are unaware of the treatment group or ratings by family members may help mitigate against the effects of patient compliance.

Other methodological difficulties in some studies are the lack of clinical experience of therapists (Zeiss, Lewinsohn, & Munoz, 1979), difficulties in monitoring the content of psychotherapy, failure to differentiate between appropriate reactive depression and serious clinical illness, and failure to assess the interaction between gender and age effects.

Role and Gender Considerations for Therapists

The male or female therapist working with women, and specifically those working with depressed women, must be (a) knowledgeable about the psychology of women and gender differences in the etiology and treatment of depression, (b) empathic to women's special needs, and (c) understanding of women's different realities and modes of expressing depression (Gilligan, 1982; Kaplan, 1984).

As Section I of this report demonstrates, depression among women tends to be associated with many gender-related biological, psychological, and social factors, among them reproductive-related events; personality variables related to instrumentality and competence; lowered self-esteem and unrealistic expectations for physical perfection; coping styles and expectancies, including helplessness and hopelessness; stress and conflict in interpersonal relationships; physical and sexual abuse; discrimination; and poverty.

The review of the literature in Section I reveals the importance of relationships in women's lives as a consistent finding in the research and treatment literature on women's depression. However, the evidence that such depression reflects a psychological orientation toward others (e.g., an expressive orientation) is mixed. A recent systems theory proposes that what happens to women in relationships, as opposed to their relationship orientation per se, is what contributes to women's risk for depression (Lerner, 1987). Further studies that simultaneously consider a woman's psychological characteristics as well as those of her relationship are needed.

Within a psychoanalytical framework, Notman (1986) identified the factors that make women vulnerable to depression as (a) differences in separation, individuation, and attachment in feminine development and early relationship dynamics with the mother that result in anxiety about loss and abandonment; (b) sensitivity to responsiveness to others in the regulation of self-esteem; (c) restricted sociocultural pathways for the expression of aggression, and the relatively fewer modes available to women for activity and mastery; (d) problems with self-esteem, in addition to the internalization of an ego ideal comprising sacrifice and service; (e) identification with a culturally devalued woman (the mother); and (f) social stereotypes that devalue women in general.

What implications do these analyses have for depressed women's treatment and specifically that of the therapist's role? Are women more effective therapists than men for treating depression? Or do the negative feminine stereotypes add to women's devaluation and stigma, making women more responsive to male therapists' authority and perceived valued position in society? Does therapist–client similarity (particularly gender) have any effect at all? Indeed, these are controversial issues that deserve closer examination.

The effect of therapist–client similarity on psychotherapy has generated a considerable body of literature (see review by Russell, 1988), and the results vary across studies. Therapist–client similarity has been alternatively defined in terms of demographics, expectations regarding therapy, personality variables, cognitive style, and personal values (Russell, 1988). The earlier studies on therapist–client similarity dealt mainly with racial and socioeconomic backgrounds. For instance, Carkhuff and Pierce (1967) found that the client's level of self-exploration was greatest when they were similar in race and social class to their therapists.

More recently, in a sociological context, Riessman (1987) stated that cultural knowledge is vital in understanding women's different narrative forms of telling their stories. She argued that gender congruency is not enough, and that women interviewing women require a sociocultural understanding of their realities in order to be effective.

Kaplan (1984) believes that female therapists working with women are more likely to achieve therapist–client empathy because they incorporate into their therapeutic role some sense of their core self (and their client's) as a relational being, and some internalized experience of being in a subordinate position. Male therapists, according to Kaplan, tend to bring to their role some sense of a core self as a separate, autonomous being and an internalized experience of being in a dominant position. Kaplan has stated that there are wide variations in the degree that each individual modifies his or her personal positions via training and personal therapy. However, she believes that female therapists may be more receptive than men to the female client's ongoing affective experience because of their (the female therapist and female client) common relational concerns and shared cultural conditioning.

Power and powerlessness are therapeutic issues for depressed women, which may be related to the therapist–client gender dyad. The learned helplessness paradigm points to empowerment as an important therapeutic issue for depressed women. Regardless of gender, when treating depressed women, therapists need to examine issues of power/powerlessness and the relation among their own gender roles, therapeutic roles, and modeling behaviors to their clients as well as their clients' expectations.

What are the implications of a history of depression for a therapist treating depressed women? To answer this question, it is helpful to view depression as a set of heterogeneous emotional experiences and illnesses including (a) a normal emotion, where fluctuations of depressive affect and mood are expected aspects of normal experience; (b) a symptom, where depressive symptoms occur as part of environmental changes and life events; and (c) a clinical psychiatric condition, or dysphoric state and symptoms, including mood or affective disorders (Klerman, 1987). Almost everyone has had personal experience with some form of depression. Within this context, Rippere and Williams (1985) compiled a series of personal accounts of depressed mental health professionals. Clinicians need to monitor their own reactions especially when working with depressed clients. If the therapist is a "wounded healer" (Maeder, 1989), he or she may be helpful in eliciting and empathizing with the client's depression because it reflects the therapist's depression; however, the depressed therapist may be unable to aid the client's movement into effective action, problem solving, and healing of the depression because the therapist has not mastered those tasks.

In sum, female and male therapists working with depressed women need to be well versed in women's realities (as women and as members of specific cultural, ethnic, racial, social, and other types of groups), as well as have understanding of the causes and treatment of depression. Some female therapists may have a special empathic knowledge that may be very helpful in treatment depression, by virtue of being female and sharing affective connectiveness with their women clients. In terms of facilitating therapeutic gains, women could potentially help repair early damage caused by faulty object relationships, in addition to acting as a positive female role model.

In terms of hindering therapeutic progress, treatment of depressed women needs to address power issues, when the female role has been associated with powerlessness and submission. Therapists of both genders need to monitor their countertransferential reactions to working with depressed women, in addition to understanding the adult developmental issues that their clients may present underlying their depressive picture. Empowerment of depressed clients by attending to their preferences regarding a therapist may be one of the most important of all.

The preceding three sections have discussed important diagnostic, methodological, and role/gender issues to be taken into consideration in treatment of depressed women. The next four sections are a review of psychotherapy, phototherapy, pharmacotherapy, and psychotherapy/pharmacotherapy combination approaches to the treatment of depression in women.

Psychotherapy

Many of the treatment approaches examined in the research literature involve highly structured therapies with predictable programs, manuals, and homework. Rehm (1989) reviewed four approaches: behavioral/activity-targeted programs, social skills programs, cognitive therapy, and self-management therapy. All four approaches were more effective than no treatment or placebos. No basic differences in outcome effectiveness were found among the four treatments. These findings confirmed the earlier results of Zeiss et al. (1979); deRubis, Hollon, Evans, and Bemis (1982); and the National Institute of Mental Health Collaborative Study of Treatment of Depression (Elkin et al., 1989).

Rehm (1989) found the absence of differences in outcome effectiveness of different therapies to be puzzling. However, the programs share strategies that appear highly effective in treating depression. They share a clear rationale and developed theory that provide depressed women with alternatives to feeling hopeless, overwhelmed, and inadequate; they include support and instillation of hope, the curative factors used in most therapies (Frank, 1974); and they provide an opportunity for an increase in morale, self-efficacy and self-regard (Zeiss et al., 1979). Rehm, therefore, suggested that larger numbers of depressed women may need to be studied before differences in specific treatment approaches can be detected. Of greatest significance is that programs seem to work because they are built around action, skill development, and progress about feedback.

Action and mastery approaches may be particularly needed by depressed women. Blechman (1981, 1985) made a convincing case for competence as one antidote to depression in some women. She pointed out that women are usually not taught as broad a range of problem-solving and coping skills as are men because women are socialized into more passive, dependent roles. She described three aspects of competence training (job skills, social skills, and family skills) that have been successful for a variety of depressed women, including those from the inner city.

Nolen-Hoeksema (1990) also stressed the importance of action and competence for women. She found that women are more likely than men to ruminate when depressed. Women think about why they are depressed and worry about the effects of their depression on others. Men are more likely than women to distract themselves when depressed, usually through engagement in some kind of activity (e.g., physical work or a sport). Because activity and distraction seem particularly important in reducing depression, structured therapy programs built around taking action, changing negative cognitions, and reducing social isolation seem particularly relevant for women. In keeping with the value of activity for depressed women, exercise, running, and weight lifting also have been found to improve self-concept in clinically depressed women (Ossip-Klein et al., 1989).

Existing outcome research does not yet answer the question of whether there is an optimal treatment for depressed women. However, clinical theory and practice offer a number of promising directions. It has already been suggested that cognitive–behavioral therapy (CBT), social skills training, and self-management programs may be effective for depressed women because of their focus on action, mastery, and distraction from depressed rumination. In addition, interpersonal therapy (IPT) may be especially helpful for women because it focuses on issues currently viewed as central to the psychology of women, that is, that relationships are core to a woman's being, meaning, and self-esteem (Gilligan, 1981; Miller, 1986). In addition, self-in-relation (SIR) theory (Surrey, 1987) says social intimacy is the profound organizer of female experience.

Women develop by experiencing their selves in relationships and gaining mutual understanding with others. Therefore, for women, perhaps more than for men, social isolation, relationship loss, and dysfunctional family relationships may precipitate, contribute to, and/or prolong depression.

Table 4 provides an outline and overview of current treatment approaches to depression in women. Five of those approaches are discussed in greater detail: IPT, CBT, behavior therapy, psychodynamic therapy, and feminist therapy.

Interpersonal Therapy

Interpersonal psychotherapy is a brief treatment designed to reduce symptoms and improve social functioning in depressed patients (Rounsaville et al., 1985). This short-term therapy focuses on current interpersonal problems that are secondary to unresolved grief, role transitions, role disputes, and social skill deficits.

Treatment. Interpersonal therapy is usually conducted over no more than 15 sessions. The clinician uses the first several sessions to assess current problems and arrive at mutually agreed upon goals of treatment with the client. The therapy, although intense and using the relationship between client and therapist as a variable, differs from other short-term dynamic psychotherapies. There is no analysis of transference, and no attention is paid to early life factors that might have been a precursor to the current depressed state of the client. Rather, the focus is on relationships in the "here and now" and on facilitating the client to develop more effective ways of relating. Sometimes IPT is used in conjunction with a regimen of antidepressant medication, because the goal of this approach is symptomatic relief, not insight into problems per se.

Weissman and her colleagues conducted a 16-week trial comparing four alternative treatment conditions: IPT, amitriptyline, combined IPT and amitriptyline, and a nonscheduled control treatment (Weissman et al., 1979, 1981). After 4 months of treatment, combined IPT and amitriptyline were found to be more efficacious than either treatment alone. Amitriptyline and IPT were about equal in effect and both were more effective than nonscheduled treatment. At 1-year follow-up there were no differential long-term effects on clinical symptoms among the treatments on clinical symptoms. Interpersonal therapy, with or without pharmacotherapy, had a positive impact on social functioning. Patients who participated in IPT were rated more positively in their social and leisure activities and parental and family member functioning than were patients in the other treatment groups.

Results from the National Institute of Mental Health Collaborative Study of the Treatment of Depression (Elkin et al., 1989) indicated that 57–69% of patients who completed a 16-week course of IPT were symptom free. Treatment effectiveness of IPT did not differ from results obtained with imipramine therapy or CBT. Unfortunately, the relative effectiveness of IPT for women versus men has not been studied systematically.

Proponents of the SIR theory argue that IPT might be a particularly effective approach to treatment with depressed women. The SIR model suggests that for women, the concept of self is not that of a completely individuated, boundaried phenomenon. Rather, women's self-awareness and self-concept are clearly connected to their emo-

Table 4
Overview of Treatment Approaches to Depression in Women

Modality	Definition	Treatment and outcome literature
Behavioral therapy	A form of psychotherapy that focuses on modifying faulty behavior rather than basic changes in the personality. Instead of probing the unconscious or exploring the patient's thoughts and feelings, behavior therapists seek to eliminate symptoms and to modify ineffective or maladaptive patterns by applying basic learning techniques and other methods.	Treatment: Hayman & Cope (1980) Outcome: Hayman & Cope (1980); La Pointe & Rimm (1980); Wolfe & Fodor (1977)
Assertiveness training	Teaches women to behave more assertively in communicating their needs and feelings. Brief treatment.	
Relaxation training	Teaches techniques to help clients learn to relax, including biofeedback and guided imagery. Brief treatment.	Treatment: Hoberman & Lewinsohn (1985) Outcome: McLean & Hakstian (1979)
Self-control therapy	Encourages depressed clients to attend to positive events, to set realistic self-expectations, to increase self-reinforcement and decrease self-punishment. Brief treatment.	Treatment: Fuchs & Rehm (1977) Outcome: Rehm, Fuchs, Roth, Kornblith, & Romano (1979); Roth, Bielski, Jones, Parker, & Osborne (1982)
Social skills training	Teaches clients communication and social interaction skills. Brief treatment.	Treatment: Bellack, Hersen, & Himmelhoch (1981); Hersen, Bellack, Himmelhoch, & Thase (1984) Outcome: Hersen, Bellack, Himmelhoch, & Thase (1984)
Cognitive therapy	A psychotherapeutic approach based on the concept that emotional problems are the result of faulty ways of thinking and distorted attitudes toward oneself and others. The therapist takes the role of an active guide who helps the patient correct and revise her perceptions and attitudes by citing	Treatment: Beck & Greenberg (1974b); Beck, Rush, Shaw & Emery (1979); Sacco & Beck (1985) Outcome: Comas-Dias (1981); La Pointe & Rimm (1980); Kovacs, Rush, Beck, & Hollon (1981); Teasdale & Fennell (1982)

Treatment	Description	References
	evidence to the contrary or eliciting it from the patient herself. The therapist uses cognitive and behavioral techniques to correct distortions of thinking associated with depression, that is, pessimism about oneself, the world, and the future. Brief treatment.	
Interpersonal psychotherapy	A form of psychotherapy in which the therapist seeks to help the patient to identify and better understand her interpersonal problems and conflicts and to develop more adaptive ways of relating to others. The therapist focuses on client's current interpersonal relationships. Helps clients learn more effective ways of relating to others and coping with conflicts in relationships. Brief, focused treatment.	Treatment: Klerman, Weissman, Rounsaville, & Chevron (1984) Outcome: Klerman & Weissman (1987); Weissman et al., (1979); Weissman, Klerman, Prusoff, Sholomskas, & Padian (1981)
Psychodynamic psychotherapy	Any form or technique of psychotherapy that focuses on the underlying, often unconscious factors (drives and experiences) that determine behavior and adjustment.	
Long-term analytic treatment	Focuses on unresolved internal conflicts, often originating in childhood family relationships as the basis for self-esteem deficits, repetitive unsatisfying relationships, and depressed mood; open-ended, often lengthy. No specific treatment protocol for depression.	Treatment: Bemporad (1985); Kaplan & Yasinsky (1980) Outcome: Research confirming the efficacy of long-term psychoanalytic treatment with depressed women is not available.
Brief dynamic psychotherapy	Focuses on a single theme, frequently unresolved conflict. Therapist actively guides insight work into the origins of the conflict in childhood, repetitions in current relationships, as well as the transference relationships. Time-limited therapy.	Treatment: Rosenberg (1985); Strupp (1982) Outcome: Hersen, Bellack, Himmelhoch, & Thase (1984); Horowitz, Marmar, Weiss, DeWitt, & Rosenbaum (1984); McLean & Hakstian (1979)

Table 4
(continued)

Modality	Definition	Treatment and outcome literature
Feminist therapy	A form of psychotherapy that views symptoms as a reaction to cultural oppression rather than simply as an intrapsychic phenomenon. It focuses on empowerment of the clients. Clients are helped to understand that depression stems, in part, from the cultural role of women in society. Typically open ended.	Treatment: Brody (1984); Gilbert (1980) Outcome: Johnson (1976); Mareeek, Kravetz, & Finn (1979)
Marital and family therapy	Treatment of marital partners or parents and children. Wide range of treatment strategies, including insight-oriented and systems-oriented therapy, communication skills training, and reinforcement strategies. May be time limited or open ended.	Treatment: Gurman & Klein (1980); Haas, Clarkin, & Glick (1985); Lerner (1987) Outcome: Friedman (1975); Gurman & Kniskern (1978); Gurman & Kniskern, (1981)
Group therapy	Psychotherapy in a group setting. Typically led by a trained therapist. May be interpersonally oriented, behaviorally oriented, or insight oriented. Provides cohesiveness and support, sharing of feelings and experiences, feedback about interpersonal skills, and problem solving.	Treatment: Brody (1987); Yalom (1975) Outcome: Covi, Lipman, Derogatis, Smith, & Patterson (1974); Jarvik, Mintz, Steuer, & Garner (1982)
Support	Women's peer self-help and consciousness-raising groups. Women provide support for each other in a setting that encourages sharing feelings and innovative problem solving. May be leader led or leaderless. Typically open ended.	Treatment: Kirsh (1974); Kravetz (1976) Outcome: Barrett (1978); Follingstad, Robinson, & Pugh (1977)
Pharmacotherapy	The use of pharmacological agents in the treatment of mental disorders in conjunction with psychotherapy.	Treatment: Noll, Davis, & DeLeon-Jones (1985) Outcome: Friedman (1975); Hersen, Bellack, Himmelhoch, & Thase (1984); Hollister (1978); Klerman, DiMascio,

Treatment	Description	References
		Weissman, Prusoff, & Paykel (1974); Murphy, Simons, Wetzel, & Lustman (1984); Weissman et al. (1979); Wilson (1982)
Electroconvulsive treatment	A painless form of electric therapy. The patient is prepared by administration of barbiturate anesthesia and injection of a chemical relaxant. An electric current is then applied for a fraction of a second through electrodes placed on the temples, which immediately produces a two-stage seizure (tonic and clonic). The usual treatment is bilateral, but unilateral stimulation of a nondominant hemisphere has been introduced in order to shorten the period of memory loss that follows the treatment.	Treatment: Noll et al. (1985) Outcome: Paul et al. (1981); Scovern & Kilman (1980)
Aerobic exercise	Daily involvement in any exercise that elevates the heartbeat.	Treatment: Doyne, Chambless, & Beutler (1983) Outcome: Folkins & Sime (1981)
Phototherapy	A form of treatment that consists of exposure to bright artificial light of higher intensity than is usually present in the home or workplace.	Treatment: Rosenthal et al. (1984) Outcome: Jacobsen & Rosenthal (1985)
Interventions for premenstrual syndrome	A variety of treatments have been used. See Harrison (1985) for description.	Treatment: Clare (1979); Davis (1985); Harrison (1985) Outcome: Harrison (1985)

tional and interpersonal relationships. Female development leads to ego boundaries that are fluid and permeable, with a heightened capacity for empathy and sense of self characterized by a certain amount of projective identification (e.g., experiencing as one's own the affects of another with whom one is empathetically relating).

The SIR model has been proposed as an example of a healthy alternative perspective on personality development that deemphasizes the importance of separation and individuation for normal development, and reconceptualizes normal development as the capacity for empathic relationships that grows more complex and richer over time (see also Gilligan, 1982).

Depressed women and men tend to withdraw from interpersonal relationships as a result of distress, lowered self-esteem, and/or loss of interest in the external world. Often, depressed people are also unpleasant to be around over long periods of time because they provide little in the way of interactive rewards for those around them. For example, depressed women maintain less eye contact than nondepressed women. They speak less, more softly, and monotonously, and take longer to respond. Their behavior is self-focused and negative, and they communicate a helplessness that suggests the other person just is not doing enough. The depressed woman's demands for support may gradually become aversive to others who become increasingly annoyed and frustrated with her. The depressed woman becomes aware of the negative reaction, feels worse, and becomes more needy. At the extreme, people withdraw completely or the depressed woman is withdrawn from the environment and hospitalized (Coyne, 1976).

For depressed women, such relational dysfunction may have a particularly negative impact. If relational capacities in women are linked to women's core sense of self, then impaired relational abilities will have a profoundly negative effect on how a woman sees and values herself. Women are often assigned the role of emotional caretakers who do the emotional and relational work of marriage or parenthood (Bernard, 1971; Blumstein & Schwartz, 1983). Thus, women may be more likely to be responded to in a hostile or punitive manner by family and friends when they become depressed and cease to fulfill this nurturing role.

Because of the special relevance of relationships and relational functioning to women, IPT may be an especially useful strategy for treatment of depression in women. IPT offers specific and symptom-focused relief for relational dysfunctions in the life of the depressed person. It would be likely that for depressed women, the ability to regain good quality relational functioning would be a particularly important aspect of empowerment and recovery from depression, and of more importance to the depressed women than the remission of other symptoms of depression. By focusing on the improvement of regeneration of damaged interpersonal skills, IPT may be especially effective for women because it empowers them to use a potential repertoire of relational talents that have been developed from birth.

There are several problems with IPT. It does not offer the client a critical examination of the social context in which he or she functions. IPT does not question the appropriateness of the relational demands placed on a client; rather, the focus is on improving the client's ability to respond to these demands. Such a value-neutral perspective on treatment, although utilitarian in ameliorating a depressed woman's symptoms, does not call into question whether aspects of the roles assigned to the woman in her particular cultural matrix are potential risks for the recurrence of depression. An examination of the relation between societal expectations and women's depression may be an important adjunct to IPT.

Another concern raised by some clinicians is that symptomatic relief may appear in 16 weeks but seeing differential effects of IPT on patients' social skills may take as long as 6 months to a year, so treatment may not be quite as short-term as originally reported or expected.

A third problem with IPT is that training is not readily available in clinical training programs in training workshops. IPT has been used more as a research tool at this point than as a known treatment strategy for depression. Clinicians of all disciplines may need to be aware of the utility of IPT and how to practice it if they are treating depressed women.

Cognitive–Behavioral Therapy

Cognitive–behavioral therapy (CBT) is a short-term, structured, psychoeducational approach to the treatment of depression (Beck, Rush, Shaw, & Emery, 1979). The therapy is based on the assumption that emotions and behavior are determined to a great extent by the way the individual views the world. Depression is thus viewed as essentially a thinking disorder (Beck, 1967). Cognitive techniques are used to correct the distorted thinking that characterizes depression, including negative, pessimistic views about the self, the world, and the future.

Kovacs, Rush, Beck, and Hollon (1981) reported greater symptomatic improvement for patients treated with cognitive therapy than imipramine hydrochloride at the end of 3 months of treatment and at a 1-year follow-up. In contrast, Murphy (1984) and his colleagues treated 70 depressed patients with CBT, nortriptyline hydrochloride, or a combination of the two for 12 weeks. Significant improvement was noted at the end of treatment and at 1-month follow-up, but therapeutic gains did not differ as a function of treatment modality.

Paykel (1989) noted that his review of published studies on the treatment of depression suggests that CBT may cut down the rate of depression relapse. On follow-up for 6–24 months, relapse rates were much lower in the CBT group (12–25%) than in those who received tricyclic antidepressants (TCAs) (66–78%). Follow-up studies (e.g., Kovacs et al., 1981) failed to find this benefit for relapse rates.

Treatment. The depressed woman, according to CBT theory, typically assumes excessive responsibility for negative events in her life. She also underestimates the power she has to influence those events (Beck & Greenberg, 1974a). Thus, the depressed woman overestimates her responsibility in a relationship and at the same time underestimates her ability to affect important outcomes.

The relation between distorted negative thoughts and depression in women is compounded because of cultural distortions ("You're no one unless you're loved") and gender role stereotypes (Steinmann, 1974). Many of the symptoms of depression, such as apathy, increased insecurity, and dependency, are stereotypical characteristics of the female gender.

The CBT approach is geared to helping the woman regain a sense of power and mastery over her own life by learning to control her cognitions (Emery, 1982). An active and direct approach is used throughout therapy in the context of a collaborative relationship between the therapist and the depressed woman (Beck & Emery, 1985). The three questions a therapist frequently asks clients about their interpretations of events are What's the evidence that the thought is true? What's another way of looking at it? Even if it is true, how bad are the consequences?

To gain a sense of power, the woman learns to cognitively and behaviorally master her symptoms (Emery, 1988). Simply presenting depression as a problem of faulty thinking (Burns, 1980) can provide relief to the depressed woman. The therapist helps the depressed woman increase her sense of power by showing her how to minimize unpleasant activities. She learns how to avoid aversive situations, how to plan and organize her time, and how to be more assertive with unreasonable requests. To gain greater self-mastery, the woman is encouraged to schedule activities and break tasks into small, manageable steps. Women start to see the symptoms of depression as problems to master and transcend, not as permanent character traits or personality flaws.

The first cluster of symptoms targeted for treatment is emotional. The woman learns (a) that her negative feelings have no life of their own, (b) that her negative feelings (sadness, loneliness, guilt, and anxiety) are caused by her own thinking and she has the innate ability to think differently, and (c) that alternatives to her negative distorted thoughts can be developed by questioning their validity.

As the symptoms of depression abate, the therapist targets the dysfunctional beliefs that lead to depression in the first place. Three themes helpful to working with depressed women are the issues of responsibility, acceptance, and choice. The depressed woman tends to hold others responsible for her feelings and to feel responsible for others (Bepko & Krestan, 1985). Once women stop holding others responsible for how they are feeling, they usually find that intimacy with others increases. Cognitive and behavioral techniques are often used concurrently. Behavioral techniques are described in greater detail in the next section.

The second cluster of symptoms targeted for treatment is behavioral (withdrawal, nonassertiveness, and lack of pleasurable activities). The aim is to help the woman become more active and powerful in her everyday life. In addition to pointing out the advantage of becoming more active, the therapist sets up behavioral experiments. In this procedure the woman's negative predictions about tasks to be performed are elicited ("It's too hard," "I don't think I can do it," and "I won't enjoy it"). The therapist has the woman conduct experiments (by doing the tasks) to see if her thoughts are true or not.

Behavioral Therapy

Behavioral therapy treatments of depression encompass a broad spectrum of strategies and techniques derived from behavioral principles. In general, Hoberman and Lewinsohn (1985) viewed depression as the consequence of a low rate of response-contingent positive reinforcement. Deficiencies in social skills and a lack of satisfaction in activities are seen as antecedents to the low rate of positive reinforcement obtained by depressed women and men. Alternatively, McLean and Hakstian (1979) viewed depression as the result of ineffective coping techniques in attempting to remedy life problems. Some of the behavioral treatments for depression include training in social skills, assertiveness, and relaxation, and increasing pleasant activities in one's life. Behavioral techniques are often used in combination with cognitive interventions, such as decreasing negative thoughts. These interventions may be used singly or in combination, as in Lewinsohn's "Coping with Depression" course, which combines all of the aforementioned interventions (Steinmetz et al., 1983). The Social Skills Training Treatment for Depression (Becker, Helmberg, & Bellack, 1987) assesses the client's range of social skills and offers direct behavioral training, self-evaluation, and self-reinforcement strategies.

In one of the few studies to examine the differential treatment response of depressed men and women, Wilson (1982) compared three therapies (increasing positive activities, relaxation training, and minimal contact) in combination with either amitriptyline or placebo medication. Her sample included 42 women and 22 men. After 2 months of treatment, marked improvement was observed on measures of depression and anxiety. Improvement was independent of type of treatment. Significantly greater improvement was noted at midtreatment for amitriptyline and behavioral therapies. However, by the end of treatment and at a 6-month follow-up period, treatments were not differentially effective. Improvement also was noted for patients receiving minimal contact (two 1-hr therapy sessions) plus placebo. The treatment responses for female and male depressed patients were comparable.

Studies have also evaluated the effects of assertiveness training for depression in women. In a study of 26 moderately depressed women, Hayman and Cope (1980) compared assertiveness training to a delayed treatment control. Women receiving active treatment were more assertive and engaged in significantly more activities than did controls. However, women in both the assertiveness training and delayed treatment groups reported a significant decrease in depression. Levels of depression for women in active treatment continued to decline at 2-month follow-up. The results of these two studies by Hayman and Cope (1980) and Wilson (1982) suggested that levels of depression may improve substantially while women are waiting for treatment or receiving minimal treatment.

In another study comparing the efficacy of four treatments, McLean and Hakstian (1979) developed a unique hierarchy of treatment goals for each patient in their behavioral intervention. Using graduated practice and modeling techniques, therapists focused on goal attainment with respect to communication, social interaction, assertiveness, problem solving, and other skills. The authors compared a 10-week course of behavioral treatment with amitriptyline, insight-oriented psychotherapy, and relaxation training. Seventy-two percent of the 178 patients were women. Results showed behavioral therapy to be superior to the other interventions at the end of treatment and marginally superior at the 3-month follow-up.

Cognitive and behavioral therapies may be particularly important for depressed women because they teach women to confront and overcome the passive, dependent role they may have been taught since childhood and that may be feeding their depressions.

Psychodynamic Therapy

The psychotherapies examined most frequently in research on depression include the already described IPT, CBT, and behavioral psychotherapies. They are highly structured and easy to replicate, and consequently are most frequently chosen for research studies. It is important to note, however, that in the United States, the most common forms of therapies derive from psychodynamic theories (Klerman, 1987) and are therefore widely applied to depressed patients within clinical practice. As noted previously, IPT is a nontraditional form of dynamic psychotherapy that was specifically developed to treat depression within a short time period.

Although psychodynamic psychotherapy tends to be open ended or more long term than IPT, CBT, and behavioral therapy, other brief forms of psychotherapy have been developed (Mann, 1973; Strupp & Binder, 1984) and codified into treatment manuals (e.g., supportive and expressive treatment; Luborsky, 1984). Unfortunately although the psychodynamic therapies could be applicable to some forms of depression, there are few controlled studies of the model's efficacy in treating depression and such studies need to be conducted and reported (Klerman, 1987). Because of the scarcity of research, this report does not focus on traditional psychodynamically oriented psychotherapies.

Feminist Therapy

Over the past two decades, practitioners from many different theoretical perspectives have proposed the use of a feminist perspective in treatment (Dutton-Douglas & Walker, 1989). Feminist therapy is usually seen as a philosophy of psychotherapy rather than as a prescription of technique (Brown, 1984). Consequently, a feminist therapy perspective can be interwoven into most approaches to treatment, including CBT (Fodor, 1989), psychodynamic therapy (Eichenbaum & Orbach, 1983), and family therapy (Bograd, 1989; Luepnitz, 1988).

A feminist philosophy of treatment believes that certain principles should guide the therapist both in diagnosis of the problem and in decisions regarding treatment. First, women's experiences in a given culture are seen as socially constructed and devalued as a result of pervasive sexism that affects women's lives in both subtle and overt ways. Consequently, any understanding of women must take this sociocultural matrix into account. Women are perceived as an oppressed class, with some women (e.g., women of color, lesbians, women with disabilities, poor women, older women, and immigrant women) experiencing greater oppression because of their membership in other devalued nondominant groups.

Second, feminist therapists believe in the importance of attending to power relationships in therapy (Feminist Therapy Institute, 1987). An emphasis is placed on developing strategies for treatment that will lead to a more egalitarian relationship. These include a consumer orientation to psychotherapy in which the client is empowered to ask questions and challenge interventions made by the therapist (Brown, 1982), is on a first-name basis with the therapist, and is viewed as possessing important expert information about her own problems and solutions.

These perspectives can be used by therapists in many contexts. Because the feminist politic of feminist therapy is expressed in its approach to the analysis of presenting problems and the process of psychotherapy, rather than as overtly political behavior as generally understood, recipients of feminist therapy can benefit from it whether they hold feminist values or not. It works as well with men (Ganley, 1989) as with women (Rosewater, 1989).

Feminist therapy perspectives, when interwoven with specific treatments for depression, may make those treatments especially efficacious for women. Because feminist therapists raise questions for themselves and their clients about the gender-specific nature of their problems, and because there is an emphasis on empowering clients, thus increasing their instrumentality and sense of self-worth, depressed women may benefit more from the addition of a feminist therapy perspective to CBT or ITP than if either of these treatments occurs without this analysis. Fodor (1989) specifically described how feminist analysis strengthens CBT. A feminist therapy perspective, addressing as it does the social and cultural aspects of distress as well as the intrapsychic ones (Lerman, 1987), can also be of particular use for depressed women who are in multiply disenfranchised groups such as lesbians (Brown, 1989), divorced or single mothers (Rawlings & Graham, 1989), women of color (Mays & Comas-Diaz, 1989), and older women (Midiarsky, 1989). Luepnitz (1988) demonstrated how a feminist perspective also can enhance family therapy for depressed women.

Phototherapy

Phototherapy is used to treat individuals who have seasonal affective disorder (SAD). Seasonal affective disorder is a cyclic illness characterized by recurrent episodes of depression in fall/winter alternating with periods of euthymia (normal mood) or hypomania (mild elation and behavioral activation) in spring/summer (Rosenthal, Sack, Gillin, et al., 1984). It is four times more common in women than in men, yet health and mental health practitioners often overlook this possibility in diagnosing women's depression. Seasonal affective disorder usually begins when a woman is in her 20s or 30s. The *DSM-III-R* (American Psychiatric Association, 1987) diagnostic criteria for major depression with a seasonal pattern are

1. a regular temporal relation between the onset of an episode of bipolar disorder or recurrent major depression and a particular 60-day period of the year (e.g., regular appearance of depression between the beginning of October and the end of November);
2. full remissions (or a change from depression to mania or hypomania) also occurring within a particular 60-day period (e.g., depression disappear from mid-February to mid-April);
3. at least three episodes of temporal seasonal mood disturbance in 3 separate years, with at least 2 of the years being consecutive; and
4. seasonal episodes of mood disturbance outnumber any nonseasonal episodes by more than three to one. (p. 224)

In addition, many SAD patients report daytime drowsiness and carbohydrate cravings (Jacobsen et al., 1987).

Proper diagnosis is critical, and misdiagnosis can be quite problematic because 88% of SAD patients report disability at work and 94% have problems in their relationships. Daytime sleepiness associated with SAD also is related to multiple work accidents (Lavie, Kremerman, & Wiel, 1982), so proper diagnosis and treatment of SAD also have public health implications.

As previously reported, depression affects biological functioning in a number of areas for women. Jacobsen et al. (1987) found that many women with SAD show an increase in premenstrual symptoms in the winter.

The treatment of choice for SAD is phototherapy, in which patients are exposed to very bright light two times a day. Such treatment is nonintrusive, inexpensive, and effective. Either fluorescent light or incandescent light can be used. In one study using phototherapy, depression in SAD patients was lifted in 3 days; however, when treatment was discontinued, the depression returned 3 days later (Lobel & Hirschfeld, 1985). A number of other studies have confirmed that phototherapy is very effective in treating SAD patients (James, Wehr, Sack, Parry, & Rosenthal, 1985; Rosenthal, Sack, James, et al., 1984).

Pharmacotherapy

Major advances have been made in the pharmacological treatment of major depressive disorders during the last decade. Both traditional antidepressants (TCAs and mono-amine oxidase inhibitors [MAOIs]) and the newer so-called second-generation anti-depressants have been reported to be effective treatments for patients with major depressive disorder, particularly those with endogenous depression. It has been esti-mated that 60–65% of depressed patients show a definitive improvement with phar-macological treatment (Sacco & Beck, 1985). Specific gender differences are examined in the next section, but the data suggest that these pharmacological treatments are, at least partially effective for women, especially those with major depressive disorders.

Tricyclic Antidepressants

TCAs, named for their three-ring chemical structure, remained the treatment of first choice for patients with endogenous depression (manifested by a cluster of the more biological symptoms such as sleep disturbance and weight loss) (Schatzberg & Cole, 1986) until 1987. Between 1987 and 1990, fluoxetine became the leading choice of antidepressants for most forms of depression (McGrath, 1990). Approximately 60–95% of depressed patients reported in the literature show a therapeutic response to TCA treatment (Noll, Davis, & De Leon-Jones, 1985). There are currently seven TCAs on the U.S. market: amitriptyline, desipramine, doxepin, imipramine, nortriptyline, pro-triptyline, and trimipramine. All the TCAs have anticholinergic side effects, including dry mouth, constipation, urinary hesitancy, blurred vision, and confusion (Schatzberg & Cole, 1986). Some TCAs, however, are more sedating (particularly amitriptyline), whereas others are usually more activating (desipramine and protriptyline) (Noll et al., 1985). Elderly patients have greater difficulty tolerating anticholinergic side effects. Trimipramine (Surmontil) appears to be particularly useful in the treatment of this population because of its relatively low side effect profile.

Dosage is a critical issue in the use of the TCAs. Too low a dosage can lead to drug ineffectiveness, but too high a dosage can result in toxicity or even fatality (Noll et al., 1985). Increasingly, TCA plasma levels are being obtained in order to monitor compliance, improve clinical response, and avoid drug toxicity (Preskorn, 1989). Blood levels are more useful for some TCAs, for example, nortriptyline, which has a well-defined "therapeutic window," than for others, such as fluoxetine, which has no defined therapeutic levels. Tricyclic antidepressant blood levels are most useful when obtained in patients with endogenous depression because there is little or no relation between TCA level and clinical response in patients with nonendogenous depression or dysthymia (Schatzberg & Cole, 1986).

Monoamine Oxidase Inhibitors

The MAOIs (isocarboxazid, pargyline, pheneizine, and tranylcypromine) are indicated for depression that is refractory to treatment with TCAs. The MAOIs are clearly effective in patients with panic attacks or with anxious or atypical depressions (Schatzberg & Cole, 1986). There has been debate regarding the effectiveness of the MAOIs in the treatment of patients with endogenous depression. Treatment of these patients with the MAOIs may require higher dosages than was previously thought necessary (Schatzberg & Cole, 1986). Both phenelzine and tranylcypromine, however, have been reported to be effective in the treatment of endogenous depression (Noll et al., 1985).

For many years the MAOIs were rarely prescribed because of the potentially dangerous side effects. The MAOIs are known to interact with foods rich in the amino acid tyramine and with cold remedies. These interactions can potentially result in "hypertensive crises with violent headaches, occasional cerebrovascular headaches or hyperpyrexic states leading to coma" (Schatzberg & Cole, 1986). The most common side effect, however, is dizziness, particularly of the orthostatic hypotensive type. Other reported side effects are sedation, dry mouth, and occasionally other anticholinergic effects. In women in particular decreased sexual drive and anorgasmia accompanied by increased appetite and weight gain have been observed (Noll et al., 1985).

Newer Antidepressants

Several of the newer antidepressants have developed out of the increased interest in the role of serotonin in the pathophysiology of depressive disorders. Fluoxetine (Prozac), a drug released on the U.S. market in January 1987, has been found to be more effective than placebo and comparable in efficacy to the TCAs amitriptyline, doxepin, and imipramine (Schatzberg et al., 1987). Table 5 presents a comparison of the major antidepressants.

The side effect profile of fluoxetine is generally more favorable than that of the TCAs. It produces fewer anticholinergic side effects such as dry mouth, dizziness, and blurred vision. The major side effects of fluoxetine are nausea, tremor, drowsiness, sweating, headache, insomnia, and nervousness. A significant advantage of fluoxetine is that unlike most TCAs, it appears to facilitate weight loss of a few pounds rather than promote weight gain. It also appears to be relatively safe in overdosages (Schatzberg & Cole, 1986).

These advantages have made fluoxetine the most widely prescribed antidepressant in the United States, a mere 3 years after its public introduction in 1987. More than six million prescriptions for fluoxetine were written in 1989, twice as many as the next

Table 5
Drugs That Fight Depression

	Prozac	Tricyclic Antidepressants	Inhibitors
Action	Seems to block reabsorption of serotonin, a neurotransmitter that carries signals in the brain, prolonging its effect.	Primarily block re-absorption of norepinephrine, the neurotransmitter. May also affect serotonin.	Inhibit an enzyme, monoamine oxidase, that breaks down various neurotransmitters.
Generic names and proprietary names	Fluoxetine (Prozac)	Amitriptyline (Elavil, Endep); nortriptyline (Aventyl, Pamelor); protriptyline (Vivactil); desipramine (Norpramin, Pertrofran); doxepin (Adapin, Sinequan); imipramine (Tofranil, Imavate)	Tranylcypromine (Parnate); phenelzine (Nardil)
Cost	Up to $2 a pill; a month's supply might be about $70.	Some older generic drugs cost less than $10 a month but some proprietary forms can be almost as expensive as Prozac.	About one-eighth to one-tenth as much as Prozac.
Major side effects	Comparatively less likely to cause side effects, but in a minority of cases may trigger agitation, mania and, rarely, a preoccupation with suicide.	Can include dry mouth, constipation, urinary difficulties, individual drugs may have others, like weight gain, dizzy spells or sedation.	Can include sudden rises in blood pressure if cheeses, wines and certain other foods are eaten, and dizzy spells. Nardil can also cause sedation, weight gain and insomnia.

Note. From *Drug Topics Red Book* (1990, March 19). Copyright 1990 by Medical Economics Company. Reprinted by permission.

most popular antidepressant, nortriptyline. Early research and current clinical practice suggest fluoxetine may also be helpful in treatment bulimia, obsessive–compulsive disorders, and depressions unresponsive to other antidepressants. The problems with fluoxetine, however, are becoming more apparent. Rather than just tremors and a caffeinelike high, a minority of patients (approximately 15%) suffer from intense agitation, even mania; more negative effect; and apparently medically induced suicidal thoughts and obsessions (Angier, 1990; McGrath, 1990). More reports are surfacing of greatly increased suicide risk for some patients on fluoxetine, and there are reports of tardive dyskinesia resulting in permanent neurological damage (Citizens' Commission on Human Rights, 1990). The Citizens' Commission on Human Rights (1990) reported that in the last 2 years, the Food and Drug Administration has received more than two times the number of complaints regarding severe side effects from fluoxetine than it has in 20 years for Elavil, the other popular antidepressant. Fluoxetine seems helpful for the majority of patients but seems to have severe side effects for a significant minority.

Because fluoxetine is a serotonin reuptake inhibitor, it may be prolonging the effect of serotonin in some patients and creating more violence and aggression when it becomes too unbalanced. Clinicians need to be aware of these problems with fluoxetine because this drug will be prescribed for many depressed women, often by a physician other than a psychiatrist. Other important considerations include the following: (a) Fluoxetine is several times more expensive (about $1.50–$2.00 per pill) than the older generic antidepressants, which is a real problem for many women with limited economic resources, and (b) unprecedented media attention has been given to fluoxetine as a kind of "happy pill for the 1990s," (Eli Lilly, the manufacturer of fluoxetine, has staged one of the strongest and most effective marketing campaigns ever launched for an antidepressant). Women may be more vulnerable to its claims because they are more frequently prescribed antidepressants.

Trazodone (Desyrel) has been available on the U.S. market and widely prescribed since 1982 (Rudorfer & Potter, 1989). Trazodone appears to be most effective in outpatients with mild to moderate depression and anxiety, particularly those with difficulty falling asleep. In clinical trials it has been found to be comparable in efficacy to the TCAs and more effective than placebo. The efficacy of trazodone may be reduced if too high a dosage is prescribed or if the dosage is increased too quickly (Schatzberg et al., 1987).

Trazodone can be quite sedating, and when taken on an empty stomach can produce acute dizziness and fainting. The drug is not anticholinergic, however, and thus does not share many of the side effects of the TCAs.

Two of the newer drugs, amoxapine (Asendin) and maprotiline (Ludiomil), have biochemical effects similar to those of the TCAs but differ in that they have four-ringed structure. Amoxapine is known for its rapid onset of response, sometimes working within 4–7 days (Rudorfer & Potter, 1989). Maprotiline has recently come to the attention of researchers because an increased incidence of seizures has been reported in patients using this drug. Prolonged treatment, rapid dose escalation, coadministration of neuroleptics, and rapid withdrawal of benzodiazepines appear to be risk factors for the occurrence of seizures (Rudorfer & Potter, 1989).

Another new drug, alprazolam (Xanax), has been approved since 1981 for use in patients with anxiety or anxiety associated with depression, and also has been studied in patients with major depressive disorder. Alprazolam is similar to diazepam but, unlike typical benzodiazepines, appears to affect noradrenergic systems. Alprazolam seems to have strong antipanic effects, but has only moderate antidepressant effects. Compared with imipramine and doxepin in mildly to moderately depressed outpatients, alprazolam appears to be reasonably effective. However, the effects in seriously endogenous patients are inconsistent. For this reason alprazolam's usefulness as a primary treatment for this population is limited.

The most common side effect of alprazolam is sedation, but generally an effective dosage can be found that is not excessively sedating. Typically, patients feel relatively free of side effects on alprazolam; however, used on a regular basis for several weeks or more, alprazolam is dependency producing or addicting. There is great debate about whether to use alprazolam, given that it is highly efficacious against panic but addictive. Some clinicians feel that for those patients whose lives are impaired by panic, phobias, and agoraphobia, the benefits of alprazolam in relieving symptoms make alprazolam worth the addictive risk. Other clinicians feel that nonaddictive alternatives (TCAs and MAOIs) should be used rather than alprazolam. Alprazolam can be used on an as-needed basis for occasional panic attacks, whereas antidepressants must be used on a regular basis.

Clonazepam is a longer acting benzodiazepine with antipanic effects similar to those of alprazolam. For patients who experience a "roller coaster" effect between alprazolam administrations, a switch to clonazepam can produce a more even effect.

Benzodiazepine withdrawal produces a number of symptoms including disrupted sleep, anxiety, irritability, and lability. Even with very gradual tapering off of the benzodiazepine, the benzodiazepine-dependent patient often will experience these symptoms for days or weeks and so must have a commitment to get off the medication and work in conjunction with the treating physician. Abrupt discontinuation is not recommended because of significant discomfort and, more important, because of the dangerous risk of seizure.

Panic and agoraphobia are more common in women, so these issues are particularly pertinent in the treatment of women. Cognitive, behavioral, and contextual treatments of panic are important and effective. These approaches used in combination with medication can help to minimize the amount of medication needed.

Several other new antidepressants are currently being studied. One that came on the market in the United States. In early 1990 is buproprion (Wellbutrin). Buproprion is a unicyclic antidepressant with a chemical structure unrelated to any other. It appears to be effective inpatients with depression, including some patients whose depression is not responsive to other classes of antidepressants. It appears not to be effective in patients with panic-related disorders. It is being marketed as having fewer side effects than other antidepressants. In fact, it is not anticholinergic and so has fewer specific side effects. However, it is "activating" and causes agitation in some patients. Nausea has been reported occasionally, and seizures have been reported rarely (Schatzberg & Cole, 1986).

In sum, it is not clear whether the new antidepressants are more effective overall than previous pharmacological agents. They do, however, offer some advantages in terms of alternative biological actions and fewer side effects overall or fewer of specific side effects for most patients. For patients who cannot tolerate or have not responded to the more traditional antidepressants, these newer medications could prove very valuable.

The development of new antidepressants raises two intriguing questions: Do these drugs work differently for women than for men? What are the ramifications of widespread use of antidepressants for depressed women? There are currently more than 30 antidepressants from which to choose and some 150 are presently in development. The current market for antidepressants is $700 million, and it will rise to $1,800 million in 1995, making antidepressants one of the strongest growth stocks in pharmaceuticals (Smith, Adkins, & Walton, 1988). Because of these kinds of economic pressures and women's greater use of prescription drugs in general and antidepressants in particular (Cafferata, Kasper, & Bernstein, 1983; Cooperstock & Sims, 1971; Fidel, 1982), depressed women may be the most vulnerable to economic exploitation by overprescribing antidepressants.

On the other hand, underprescribing antidepressants because of a lack of education among clinicians and other health professionals can be a health hazard for those who are suicidal or significantly impaired psychologically and/or organically by their depression. Misdiagnosis and improper dosages of antidepressants are real dangers for many women. Seventy percent of prescriptions are written by nonpsychiatrists, and it is estimated that 30–50% of depressions are improperly diagnosed by these physicians (Smith, et al., 1988; Zetin, Sklansky, & Cranier, 1984). Primary care physicians tend to prescribe antianxiety drugs rather than antidepressants for depression in women (Klerman, 1986; McGrath, 1988).

Attention to proper diagnosis and medication dosages and avoidance of reinforcing dependency and passivity are very important considerations for physicians treating depressed women, because drugs are prescribed for women and women use prescription drugs at rates significantly higher than men (Cafferata et al., 1983; Cooperstock & Sims, 1971; Fidel, 1982). In 1984, 64% of the 131 million prescriptions in the United States were for women. Sixty-eight percent of prescriptions for heterocyclic antidepressants and 72% of prescriptions for antidepressant tranquilizers (e.g., Triavil, a combination of Trilafon, a neuroleptic, and Elavil, a TCA) went to women. Women also have a greater number of concurrent medications compared with men (Baum, Kennedy, Knapp, Juergens, & Faich, 1988). Also, compliance is more of a problem when drugs are prescribed independently of psychotherapy. Many clients do not follow the prescription instructions and may be more likely to terminate the medication prematurely. In one study, 67% of the patients dropped out prematurely when the treatment for depression was by drug therapy alone (Weissman et al., 1979).

Therefore, it is particularly important for clinicians to work with psychiatrists over time to match particular drugs and dosages with the changing needs of their mutual female patients. As part of the partnership, clinicians also need to take an extensive drug use history (prescription and nonprescription drugs) as an intrinsic part of developing a therapy treatment plan. Many drugs have depressive side effects (i.e., antihypertensives, antiparkinsonism agents, and certain hormones), and prescription drug abuse is not uncommon among depressed women. In addition, TCAs are one of the drugs used in most completed suicide attempts (Krenzelok & Anderson, 1983).

Despite the greater prevalence of depressive symptoms and syndromes among women (Blazer et al., 1988; Wehr, Sack, Rosenthal, & Cowdry, 1988) and the fact that most prescriptions for antidepressant medication are written for women (Baum et al.,

1988), the Task Force found remarkably few studies examining the relation of gender differences to medication effects. The review process for new drugs has three phases. Female subjects of reproductive age are excluded from Phase 1 (first phase involving humans with the main purpose of determining toxicity) of the review process. They are included in Phase 2 (trial phase that addresses questions of dosage, route of administration, and evidence of Treatment × Condition interaction) and Phase 3 (final human trial phase that focuses primarily on comparison of experimental treatment with standard or traditional therapies), with certain limitations (Dannello, 1986). Studies of drugs in basic clinical settings often fail to analyze data for gender effects, or even to specify the gender composition of subjects, thereby hampering meta-analysis of gender effects. Studies of drugs involving female patient and control groups infrequently include a male control group. For all of these reasons opportunities to compare gender effects of medications are lost. This indicates a gender-related blind spot (Hamilton, 1986a). This blind spot involves the assumptions that gender differences are trivial, that studying such differences will not contribute to understanding the disease process, and that studying such differences will not help us better match the specific treatments to the unique needs of women or men. The index of a leading psychopharmacology text lists only two citations under "gender" in its more than 1,000 pages and downplays gender differences in those citations (American College of Neuropsychopharmacology, 1987).

Despite the relative neglect of gender differences as a subject of study, there are a number of ways in which gender would be expected to interact in a complicated manner with pharmacological treatment of depression. In fact empirical studies do show more adverse effects from medication in women than men (Bottinger, Furhoff, & Holmberg, 1979; Domincq, Naranjo, Ruiz, & Busto, 1980; Hurwitz, 1969). Some psychotropic medications (Greenblatt et al., 1985; Preskorn & Mas, 1985; Wilson & Roy, 1986), although not all (American College of Neuropsychopharmacology, 1987; Young, 1986), have slower metabolism and longer clearance times in women. Age, body weight and composition, and reproductive events could all influence medication effects differently for men and women.

The age effect on drug metabolism is significant for a number of drugs. Because more of the elderly are women, the effect of age on medication affects women disproportionately (Gibaldi, 1984).

In the American population substantially more obese persons are women. Adipose tissue has a complicated effect on drug metabolism, affecting particularly those drugs that are metabolized by the liver and having essentially no effect on medications without hepatic metabolism (Gibaldi, 1984).

In animals, cyclical changes in brain neurotransmitter levels over the course of the estrous cycle suggest that antidepressant medication might have differential effects during different phases of the menstrual cycle (Kendall, Stancel, & Enna, 1982).

The research also fails to adequately address the interaction between antidepressants and reproductive events unique to women including menstrual cycles, pregnancy and postpartum, and menopause. For example, remarkably few reports have addressed tailoring psychotropic medication dosage to the menstrual cycle phase, although a few reports suggest it may help to optimize pharmacological treatment of some women (Conrad & Hamilton, 1986; Jensvold, Reed, & Jarrett, in press). Lithium treatment in manic depression may be more effective if it is readjusted depending on the phase of a woman's menstrual cycle. The most common reason for lithium withdrawal is the desire to become pregnant (Goodwin & Jameson, 1990), yet physicians are often unaware that their patients plan to discontinue lithium or have already stopped because of their decisions about reproduction (K. R. Jameson, personal communication, 1990).

Women are the exclusive consumers of oral contraceptive medications, which have both psychotropic effects (causing depressive symptoms in some women who take them) and drug interaction effects (altering binding protein availability and thereby altering availability of the active forms of some medications) (Jensvold, 1989). For these reasons, oral contraceptive status must be taken into account in evaluating women with depressive symptoms.

Women are the primary consumers of other medications that also can have psychotropic effects and can complicate treatment of depression; for example, phenylpropanolamine is the active ingredient in a number of diet pills. The use of diet pills by women with depressive symptoms is a potential public health problem about which very little is known, and the effects of the substances deserve further study.

Comorbidity is an important concern in treating depression. Women have more cases of certain medical illnesses associated with depression, especially autoimmune diseases, including thyroid disease, lupus erythematosis, and Addison's disease, and more cases of certain psychiatric illnesses associated with depression, including anorexia nervosa and bulimia. Comorbidity is important for several reasons: (a) It may decrease the ability to attain therapeutic dosages of antidepressant medications (Black, Winokur, Bell, Nasrallah, & Hulbert, 1988), (b) physiological changes due to concurrent disorders may complicate treatment of depression, (c) drug interactions with concurrent medications may also complicate treatment of depression, and (d) presence of comorbid conditions may worsen, or improve, the prognosis of treatment of the depression (Black et al., 1988).

Substance abuse and depression often coexist. Substance-abusing women may have different motivations for drug use, experience different effects from the drugs, and have different prognoses than men. For example, in a study of cocaine abuse patterns (Griffin, Weiss, Mirin, & Lange, 1989), women expressed less guilt and were more likely to cite a specific reason for their cocaine use, whereas men's cocaine abuse was more likely to be part of an antisocial pattern of behavior. Cocaine-abusing women were more depressed than cocaine-abusing men and had poorer outcome following treatment of their substance abuse. Treatment of depression improved chances for successful treatment of the substance abuse, particularly in women.

This research led the Task Force to recommend strongly that it is important to study both sexes and to analyze data by gender in the study of depression. Clients must still be treated on an individualized basis, but a knowledge of gender norms and pharmacotherapy selected with these norms in mind can optimize treatment for the individual and better address the unique needs of women.

Combined Psychotherapy/Pharmacotherapy

Conte et al. (1986) reviewed 17 controlled studies published between 1974 and 1984. Results of the review indicated that for outpatients treated for unipolar depression, a drugs/psychotherapy combination was appreciably more effective than placebo conditions, but only marginally superior to psychotherapy or pharmacotherapy alone. In no case was combined treatment worse than other treatments, which suggests that use of antidepressant medication in conjunction with psychotherapy does not compromise the effectiveness of the psychotherapy. In fact, medication may help some patients use therapy by relieving disabling anxiety or depression. The patient can then concentrate available energy on understanding and solving problems (Friedman, 1975). However, Conte et al. reported that the combined condition was superior to other treatment conditions for patients with endogenous depression, but found no significant differences between conditions for situational depression.

Steinbrueck, Maxwell, and Howard (1983) used meta-analysis as developed by Smith and Glass (1977) to assess treatment effectiveness of drug therapy and psychotherapy in adults with unipolar depression. Outcome measures from 56 studies were standardized to make them comparable. The evidence suggested that psychotherapy was superior to drug therapy. The particular type of psychotherapy used did not contribute to the effect obtained, but treatments with longer durations showed greater treatment effects.

In terms of specific therapeutic approaches, several studies indicate CBT and antidepressants are more effective in tandem, but several other studies negate these findings. Overall, CBT seems equal or superior to TCAs (Rehm, 1989) for mild to moderate depressions, but TCAs may produce quicker results with the vegetative and somatic symptoms of the major depressions.

It is interesting that there are few outcome studies of persons with bipolar disorder in the psychotherapy outcome literature (Rehm, 1989). A new publication entitled *Manic Depressive Illness* by Goodwin and Jamison (1990) summarizes the existing research and treatment information for these conditions. The assumption seems to be that bipolar states are biological conditions and are effectively treated by lithium, so the impact of stress and gender role socialization as contributors to bipolar states has been ignored in both research and treatment. Although there appears to be no gender difference in overall rates of bipolar disorder, gender may play a role in the course and recovery of depression. The Task Force recommends that more outcome research on bipolar conditions also be conducted to fill in an important gap in the field.

Another important consideration with use of antidepressants is patient compliance with treatment. Whereas there are lower dropout rates for CBT, the rates of refusal and discontinuance of TCAs are quite high. As previously noted, Weissman et al. (1979) reported that 67% of patients assigned to their medication condition dropped out of treatment. Higher rates of refusal for TCAS than for psychotherapy were reported by other researchers as well (Hersen et al., 1984; Kovacs et al., 1981; Weissman et al., 1981). Furthermore, TCAs may not provide effective protection against a recurrence of depressive symptoms once they have been discontinued.

A subgroup of patients treated for depression remain chronically depressed. Chronicity is defined as the presence of continuing symptoms without a sustained symptom-free interval. Approximately 8–16% of patients remain depressed despite treatment interventions (Murphy, Woodruff, Herjanic, & Super, 1974; Weissman et al., 1976, 1981). Wilson (1982) reported that recovery was incomplete for a substantial number of patients in his study. Forty-two percent continued to be at least mildly depressed at posttreatment. Recurrence of depression was reported for 28% of the patients. Hersen et al. (1984) considered only 42% of patients to be significantly improved after a 6-month maintenance period. Hersen et al. noted that their standards for improvement were quite rigorous.

Improvement as a consequence of short-term therapy may only be transitory. Therapy may be too brief to produce enduring change or may require supplementation by booster sessions (Gonzales et al., 1985). Researchers who evaluated cognitive, behavioral, interpersonal, and pharmacological treatments revealed similar results with respect to the recurrence of depression and/or the failure of a subgroup of patients to recover fully as a consequence of treatment (Gonzales et al., 1985; Kovacs et al., 1981; Murphy et al., 1981). The research literature thus suggests that a proportion of patients (25–75%) who have been treated with brief psychotherapy or medication will experience symptoms of depression within a year and need further treatment. Short-term therapies may offer temporary symptomatic relief (Kovacs et al., 1981) but may not prevent the recurrence of depression. The challenge for the future, according to McLean and Hakstian (1979), is to develop ways to preserve clinical improvement by means of effective maintenance treatment.

Recommendations for Treatment

The Task Force identified a number of areas in which improved treatment and research on treatment outcome in depression in women are critically needed. Controlled outcome research that compares treatment results for women and men is vital to help identify treatment approaches that are beneficial to women. To be most effective, this research should include researchers and practitioners working together to identify characteristics of optimal treatments for the different depressions found in individual women. Understanding how to ameliorate the negative effects of gender roles and stereotypes is essential if optimal treatment outcomes are to be attained. The following specific recommendations are divided into diagnostic, methodological, role/gender, and treatment issues.

Diagnostic Issues

Fundamental requirements for assessing and treating women's depression include addressing gender issues, considering specific risk factors in the development of depressive symptoms for women, and developing a complete picture of the social and interpersonal context in which such experiences have occurred. The Task Force recommends that

1. clinicians be aware of their own stereotypes and biases related to gender and the effect such stereotypes and values may have on the assessment and treatment of female patients.
2. mental health professionals ask specific questions about physical and sexual abuse, both current and past, as a routine part of screening new clients;
3. clinicians conduct gender role analyses and obtain reproductive life histories for depressed clients;

4. primary care physicians be trained to recognize and diagnose depression and to make appropriate referrals; and
5. physicians who treat women with depression be alert to proper diagnoses and dosages of medications and avoid reinforcement of dependency and passivity in the clients.

Methodological Issues

In addition to the methodological issues raised in Section I, the Task Force underscores the need to advance methodology in treatment research. It recommends that

1. multimodal strategies be used in the assessment, treatment, and evaluation of treatment of the depressions in women;
2. greater attention be given to patients who drop out of outcome research studies;
3. issues related to depressive relapse and relapse prevention be examined and attended to by researchers and practitioners;
4. studies of treatment outcome more clearly specify the diagnoses of clients participating; and
5. outcome studies be conducted to determine the effectiveness of therapies that are frequently used to treat depression but have not been subjected to outcome research (e.g., feminist and psychoanalytic therapies).

Role/Gender Issues

All therapists must understand the risk factors and treatments of the depressions. The Task Force underscores the additional need for male and female therapists working with depressed women to be well versed in the realities of their lives (including those associated with membership in specific cultural, ethnic, racial, social, and other special populations). The Task Force recommends that

1. gender- and culture-aware assessment and treatment strategies be used and treatment outcome research on those psychotherapies that specifically use gender role analyses be used;
2. action and mastery components in treating depressed women regardless of treatment model used be facilitated; and
3. psychotherapy treatments be expanded to include examination of the relation between societal expectations and women's depression.

Treatment Issues

The Task Force underscores the need for mental health professionals to recognize women's diverse psychosocial and cultural realities as they diagnose and treat women for depression. It recommends that

1. longitudinal, controlled treatment outcome research on the effectiveness of short- and long-term treatments for the different subtypes of depression in women be conducted;

2. nonmedical mental health specialists working with depressed women develop a working relationship with a psychiatrist for purposes of coordinating psychopharmacological treatment;

3. clinicians become familiar with current knowledge on side effects of psychopharmacological treatment for the depressions and, when they use medications, monitor their clients closely for side effects;

4. practitioners be trained to use conceptual and practical eclecticism when necessary to meet the unique needs of individual clients;

5. curricula be developed in professional education to include training in a variety of specific techniques known to ameliorate depression;

6. depressed women be encouraged and taught to become effective consumers by psychotherapy services; and

7. public education be conducted with the aim of destigmatizing depression and the use of depression medication.

III

Special Female Populations: Risk Factors and Treatment Issues in Depression

All women may be directly or indirectly affected by gender role stereotyping, discrimination, powerlessness, and devaluation associated with women's roles. Sexual harassment, rape, and sexual abuse are not limited by such things as age, race/ethnicity, socioeconomic status, or disability. In discussing risk factors and treatment needs of depressed women, it is important to remember that women are not a homogeneous population. For example, race/ethnicity, age, professional status, lesbianism, physical abuse, poverty, presence of an eating disorder, and substance abuse are all characteristics that are associated with depression. Such characteristics can be used to identify populations of women who may be at higher risk for depression and who have special treatment needs.

This section examines depression in nine special populations: ethnic minority women (including African American/Black, Hispanic/Latina, Asian American, and Native American women), female adolescents, older women, professional women, lesbians, women who are physically abused, women living in poverty, women with eating disorders, and women who are substance abusers.

Ethnic Minority Women

Depression is the leading diagnosis for women, and ethnic minority women are no exception (Russo et al., 1987; Russo & Olmedo, 1983). As Russo (1987) has pointed out, gender must be conceptualized as a dynamic concept that itself varies across social classes and ethnic groups. Cultural backgrounds of ethnic minority women may vary in cultural role prescriptions that relate to depression in a variety of ways. For example, some ethnic minorities, particularly some Asian American and Native American cultures, have cultural norms of passivity, deference, and courtesy for both sexes that reinforce gender stereotypes for ethnic minority women in those cultures. Such women may experience particular problems and conflicts in asserting themselves, especially around issues of power (perceived and/or real).

Nonetheless, there is little information about how differences in gender and sex role stereotypes and expectations might result in different patterns of etiology, diagnosis, or treatment of depression in women of diverse ethnic groups. The gender and ethnic differences reported in utilization statistics may reflect many factors, including differences in rates of mental disorder, diagnostic practices, and types of treatment in women and members of ethnic minority groups. Research and mental health training on minority mental health are needed, particularly with regard to processes of immigration and acculturation, which may involve greater cultural contrasts and dilemmas for women.

Mental health professionals must be made aware of the dangers of generalizing from the experiences of one ethnic group to another, especially among diverse ethnic groups with an implicitly homogeneous label, such as "Hispanic," "Asian American," or "Native American." Unfortunately, there has been little comparative work to differentiate among shared and unique qualities of ethnic minority women's experiences that contribute to risk for depression. Ethnic minority women are more likely than Anglo women to share a number of socioeconomic risk factors for depression, including racial/ethnic discrimination, lower educational and income levels, segregation into low-status and high-stress jobs, unemployment, poor health, larger family sizes, marital dissolution, and single parenthood. Thus, although the discussions below highlight issues and findings with implications for research and treatment, they should not be interpreted as necessarily unique to the population being discussed.

African Americans/Blacks

African American/Black women face a number of mental-health-related issues based on their experience with racism and on the historical, cultural, and structural position of Black people in American society. Many of these mental health issues are reflected in increased risk for stress, alcoholism, drug abuse, and suicide (Smith, 1985). Steele (1978) studied the relation of depression in upper and middle class adults to race, gender, social class, and social mobility in 34 Black women, 32 Black men, 31 White women, and 37 White men. Findings indicated that female status, lower social class, and downward social mobility were related to greater depression.

Misdiagnosis is a concern among ethnic minority groups in general. As mentioned in Section I, Loring and Powell's (1988) analogue study found a tendency among male psychiatrists to misdiagnose undifferentiated schizophrenia with a dependent personality disorder as depression in both Black and White female patients. Bell and Mehta (1980) cited reports of misdiagnosis of manic depression and other affective disorders among Blacks. In a survey of therapists working with Black patients, Jones and Gray (1984) found that affective nonpsychotic disorders were the most frequent diagnoses for Black women, followed by anxiety disorders (the diagnoses were reversed for Black men). Depression and family problems were the most frequent complaints cited by Black women (depression and work-related problems were cited most often by Black men). A study of the use of outpatient psychiatric services (Russo & Olmedo, 1983) found depression to be the leading diagnosis for all women, but the rate for Black women was 42% higher than that of White women. Among patients with a primary diagnosis of depressive disorder, more Black women than White women were likely to receive drug therapy (56% vs. 36%) and family therapy (11% vs. 6%). The proportion of women receiving group therapy was about the same in both groups (6% vs. 8%). Depressed Black women were less likely than White women to fall into the category "no treatment rendered" (14% vs. 26%).

Whether such differences in treatment are appropriate adaptations to the situations of Black women is unknown.

Hispanics/Latinas

As Amaro et al. (1987) pointed out, the umbrella label *Hispanic* is applied to groups with distinct historical, political, economic, and racial differences. They reviewed the familial and socioeconomic circumstances of Hispanic women in the United States that constitute risk factors for women's depression. Hispanic women, as a whole, were found to be overrepresented among lower socioeconomic classes and younger ages, and to have living arrangements incongruent with gender stereotypes of the Hispanic woman. One in seven Hispanic women over age 15 was separated or divorced in 1981, and more than one out of two had no husband present.

Migration and the subsequent culture shock may engender anxiety. Other research seems to substantiate these clinical observations and theoretical analyses. Salgado de Snyder (1987) studied depressive symptomatology among married Mexican immigrant women. Using the Spanish version of the Center for Epidemiologic Studies Depression Scale, Snyder found that women who experienced discrimination, gender role conflicts, and concern about starting a family in the United States in the preceding 3-month period had significantly higher depression scores than women not experiencing those situations. In other words, women suffering from cultural conflicts due to the immigration and cultural adjustment experience reported higher depression than those women without such conflicts.

Hernandez (1986) discussed depression among Mexican women within an intergenerational and historical framework, and theorized that traditional cultural expectations may predispose women to depression. Such expectations include passivity, manipulation, seduction, and obligation. Women are expected to be responsible for the outcome of their marriages and unassertive toward father, husband, and other figures of authority. The cultural intolerance for differences, distrust, and confusion about sexuality has a further impact on Mexican women. Traditional cultural expectations do not allow cooperative fulfilling heterosexual relationships to develop. Confronted with motherhood, Mexican women may become overly involved with their children as a means of coping with their own inability to obtain self-gratification. Hernandez concluded that many Mexican women transmit this psychocultural vulnerability to depression to their daughters.

In another study examining the depressive characteristics of low-income Mexican American and Black women living in a southwestern city, Quesada, Spears, and Ramos (1978) found that women expressed more depressive symptoms as they became aware of better socioeconomic opportunities and the structural barriers to a better way of life. Interestingly, marital status was not found to be a good predictor of depression among the poor who were studied, but social alienation predicted personal depression in Mexican American women. These findings appear to be related to the cultural value that Hispanics place on familism, or on being a member of an extended network such as family and/or community.

Comas-Diaz (1981) found that female Puerto Ricans in the United States are exposed to a multiplicity of stressful situations, including disintegration of family values, poverty, discrimination, and the pressures of acculturation. These stresses may be translated into feelings of powerlessness, low self-esteem, loss of identity, and depression. Torres-Matrullo (1976) found a high prevalence of nervousness, psychosomatic complaints, and depression among nonpsychiatric Puerto Rican women living in the United States. Caste, Blodgett, and Rubinow (1978) found a high incidence of suicidal thoughts among Puerto Rican women compared with Anglo, Black, and Puerto Rican men. Similarly, Bluestone and Purdy (1977) asserted that among Puerto Rican women in the United States, suicide attempts provide an outlet for culturally and environmentally generated anger and frustration.

Canino et al. (1987) found gender differences in an examination of risk factors associated with depression in a sample of Puerto Rican residents and discussed those differences from a gender role perspective. Specifically, Puerto Rican women, after controlling for demographic, social role, and health variables, reported significantly higher rates of depressive symptomatology than men. These findings are relevant because a significant number of Puerto Rican women residing in Puerto Rico tend to migrate and reverse migrate to and from mainland.

Access to mental health services has been identified as a major issue for Hispanics in a number of reports on Hispanic mental health (e.g., U.S. Department of Health and Human Services, 1985). Examination of gender differences in the use of mental health inpatient statistics by Hispanics and non-Hispanics, however, suggests that Hispanic *women* more than Hispanic men are underrepresented in mental health facilities, at least in inpatient facilities. Further, this underrepresentation appears related to marital status. Such findings underscore the importance of gender-comparative research when the relation between depression and family roles and values is studied.

Further, given the many differences in risk factors for depression between Hispanics and Whites, it is important to control for economic, social class, and age differences before interpreting Hispanic/White differences in depression as reflecting differences in cultural values. As Amaro et al. (1987) cautioned, all too often "Hispanic cultural values" and acculturation are invoked to explain Hispanic women's behaviors without adequate examination of more proximal variables such as socioeconomic status and life cycle stage.

Asian Americans

The term *Asian American* (which here includes Pacific Islander) also embraces ethnic groups of diverse cultural character and with distinct histories of immigration and acculturation in the United States. Lott (1990) has pointed out that the educational and economic profile of some Asian groups compares favorably with that of White women, partially because of U.S. immigration policies that favor college-educated professionals. High educational attainment is not uniform among all Asian women or all Asian groups, however. For example, in 1980, one third of Vietnamese women; one fourth of Chinese women; and one fifth of Guamanian, Filipino, Samoan, and Korean women had completed 8 or fewer years of education (Lott, 1990).

Further, despite their cultural diversity, Asian American women must also contend with racial and ethnic discrimination and gender stereotyping. Asian American women are held up as models for docility and subservience, and paradoxically are stereotyped as both erotic and sexless (Lott, 1990).

Gender-related risk factors, such as low self-esteem, are also problems for Asian women. In a study conducted in San Francisco's Chinatown, Loo and Ong (1982) found that women, compared with men, had lower self-esteem, blamed their race more than the American system for Chinese problems in America, and were inclined to handle difficult situations by being accommodating versus assertive. Loo (1988) also found a greater predisposition to depression among the Chinese women compared with their male counterparts. Further research is needed to ascertain how factors underlying this gender difference in depression compare with those underlying such gender differences in other ethnic groups. It will be important to separate factors related to psychological and social roles for women in Chinese American society and culture from gender-related life circumstances associated with negative events such as discrimination, violence, and poverty.

Other recent studies indicate that many Southeast Asian refugees suffer from depression and posttraumatic stress disòrder (Kinsey, Fredrickson, Fleck, & Karls, 1984; Mollica, Wyshack, Coelho, & Lavelle, 1985; Mollica, Wyshack, & Lavelle, 1987). Female Southeast Asian refugees have special treatment needs because many of them have been sexually abused (Refugee Women Development Project, 1985). According to Mollica and Lavelle (1988), rape is a secret issue surrounded by an extreme reticence to reveal details during evaluation and treatment. They recommended that clinicians treating this population make clear that it is critical to be able to discuss rape and sexual abuse and that all information given will be kept confidential by the clinician.

Native Americans

Native American women (including Alaskan Natives) are among the least visible and least researched sectors in U.S. society (Snipp, 1990). Native Americans have a unique political status because of their history of treaties that establish the federal government's responsibility for their welfare. In 1955, the Indian Health Service was established to provide a comprehensive health care delivery system for Native American members of tribal organizations living on or near Native American reservations. Access to and quality of that agency's services for women should be evaluated.

There is a dearth of empirical research focused on Native American women's mental health (LaFromboise & Ozer, in press). Further, most of the available information stems from government-based agencies that are not necessarily sensitive to a Native American perspective. This situation notwithstanding, the health and mental health status of Native American women is bleak. For instance, the U.S. Department of Health and Human Services (1988) reported that compared with other American women, the death rate for Native American women is 6 times higher for alcoholism (10 times higher for ages 25–45), 5 times higher for cirrhosis/liver disease, 3 times higher for homicide, 3 times higher for accidental death (for ages 15–54), and 3 times higher for motor vehicle accidents. Moreover, suicide is twice as high among both Native American women and men than among the general American population (May, 1987).

Native American women are at risk for many factors associated with depression, including poverty, lack of education, and larger numbers of children. According to Snipp (1990), in 1979, the latest year for which detailed data are available, the poverty rate of Native Americans was nearly 28%, and 45% of poor families were headed by single women. A 1984 study of characteristics of births found that Native American births were more likely to be to teenagers than were White births (20% vs. 11%, respectively). Black births were most likely to occur to teenagers (24%). Both Native American and Black mothers were less educated than White mothers. They were also more likely than White mothers to have no prenatal care or to delay prenatal care until after the 4th month of pregnancy (Taffel, 1987).

The prevalence of depression among Native Americans has been the focus of a number of empirical studies. The results of these studies have attested to the high depression rates among several Native American communities (Shore & Manson, 1981; Shore, Manson, Bloom, Keepers, & Neligh, 1987). Moreover, the rates of depression within select Native American Indian communities may be significantly higher than previously reported (Manson, Shore, & Bloom, 1985). In addition, female high school students in tribal-operated boarding schools appear to be more prone to depression and phobic reactions (mainly performance anxiety) than their male counterparts (LaFromboise & Ozer, in press). However, the U.S. Department of Health & Human Services (1988) reported low rates of psychiatric treatment for women. Specifically, the Social and Mental Health Services of the Indian Health Service identified the percentage of problem categories presented by Native American women requesting mental health services as alcohol misuse in the family, 82%; adult–child relationships, 78%; grief reactions, 77%; child management/abuse, 72%; and marital conflict, 72%.

Among the many Native American women who suffer from depression, there appear to be two major problems. First, the U.S. Department of Health & Human Services (1988) reported that a significant number of Native American women seeking mental health services have experienced incest, rape, and sexual assault. Second, these women, relying on their own coping skills, may be at risk by self-medicating with alcohol and drugs in response to these stressors (Heath, 1983). Given the prevalence of these problems, depression treatment for Native American women needs to include assessment and treatment of violence (sexual, physical, and other) and alcohol and drug use/abuse.

Treatment Implications

The cultural context needs to be considered when assessing and treating depression among ethnic minority women. The measures used to assess depression among ethnic minority women need to be culturally syntonic. For example, Shore et al. (1987) found similar symptom patterns among Native American patients from three tribes. However, the tribal-specific lexicons significantly differed between them. Similarly, the Hopkins Symptom Checklist-25 (HSCL-25), a measure of depression and anxiety, has been modified into three different Indo-Chinese versions (Mollica, Wyshak, de Marneffe, Khuon, & Lavelle, 1987). The HSCL-25 is readily accepted among Southeast Asian refugee patients because it resembles a medical test (Mollica & Lavelle, 1988).

Such a style is more consistent with some Asian groups' expression of depression through somatic symptomatology (Kleinman, 1980; Marsella, 1977).

Similarly, the new Lao Depression Inventory was developed and validated with 216 Laotian refugees. It is administered in either English or Lao and has an accuracy rate of approximately 90% in diagnosing depression in the validation group (Davidson-Muskilhn & Golden, 1989).

Although several theoretical orientations such as behavioral (Strumphauzer & Davis, 1983), cognitive behavioral (Comas-Diaz, 1981), dynamically oriented (Olarte & Lenz, 1984), interpersonal (Comas-Diaz, 1988), and feminist (Comas-Diaz, 1987) psychotherapies have been used successfully with some ethnic minority women, they need to be culturally grounded in order to be effective. For instance, because of the community-based definition of self, many traditional therapeutic interventions emphasizing individual volition and responsibility (internal locus of control) may prove inappropriate without a cultural translation.

Cultural translation is also necessary in assessing attitudes toward suicide and suicidal intent. For example, a recent study comparing suicidal patients from the People's Republic of China with matched suicidal patients in the United States found that the Chinese patients viewed suicide as a less effective means of solving problems and were less likely to communicate suicidal intent (Chiles et al., 1989). Culturally relevant treatment also may include a translation of those White American middle class behaviors that have no cultural counterpart in behaviors of ethnic groups. For example, among some Asian American and Hispanic/Latino cultures, the concept of assertive behavior for women is an alien one. The lack of assertiveness, therefore, could be associated with depression. An example of this has been provided by Comas-Diaz and Duncan (1985), who added a cultural component to the regular assertiveness training designing a treatment package for unassertive Hispanic (Puerto Rican) women. They found that the cultural component facilitated the training and proved successful in increasing the assertiveness of the Puerto Rican women.

Cultural and racial identity issues have been identified as crucial elements of psychotherapy with ethnic minority patients (Atkinson, Morten, & Wing, 1979). Identity issues, therefore, acquire inordinate importance in the treatment of depressed ethnic minority women. As indicated before, culturally sanctioned subordinate gender roles may predispose ethnic minority women to depression. Therefore, decisions in regard to treatment need to address the ensuing low self-esteem among ethnic minority women with their diverse identities: gender, ethnic, racial, cultural, and societal, among many others. In sum, the treatment of depressed ethnic minority women requires a comprehensive approach including interventions in the biological, psychotherapeutic, social, and ethnocultural arenas.

Female Adolescents

Extensive research indicates that the rates of depressive symptoms rise substantially from childhood into adolescence (Nolen-Hoeksema, 1990). Reported incidence of depression in adolescent clinical populations range from 3% to 33% (Robins, Alessi, Yanchyshyn & Colfer, 1982); however, data from normative populations are scarce.

A number of factors have been found to correlate with depression among adolescents. Simons and Miller (1987) found low parental support to be a significant predictor of depression in adolescents. Kandel and Davies (1982) gathered data on 8,000 adolescents and their parents and found a number of factors associated with depressed mood in adolescents. These included low self-esteem, low levels of attachment to either parents or peers or both, noninterference or the reverse, authoritarian families, and depressed parents. Several studies also indicate that an unstable family life was a major factor in 50–80% of all adolescent suicides (Crook & Raskin, 1975; Dorpat, Jackson, & Ripley, 1965; Schrut, 1968).

Suicide is correlated with depression in adolescents. Approximately 5,000 young people commit suicide each year, with as many as 300,000–400,000 attempts every year in the U.S. general population (Evans & Farberow, 1988). The Report of the Secretary's Task Force on Youth Suicide (Alcohol, Drug Abuse and Mental Health Administration, 1989) noted that in the last 30 years, rates of suicide for young people 15 to 24 years of age have almost tripled. In addition, a single adolescent suicide may be followed by a "cluster" effect in which one suicide is followed by other attempts (and some completions) from youths in the same community.

The literature for depression in female adolescents, although scant, is consistent in revealing that girls ages 14–18 experience a chronically higher incidence of depression than do their male peers (Kandel & Davies, 1982), and, although they have fewer suicide completions, they do have more attempts than boys their age (Pezel & Riddle, 1981). Interestingly, the greater preponderance of depression in female compared with male adolescents does not appear to emerge until middle to late adolescence (Nolen-Hoeksema, 1990). Before this age, boys are just as likely, even perhaps slightly more likely, to be depressed as girls.

Why is there a gender difference? Many etiological explanations have been proposed, including genetic, endocrinological, sociological, and psychological. Dornbusch et al. (1984) found that the normal physical changes of puberty decreased female adolescents' satisfaction with their bodies, whereas the reverse was true for male adolescents. In addition, Lerner and Karabenick (1974) found that satisfaction with one's own body appears to be more closely related to self-esteem and well-being in female adolescents than in male adolescents. Confirming these studies, Gilligan et al. (1989) found that girls are more disparaging than boys in appraising themselves and reveal more disturbances in self-image.

In line with these findings, McCarthy (1989) has proposed that dissatisfaction with body maturation and its relation to low self-esteem may account for the incidence of gender differences in depression in early adolescence. In his review of the literature on cultural differences in images of the ideal female body shape, gender differences in depression, and rates of eating disorders, McCarthy found that cultures that idealize a prepubescent thin body shape for girls tend also to have high rates of eating disorders and higher rates of depression in women than in men. Therefore, female adolescents' dissatisfaction with their bodies may come from an awareness of the conflict between society's obsession with a thin body shape for women and the fact that they are gaining weight as their bodies mature.

There is also increasing evidence that female adolescents may view their own competence as a liability in relationships with their peers, particularly male adolescents.

In an early study, Coleman (1961) found that female adolescents do not want to be recognized for their intelligence. Female adolescents may accurately perceive rejection if they violate the prescribed normative behavior and act competent and assertive. In *Sex Differences in Depression,* Nolen-Hoeksema (1990) quotes Block and Gjerde's (in press) finding of a significant positive relation between intelligence and depression in female adolescents but a small negative correlation in male adolescents. Girgus (1989) found that female adolescents who engage in more feminine-stereotyped activities (e.g., shopping, hairstyling and makeup, cooking, or sewing) are more depressed than their male adolescent peers. Thus, it appears as though female adolescents are in double jeopardy. Instrumentality and competence lower the risk for depression over the life cycle. However, if female adolescents are instrumental and competent in their activities and interactions, they are at increased risk for rejection by their peers, which may increase risk for depression.

An important area for consideration of the increase in rates of depression in female adolescents is the overwhelming evidence that the rate of sexual abuse of girls increases significantly in early adolescence (Russell, 1984). In a random sample of 930 adult women, Russell (1984) found that before the age of 17, 12% had experienced some type of serious intrafamilial sexual abuse and 26% had experienced serious abuse from someone not in their family. A pattern of gender differences in abuse is evident in light of the fact that girls are two to three times more likely than boys to be the victim of sexual abuse (Finkelhor, 1979).

Carmen et al. (1984) examined psychiatric inpatient records of 188 adult and adolescent male and female patients discharged from an adult inpatient unit during an 18-month period. They found that 43% of the patients had histories of physical or sexual abuse or both. Fifty-three percent of the female patients as compared with 23% of the male patients had been abused. Seventy-five percent of the 28 adolescents compared with 39% of the adults had been abused.

Treatment Implications

As noted earlier in this report, the literature focusing on outcome of therapeutic interventions with depressed women is rather modest, and few outcome studies have compared the treatment responses of men and women or addressed the issue of differential effectiveness of treatment strategies for depressed female adolescents. It should not be surprising, therefore, that the literature on treatment outcomes for depressed female adolescents is almost nonexistent.

The uniqueness of the adolescent stage of development suggests that therapists go beyond solely providing treatment for "depressed adolescents." Therapists must also address issues raised by the context of the systems in which adolescents operate. At times this may require intervention into the systems themselves. Some of the systems issues to be evaluated for a depressed adolescent include the following:

1. individual, peer, and family reactions to the physiological changes and concurrent development or lack of development of self-esteem based on these changes;
2. the adolescent's management of her transitional power position (beyond total dependence but not yet total independence) in her family and the world;

3. the variety of different systems in which the adolescent must (not necessarily by choice) operate (school, work, family, peer group, and community)—they have fewer options than most adults and typically have a restricted freedom of movement;
4. the lack of an established identity that makes their self-esteem highly vulnerable and sensitive to everything that affects them; and
5. their reliance on their "family," which they did not choose but on which they must rely for survival.

The establishment of a trusting and confidential relationship remains the backbone of treatment. Once this is accomplished, however, a rather immediate shift may need to be made to whatever systems intervention will produce some change in the status quo. Anderson (1981) emphasized the family as an extremely important factor in the functioning of an adolescent. The family may need to be part *of* the treatment; the family's function is more than bringing the adolescent *for* treatment. Parents can benefit from a variety of educational and instructive interventions with regard to fostering self-esteem and confidence in their adolescents, as well as overcoming their own feelings of "hopelessness and helplessness" in the face of their family situation. In developing family interventions, the prevalence of family violence and sexual abuse and its effects on gender differences in adolescent depression should be kept in mind.

School failure is often a concomitant of adolescent depression. Holinger and Offer (1981) noted that when youths view peers as functioning at a more competent level than themselves they experience a significant loss of self-esteem. Interventions with the school regarding possible learning disabilities, poor class placements, and the like can often provide a significant vehicle for change in the adolescent's school life. High-quality educational programs designed to help adolescents deal with their sexuality, develop responsible sexual behavior, and avoid unplanned pregnancies may be particularly important for preventing depression in female adolescents, who disproportionally bear the physical, psychological, social, and economic stresses of teenage pregnancy.

Research on depression in adolescents needs to take into account factors associated with gender including (a) body image concerns of female adolescents, (b) conflicts between relationships and autonomy for female adolescents, (c) the import of more rigid gender role norms on the self-esteem and personal integrity of female adolescents, and (d) strategies for reducing depression in female adolescents. In addition, reward systems need to be developed for reinforcing competence in female adolescents. These may take the form of education and training for parents and schools, and also raising the awareness of society at large. With regard to the latter, the media could be very influential in promoting images of intelligent, competent, and popular female adolescents, so that they may serve as positive role models for our youth.

Older Women

Depression among older adults is an area of enormous need for research and development of specific treatment strategies. Because women are overrepresented in the aging population, this problem is of special concern. It is unclear how many older women are depressed. Few studies have been conducted, and methodological difficulties are compounded by the fact that depression is often concurrent with or caused by a variety of medications or physical illnesses.

Estimates of depression in older adults range from 10% to 65%. Estimates of depression in older women range from less than 2% to more than 50% (Formanek & Gurian, 1987). Several studies indicate that the rates of depression for older men and women are approximately the same (Hale & Cochran, 1983). Similarly, women and men do not appear to differ in length of duration of depressive episodes (Lewinshon, Fenn, Stanton, & Franklin, 1986). It has been suggested that the likelihood of significant depression occurring is reduced after age 65 (Haug, Ford, & Sheafor, 1985).

Depression in older women may be related to factors different from those seen for younger women, for example, increasing poverty, isolation as adult children move away and friends and family die, changes in biochemistry as aging occurs, role changes with retirement, and moving to new locations. Two major causes for depression in older women are the loss of physical health (more than 80% of people over 65 have at least one chronic illness) and the loss of a spouse from death or divorce. Bornstein, Clayton, Halikas, Maurice, and Robins (1973) studied recently widowed women and men and found that in the month after their spouses death, 35% and 33% of the women and men, respectively met criteria for depression. In a 1-year follow-up, 17% and 19% of the women and men, respectively, continued to be depressed. There are now five times as many widows as widowers in the United States and half the women over 65 are widows. Given this, Stroebe and Stroebe (1983) suggested that the death of a spouse may not be as traumatic for women as for men; hence the nearly equal levels of depression for the recently widowed. In addition, the divorce rate for women over 60 is now approaching the rate for younger women (Dychtwald & Flower, 1989).

Treatment Implications

Proper diagnosis is essential for older depressed women. It is critical to review all medications they may be taking, ranging from prescriptions, to over-the-counter medicine, to "home" and "folk" remedies. Depression may be misdiagnosed as senile dementia, as are many other physical diseases. In many cases, treatment involves active interventions by the therapist, for example, the use of psychosocial treatment and improvement of living arrangements to reduce the isolation, economic deprivation, and age discrimination that may be contributing to the depression. Treatment also involves careful monitoring of drugs for older adults, who metabolize drugs more slowly with greater danger of drug toxicity. Tricyclic antidepressants may have cardiotoxicity. Furthermore, their long-term effect on the older adult is unknown, and they may interact negatively with other drugs being taken.

Another important issue related to depressed older women is the impact of their caretaking needs on younger women in their social support networks. Current estimates indicate that nearly 90% of all adult-children caregivers are women. The average ages of these caregivers is 57 and more than a third are 65 years or older (Dychtwald & Flower, 1989). Eighty percent of older women will need care and receive that care from their families. According to Dychtwald and Flower (1989), "The average American woman can expect to spend more years caring for her parents than she did caring for her children. . . . Average time spent [in this caretaking] was about 10 hours per week, but one in twelve spent 35 hours or more" (pp. 241, 247). The average woman may be increasingly in the position of caring for both her children and a parent, depleting her energy and using her already meager leisure time to work and care for others. This exhausting experience may contribute significantly to many women's risk for to depression.

Professional Women

Professional women are in some respects a relatively advantaged group. Women pursing professional and managerial careers typically have access to greater financial resources, are more highly educated, and have greater freedom and more options than women in other educational and socioeconomic groups. They have had the opportunities to develop competence and to achieve respect and status. In spite of these advantages, as documented in Section I of this report, professional women have a higher incidence of depression and suicide than women in the general population.

Despite the obvious advantages of professional status, career women appear to struggle with a variety of conflicts and stressors that may increase their risk for depression. Professional women may have difficulty reconciling their achievement and affiliation needs and responsibilities (Lloyd, 1983; Post, 1987). They may be rejected by men because their competence poses a threat to male self-esteem. They may worry that a high-powered career will jeopardize their marital prospects, particularly in the context of marital norms that mandate a woman's status be inferior to her husband's. Professional women have resources to purchase household help and child care. However, acceptable services may not be available, and husbands who fully share responsibility for child care and housework continue to be rare, even among dual-career families (Gilbert, 1985). Peers and/or family members may communicate direct disapproval for professional women's career aspirations and achievements as well as for their more egalitarian marital relationships. Finally, like all women, professional women are at risk for sexual harassment, rape, and domestic violence.

Single women who are self-sufficient may nonetheless struggle with dependency conflicts and unmet emotional and relational needs. Self-reliance, which is critical for professional advancement, may lead to difficulties in establishing intimate relationships that are based on interdependencies. Self-reliant women thus also experience feelings of loneliness and isolation (Post, 1982).

Further empirical research is needed to delineate the stressors, personality characteristics, psychological factors, interpersonal conflicts, and other negative life events that increase the risk of suicide and clinical depression in professional women.

Treatment Implications

One promising treatment approach combines cognitive and behavioral techniques to enable women to respect their own needs and act more assertively on behalf of those needs. Ironically, many women who are able to be assertive on behalf of others are uncomfortable with using those assertive skills on behalf of themselves. Professional women, especially those in human services occupations, often fulfill the needs of others, be they supervisors or clients, to the exclusion of their own needs. This self-sacrifice may continue until they are on the brink of exhaustion and depression. Lemkau and Landau (1986) used cognitive restructuring, self-monitoring of daily activities, role playing, and skills training in conflict resolution to help women claim the right to express and meet their own needs. This training must also include building skills in dealing with charges of "selfishness" and hostility of co-workers and family members when a woman rightfully put her needs above those of others.

For professional women who are having difficulties in establishing rewarding intimate relationships, psychotherapy based on self-in-relation theory may also provide some useful insights.

Whatever the approach, however, a feminist perspective in therapy is critical for professional women who are working in environments where power, control, and achievement are valued; competition among peers is strong; and there are few women role models or mentors. In such hostile contexts, sexual harassment and capitalizing on sexism to undermine female co-workers may be used as strategies for advancement. Feminist therapy may have a particularly important role to play in helping professional women sort out the dynamics of those hostile environments where gender stereotyping and sexism are particularly salient.

Lesbians

Research on depression among lesbians has been virtually absent. Available evidence comes indirectly from a variety of related research topics and the recent National Lesbian Health Care Survey (National Institute of Mental Health, 1987). Rothblum (1990) published one of the few major reviews on this subject; this section is drawn primarily from that review.

The National Lesbian Health Care Survey (National Institute of Mental Health, 1987) found that the most common reason for which lesbians sought counseling was depression, with half the sample seeking therapy reporting depression as the major presenting problem. In one of the few studies to assess depression among 57 lesbians and 43 unmarried heterosexual women (Saghir, Robins, Walbrann, & Gentry, 1970), 44% of the lesbians and 35% of the heterosexual women had experienced depressive episodes.

Social support appears to be an important protective factor against depression in lesbians. Research by Kurdek and Schmidtt (1987) indicated that lesbians who perceived a high level of social support were found to be less psychologically distressed. Because of widespread societal homophobia and discrimination against lesbians, many lesbians choose to keep the fact of their lesbianism hidden, or to remain in the "closet." Smith (1988) has postulated that depression and dysthymia may result from the conflict that closeted lesbians face living this double life-style. Although the coming-out process (i.e., disclosure that one is a lesbian) is stressful for many lesbians (Gartrell, 1981), there is evidence that once lesbians are out, they are at an advantage psychologically and socially (Schmidtt & Kurdek, 1987). Sources of social support that lesbians engage in are limited by their lack of disclosure regarding their sexuality. In one study only 28.4% of lesbians had come out to their mothers and even fewer (19.3%) to their fathers (Albro & Tully, 1979). Furthermore, lesbians had rarely come out to employers, colleagues at work, teachers, students, or neighbors. Kurdek (1988) reported that both lesbians and gay men listed their friends as the most frequent providers of social support, followed by their partner, family, and co-workers. Kurdek and Schmidtt (1987) found lesbians were three times more likely to rate friends rather than family members as providers of social support. This is in contrast to heterosexuals, who tended to rate friends and family members equally. Kurdek (1988) interpreted this difference to difficulty in accepting the lesbian and her partner on the part of family members, as well as the lesbian couple's need to keep distance from the family to avoid discovery of their lesbianism.

Involvement in a relationship with a partner has been found to be related to positive adjustment and mental health for lesbians. Leavy and Adams (1986) found a positive correlation between involvement in a lesbian relationship and self-esteem, self-acceptance, and social support. However, the termination of partnered relationships was a significant risk factor for depression. For women not affiliated with a lesbian network, their lesbian lover may be their only confidant. Thus, depression may be a greater risk factor for rural lesbians or lesbians who are not out to many people outside of their partner.

Since lesbian couples tend to share housework and child care (Peplau, Cochran, Rook, & Padesky, 1978), overload due to parenting responsibilities may be less of a risk factor for lesbians than for heterosexual women. However, several issues confront lesbian parents that are less frequent concerns for heterosexual parents: custody battles over competency to rear children, homophobic remarks made by others to the children, the rearing of male children, and coming out to children (Hall, 1981). Lesbian mothers lose 80% of all custody battles in lower courts (Morgan, 1984). Thus, for lesbians who do have young children, the stress may be significant.

Despite a lack of research on depression among lesbians, a number of surveys have focused on suicide and suicide attempts among lesbians and gay men. Findings indicate that White lesbians are two and a half times more likely to report having attempted suicide some time in the past than are heterosexual women (Saunders & Valente, 1987). Suicide rates among Black and Latina lesbians are 27% and 28%, respectively, and higher than those of White lesbians (16%) (National Institute of Mental Health, 1987). Lesbians who are non-White may feel isolated in the lesbian community. Research indicates that Black and Latina lesbians are at increased risk for suicide attempts and childhood sexual abuse. Yet most research has virtually ignored ethnic minority women, especially those who are lesbians in Native American tribes. The double burden of being a lesbian in this society and differing demographically from the lesbian community may increase rates of depression.

Factors that place different groups at risk for suicide include demographic factors, previous suicide attempts, alcohol and drug use, and interrupted social ties (Saunders & Valente, 1987). Buhrich and Loke (1988) found similar risk factors among gays and lesbians in Australia. They speculate that the threat of blackmail, criminal proceedings, and public exposure may increase suicide among lesbians and gay men.

Of these risk factors for suicide, alcohol use is high in the lesbian community. Fourteen percent of the sample from National Lesbian Health Care Survey (National

Institute of Mental Health, 1987) expressed worry about their use of alcohol. Saghir and Robins (1973) reported that the combination of depression, alcohol use, and previous suicide attempts among lesbians should be of particular concern.

Adolescent lesbians are three times more likely to have attempted suicide than are adult lesbians (Saunders & Valente, 1987). Kourany (1987) asked psychiatrists to speculate on reasons for increased suicide risk among lesbian and gay adolescents. About 60% of the psychiatrists reported that they had no opinion on the subject and no experience working with lesbian or gay adolescents, or that the subject matter was irrelevant to their practices. Those who did report having experience working with lesbian or gay adolescents indicated that suicide risk would be higher for reasons of depression, social isolation, rejection from family or peers, or self-hatred (Kourany, 1987).

Treatment Implications

About 80% of lesbians have consulted a counselor or therapist at some point in their lives (Albro & Tully, 1979). Although most of the lesbians in this survey reported that their therapist had been accepting of lesbianism, some indicated that the therapist was unaccepting or tried to "reorient" them to be heterosexual. Ministers were the least accepting counselors.

It is important to point out that although the *Diagnostic and Statistical Manual of Mental Disorders (Third Edition-Revised)* (American Psychiatric Association, 1987) has eliminated homosexuality as a mental illness, nearly all therapists practicing today were trained at a time when homosexuality and "ego-dystonic homosexuality" were considered mental illnesses. Furthermore, the *International Classification of Diseases* (World Health Organization, 1977) still lists both homosexuality and lesbianism as mental illnesses.

Finally, self-help groups such as Alcoholics Anonymous are the way in which many women, including lesbians, cope with distress resulting from alcohol and drugs. Nevertheless, such self-help groups consist overwhelmingly of male members and may be overtly homophobic (Glaus, 1989). Although lesbian Alcoholics Anonymous groups exist in some large urban areas, they are unavailable to most lesbians in the United States.

Research on depression among lesbians, including treatment outcome research, should be a priority for the mental health field. Problems experienced by lesbians who are members of ethnic minority groups, adolescents, older women, or women in prison need to be examined more closely. Although research on depression among lesbians remains to be done, it seems clear that eradication of homophobia and promotion of lesbian-affirmative policies would serve to decrease emotional distress, including depression.

Women Who Are Physically Abused

The relation between depression and interpersonal violence was discussed in Section I of this report. Consequently, the present discussion focuses on special issues in the treatment of victims of interpersonal violence.

Probably the most essential aspect of working with victims of interpersonal violence is the taking of a careful and thorough history. Victims of violence, especially those whose perpetrators were family members, friends, or health care providers, are highly unlikely to voluntarily reveal to a clinician that the abuse in question has occurred. When such abuse is voluntarily described, it is often done in a sketchy manner in which the client will minimize or gloss over the details of the abuse.

There are good reasons for these behaviors. Historically, the survivors of intimate interpersonal violence such as child sexual abuse, rape, and battering have been disbelieved or blamed by mental health care providers (Armstrong, 1983; Hilberman, 1980; Rush, 1980; Walker, 1979). Voluntary revelation of one's status as a victim of such assaults has commonly led to reduced quality of care and hostility from professionals.

Even when an interviewer is supportive, it is extremely painful and retraumatizing to go into the details of abuse experiences. Time, patience, and persistence on the part of a therapist will be necessary to elicit the specifics of how the victimization has occurred. Obtaining this detailed information can be essential to appropriate intervention, because certain symptoms may have a symbolic value that is known only when the complete picture of the victimization experience is developed.

Finally, many survivors of abuse, particularly early childhood physical and/or sexual abuse, may lack conscious memory of the events. Repression or dissociation are common survival strategies for young children subjected to such trauma (Bass & Davis, 1988). Clinicians should not assume that no abuse is present when none is reported. Rather, it is essential to be sensitive to possible signs and symptoms of abuse and to raise the possibility as an invitation for repressed memories of victimization to resurface. Consequently, the assessment process should not be seen as a finite one, but as a continuing effort in which new materials may emerge, particularly when the reported or suspected abuse occurred in childhood.

Treatment of victims of interpersonal violence requires the therapist to take on a role quite different from that normally prescribed in psychotherapy. For many such clients, the world has divided itself into allies and adversaries, and a neutral stance will often be interpreted as an adversarial one. Consequently, the therapist working with the survivor of interpersonal violence must be willing to adopt a more advocate-oriented position in treatment, with overt expressions of willingness to believe the painful material the client presents and a firm posture that places responsibility for the abuse on the perpetrator and not the victim. As Hilberman (1980) has pointed out, victims of violence have historically been more willing and more likely to present themselves for treatment than are the perpetrators, leading to an unfortunate trend toward victim blaming as therapists strive to "help" the victim understand how she has "unconsciously contributed" to her own victimization.

Such attitudes are not relics of the past, as demonstrated in the recent proposal by the American Psychiatric Association to develop a diagnosis of self-defeating personality disorder (American Psychiatric Association, 1987). Clinicians treating survivors of interpersonal violence must be clear in their own beliefs that *nothing* justifies a violent or abusive response. Holding such a belief is important because many survivors of violence have developed survival adaptations that render them difficult to relate to: They may be angry, indirectly hostile, withdrawn, and unrewarding for the clinician to work with, opening the door for subtle victim blaming (e.g., "If you treated him like that, no wonder he hit you").

At the same time that a therapist working with survivors of victimization must provide overt advocacy and support, she or he must also be entirely clear about the boundaries and form of the therapy relationship. Survivors of violence have had their emotional and/or physical boundaries violated and are highly susceptible to being re-victimized by a therapist who is disrespectful or sloppy with boundary maintenance. Such therapists must define the limits and norms of the therapy context and be willing to acknowledge and take responsibility for errors that may occur in the treatment process. This suggestion reflects the fact that for many victimized persons, their perception that something wrong was happening to them was denied by the perpetrator or turned against them and used as evidence of "craziness."

Therapists, in a more powerful position than their clients, will empower the survivor of interpersonal violence by taking responsibility for their inadvertent misuses of that power, rather than asking the more normative therapist question of "Why do you think that?". These issues hold doubly true when treating the victim of abuse from a therapist because, for such a person, the entry into the therapy situation itself constitutes a constant reexposure to the traumatic situation. These caveats regarding therapy with survivors of violence are not meant to imply that such treatment would be devoid of attempts at insight. Rather, what is true for many survivors of violence is that the usual approach to treatment must be tempered and blended with careful attention to the empowerment of the client and the affirmation of her perceptions (Ochberg, 1988).

Women in Poverty

Affordability and accessibility of mental health and related health services are key factors in their use. Yet most of these services require insurance and/or sufficient incomes to qualify. Poverty, social, and cultural barriers, together with an awareness and availability of services within community programs, affect how many women will actually receive these services.

Available data on poverty reflect the stark reality of many women's lives. In the United States, eight and a half million women (15% of the total female population) live in poverty. This means that they have an annual income of $5,778 or less (U.S. Census Bureau, 1987). In 1988, 53% of poor families were maintained by women with no spouse present; 75.6% of Black families headed by women were poor as compared with 43.5% of families headed by White women and 43.9% headed by Hispanic women (U.S. Census Bureau, 1987).

As described in Section I of this report, the stressors associated with living in poverty are significant and overwhelming. Although they can certainly result in depression and a need for mental health services, existing plans such as Medicaid and employer-associated insurance plans are limited in their provision of mental health care. More than 37 million Americans, many of whom are working, have no health insurance (Chollet, 1987). Only a few employer health plans provide mental benefits. For example, 64% of all employer insurance plans do not currently offer mental health benefits to employees. Medicaid-covered services are limited, often associated with poorer care, and have become increasingly less available. As the number of Americans living in poverty has increased, Medicaid coverage of individuals with incomes below the poverty level has decreased. In 1975, 63% of people living in households below the poverty level received Medicaid coverage. By 1985, the percentage dropped to 46%. It is now estimated to be 38% (National Health Care Campaign and Citizen Action, 1987). A greater proportion of Medicaid recipients are minorities and women.

Adequate data on accessibility to mental health care for this population are not readily available. In reviewing a few related studies, the lack of choice and options is of concern for many poor women. A study of female-headed families sponsored by the National Association of Social Workers found that more than half of the participants were stressed by a lack of access to preventative health care and half were stressed by the limited choice in facilities and practitioners that they could afford. Lack of available transportation was a significant barrier in managing their day-to-day needs (Miller, 1987).

High levels of depressive symptoms are reported in women with insufficient personal support, without child-rearing assistance, and experiencing chronic stress, particularly stress caused by inadequate financial resources (Belle, 1988, 1990). Inadequate income has been associated with an elevated risk for depressive symptoms over time (Kaplan et al., 1987). Poverty is associated with various factors related to depression, including single-parent status, responsibility for young children, social isolation, and lack of social support.

Taken together, these data are particularly distressing. Each year, the number of women and children in poverty appears to increase. The hopelessness and crisis-oriented nature of living in poverty not only contribute to depression and related responses, but also provide significant barriers to receiving appropriate mental health treatment and care. In providing mental health services for poor women, basic issues such as accessibility of facilities to transportation as well as the availability of child care must be addressed.

Women With Eating Disorders

In the 1980s, research accumulated suggesting that the eating disorders anorexia nervosa, bulimia, and "bulimarexia" are often related to depression (Rivinus et al., 1984; Stern et al., 1984). Depression was often observed in eating disorder patients and on follow-up with these patients (Eckert, Goldberg, Haini, Casper, & Davis, 1982; Hatsukami, Eckert, Mitchell, & Pyle, 1984; Hsu, 1980; Stern et al., 1984). There are similarities in neurochemistry between depressed women and women with eating disorders, and some bulimic women respond well to antidepressants (Biederman et al., 1984; Winokur, March, & Mendels, 1980).

However, there is no evidence of genetic transmission, and biological findings are contradictory (Finkelhor, 1987). Clearly, depression seems related to certain eating disorders; but whether it is a correlate, a cause, or a consequence is unclear. Considerably more research needs to be conducted to determine the nature of the relation between depression and eating disorders. This is a vitally important question for women and depression in the United States because of gender differences in the rate of disturbed body image and eating disorders.

Women Who Abuse Alcohol and/or Other Drugs

Experts suggest that there are 10 million alcoholics in the United States. Thirty to fifty percent of those 10 million alcoholics are estimated to be women (National Council on Alcoholism, 1987). According to available data, a significant number of women appear to be cross-addicted to alcohol and other drugs. For example, a national membership survey of Alcoholics Anonymous showed that 40% of the female membership reported addiction to another drug, and this increased to 60% for women age 30 and under (Alcoholics Anonymous, 1984).

Hesselbrock, Hesselbrock, and Workman-Daniels (1986) found that the most common lifetime diagnosis for alcoholic women was depression. Research has demonstrated significant connections between depression and alcohol. Some studies found that depression preceded heavy drinking (Beck, Steer, & McElroy, 1982; Wilsnack, Klassen, & Wilsnack, 1986). Kroft and Leichner (1987) found more depression in alcoholic women than nonalcoholic women. Depression also was found to be the strongest statistical predictor of alcohol dependence in a study of alcoholic women and matched controls (Holubowycz, 1987). Women more often than men have been found to become alcoholic following or during a depression (Goodwin, 1982).

Several studies have examined the use of alcohol by individuals attempting or completing suicide. In 20% to 37% of suicides, the victim was either drinking or had a history of alcohol abuse (Colliver & Malin, 1986; Roizen, 1982). One study reported that the proportion of women who drink and attempt suicide was lower than that for men but appeared to be steadily increasing (Kendall, 1983).

Some women may be dually diagnosed with alcoholism and depression. In these instances, antidepressants must be carefully monitored because the patient may be drinking while also taking medication. Alcohol and some drugs are depressants, and chemically dependent patients can present as depressed because of the mood-altering affects of alcohol and other drugs. After approximately 6 months of sobriety, most of the substance-related symptoms lift, and a clearer diagnosis can be made. Some substances, such as marijuana, may continue to affect body chemistry for longer periods of time. As a result, an underlying depression may not become evident for months or even a year into sobriety.

An initial assessment for substance use and abuse should aid in determining whether a substance might either mask or present as depression. Obtaining information about the length, type, and amount of usage is also important. For example, in some cases drinking is episodic or reactive and may be a time-limited response to a significant loss; in other cases it may be persistent.

Many chemically dependent individuals use alcohol and drugs to repress traumatic childhood experiences including sexual and physical abuse and incest. According to one study, up to 75% of chemically dependent women reported higher incidents of sexual abuse (Wilsnack, 1984). Other studies report a sexual abuse and incest rate among recovering women at 30% to 50%. This becomes more critical for practitioners as recovery continues. After the first year of sobriety, memory of these events can slowly begin to emerge. Eighteen months of sobriety is often a crisis point for recall. Many of these women have been self-medicating for depression with alcohol and drugs—

sometimes for years. Memories can trigger depressive episodes, cause suicidal ideation, and threaten sobriety.

According to data from a 1985 National Association of State Alcohol and Drug Abuse Directors study, only 19.7% of patients in publicly funded alcohol treatment programs were women. Most treatment programs do not provide child care; nor do they allow adequate alternatives for mothers who need to enter treatment programs. This factor alone, according to a 1986 national study (National Council on Alcoholism, 1987), has been cited as the number one unmet need of alcoholic women. Most women who enter alcohol treatment programs have serious financial problems that severely limit their treatment options to public facilities with available slots (Sandmaier, 1980).

The physiological consequences of drinking are more severe for women than for men, with women experiencing a greater prevalence of pancreatitis, cirrhosis, ulcers, and cardiovascular problems. Minority women, particularly Black and Native American women, frequently have even greater health-related problems as a result of alcoholism. Alcoholism among Hispanic women is reported to be increasing and has been identified as a serious problem. Researchers suggest that ethnic minorities may use alcohol to escape reality, depressed socioeconomic conditions, conflicts, and suppressed hostilities (Comas-Diaz, 1986). Nevertheless, relatively little research has been conducted on drinking patterns and alcoholism among Black and Hispanic populations. Several studies have reported rates of alcohol and drug abuse of approximately 30% in the gay and lesbian population (Fiffield, 1975; Morales & Graves, 1983). One fourth of all respondents to the National Lesbian Health Care Survey used alcohol more than once a week and 16% had sought counseling for alcohol and drug use (Bradford & Ryan, 1988). Earlier reports have suggested that these high rates of use are associated with stigma, lack of societal supports, and negative internalized homophobia (Smith, 1982).

Conclusion and Recommendations

In closing, it must be noted that this section provides an incomplete coverage of depression in special populations of women, not only in thoroughness of coverage but in omission of certain groups. Although the coverage is incomplete, it was considered important to highlight the groups presented, even though at this time it is beyond the resources of the Task Force to study each population in depth or include all populations desired. More research on both the specific populations covered in this report and those that have been omitted needs to be initiated and completed in the future.

Clearly, gender-related societal and cultural conditions compound risk factors for women in the special populations discussed in this report. Mental health research, training, service delivery, and prevention programs must be designed to reflect knowledge of, and sensitivity to, the effects of such conditions. The current relevant knowledge base is meager. Nonetheless, what is known has neither been fully incorporated into education and training curricula nor translated into strategies for effective treatment and prevention. Much work needs to be done. The Task Force also recommends

1. culturally sensitive research and mental health training with regard to depression in ethnic minority women, particularly factors related to racism, immigration, acculturation, and bilingualism;

2. research to identify shared and unique experiences among women of diverse ethnic groups as they relate to risk factors for depression;

3. research to understand gender and ethnic stereotyping on the part of therapists in order to develop training materials to help them understand how their beliefs and values may affect diagnosis and treatment; and

4. research specifically focused on ascertaining the appropriateness of current diagnostic categories and assessment instruments for identifying depression in women of diverse ethnic groups and over the life cycle.

The Task Force also notes the need for research on how risk factors for the depressions might differ in women of diverse race/ethnicity, age, sexual orientation, occupation, education, income, and health status, particularly with regard to

1. the nature, meaning, and outcome of reproductivity-related events;

2. distribution of depression-related personality traits and other psychological factors, including explanatory style, self-disclosure, and coping expectancies;

3. access to coping resources and support networks; and

4. interpersonal violence and sexual abuse.

With regard to treatment issues, research on how women of diverse cultural and social characteristics may differentially respond to various types of treatment is also sparse. Outcome research is needed that specifically seeks to identify optimal treatment strategies for women in the diverse populations specified in this section. The Task Force recommends that

1. research be conducted on how correlations among depression and other conditions such as eating disorders and substance abuse might differ among women of diverse race/ethnicity, age, sexual orientation, occupation, and health status;

2. depression research, intervention, and prevention programs be targeted toward female adolescents, with the dual aim of reducing current depression and preventing depression later in the life cycle;

3. medication practices be examined and monitored, particularly in the case of elderly women who may respond differentially to medication as well as require medications for multiple conditions;

4. research be conducted on how issues of therapist–client similarity might differ among women in diverse populations;

5. issues that relate to access and appropriateness of treatment in diverse populations be examined, with efforts made to reduce barriers that make services inaccessible;

6. it be recognized that ancillary services such as child care and battered women's shelters may be requisite for access to treatment for some women; and

7. efforts be made to train bilingual and multilingual therapists and staff to provide treatment to specific non-English-speaking communities.

Finally, it should be recognized that increasing the diversity of characteristics of the population of mental health professionals plays a critical role in fostering diversity of perspective and understanding of cultural differences. Equal opportunity and affirmative action in education, training, and employment of mental health researchers, service providers, and policymakers continue to be important strategies for fostering diversity in psychology.

Bibliography

Abrahams, B., Feldman, S. S., & Nash, S. C. (1978). Sex role self-concept and sex role attitudes: Enduring personality characteristics or adaptations to changing life situations? *Developmental Psychology, 14,* 393–400.

Abramson, L. Y., & Andrews, D. E. (1982). Cognitive models of depression: Implications for sex differences in vulnerability to depression. *International Journal of Mental Health, 11,* 77–94.

Abramson, L. Y., Metalsky, G. L., & Alloy, L. B. (1989). Hopelessness depression: A theory-based subtype of depression. *Psychological Review, 96,* 358–372.

Abramson, L. Y., Seligman, M. E. P., & Teasdale, J. D. (1978). Learned helplessness in humans: Critique and reformulation. *Journal of Abnormal Psychology, 87,* 102–109.

Adler, N. E. (1975a). Abortion: A social psychological perspective. *Journal of Social Issues, 35,* 100–119.

Adler, N. (1975b). Emotional responses of women following therapeutic abortion. *American Journal of Orthopsychiatry, 45,* 446–456.

Adler, N. E., David, H. P., Major, B. N., Roth, S. H., Russo, N. F., & Wyatt, G. E. (1990). Emotional responses to abortion. *Science, 248,* 41–47.

Adler, N., & Dolcini, P. (1986). Psychological issues in abortion for adolescents. In G. B. Melton (Ed.), *Adolescent abortion: Psychological and legal issues* (pp. 74–95). Lincoln, NE: University of Nebraska Press.

Akiskal, H. S. (1987). The milder spectrum of biopolar disorders: Diagnostic, characteristic, and pharmacologic. *Psychiatry Annals, 17,* 32–37.

Aksikal, H. S., Rosenthal, T. L., Haykal, R. F., Lemmi, H., Rosenthal, R. H., & Scott-Strauss, A. (1980). Characterologic depressions-clinical sleep EEG findings separating "subaffective dysthymia" from "character spectrum disorders." *Archives of General Psychiatry, 37,* 777–783.

Albro, J. C., & Tulley, C. (1979). A study of lesbian lifestyles in the homosexual micro-culture and the heterosexual macro-culture. *Journal of Homosexuality, 4,* 331–344.

Alcohol, Drug Abuse and Mental Health Administration. (1989). Report of the Secretary's Task Force on Youth Suicide. Vols. 1 & 3. Washington, D.C.: U.S. Government Printing Office.

Alcoholics Anonymous. (1984). AA surveys its membership: A demographic report. *About AA: A newsletter for professional men and women.* New York: General Service Office.

Allen, M. G. (1976). Twin studies of affective illness. *Archives of General Psychiatry, 33,* 1476–1478.

Allen, C. S., & Lewinsohn, P. M. (1981). An investigation into the observed sex differences in prevalence of unipolar depression. *Journal of Abnormal Psychology, 90,* 1–13.

Alloy, L. B., Abramson, L. Y., & Metalsky, G. I. (1988). The hopelessness theory of depression: Attributional aspects. *British Journal of Clinical Psychology, 27,* 5–21.

Alloy, L. B., Peterson, C., Abramson, L. Y., & Seligman, M. E. P. (1984). Attributional style and the generality of learned helplessness. *Journal of Personality and Social Psychology, 46,* 681–687.

Amaro, H., Russo, N. F., & Johnson, J. (1987). Family and work predictors of psychological well-being among Hispanic women professionals. *Psychology of Women Quarterly, 11,* 505–521.

Amenson, C. S., & Lewinsohn, P. M. (1981). An investigation into the observed sex differences in prevalence of unipolar depression. *Journal of Abnormal Psychology, 90,* 1–13.

American College of Neuropsychopharmacology. (1987). *Psychopharmacology: The third generation of progress.* New York: Raven Press.

American Psychiatric Association. (1980). *Diagnostic and statistical manual of mental disorders* (3rd ed.). Washington, DC: Author.

American Psychiatric Association. (1987). *Diagnostic and statistical manual of mental disorders* (3rd ed., rev.). Washington, DC: Author.

Anderson, D. R. (1981). Diagnosis and prediction of suicidal risk among adolescents. In C. F. Wells and I. R. Stuart (Eds.). *Self destructive behavior in children and adolescents.* New York: Van Nostrand Reinhold, Co.

Aneshensel, C. (1986). Marital and employment role-strain, social support, and depression among adult women. In S. Hobfoll (Ed.), *Stress, social support, and women* (pp. 99–114). Washington, DC: Hemisphere.

Angler, N. (1990, March 29). New antidepressant is acclaimed but not perfect. *New York Times,* p. B9.

Angst, J. (1978). The course of affective disorders: Typology of bipolar manic-depressive illness. *Archives of General Psychiatrica. Nervenkr.*, *226*, 65–73.

Angst, J., & Dobler-Mikola, A. (1983). *Do the diagnostic criteria determine the sex ratio in depression?* Presented at the 22nd Annual Meeting of the American College of Neuropsychopharmacology, San Juan, Puerto Rico.

Arleti, S., & Bemporad, J. (1978). *Severe and mild depression: The psychotherapeutic approach.* New York: Basic Books.

Armstrong, L. (1983). *The home front: Notes from the family war zone.* New York: McGraw-Hill.

Athanasiou, R., Oppel, W., Michelson, L., Unger, I., & Yager, M. (1973). Psychiatric sequelae to term birth and induced early and later abortion: A longitudinal study. *Family Planning Perspectives*, *5*, 227–231.

Atkinson, D. R., Morten, G., & Wing, S. D. (1979). *Counseling American minorities: A cross-cultural perspective.* Dubuque, IA: William & Brown.

Bagley, C., & Ramsey, R. (1986). Sexual abuse in childhood: Psychosocial outcomes and implications for social work practice. *Journal of Social Work and Human Sexuality*, *5*, 33–47.

Baron, R. M., & Kenny, D. A. (1986). The moderator-mediator variable distinction in social psychological research: Conceptual, strategic, and statistical considerations. *Journal of Personality and Social Psychology*, *51*, 1173–1182.

Barrett, J. (1978). Effectiveness of widows' groups in facilitating change. *Journal of Consulting and Clinical Psychology*, *46*, 20–31.

Bass, E., & Davis, L. (1988). *The courage to heal.* New York: Harper and Row.

Bassoff, E. S., & Glass, G. V. (1982). The relationship between sex roles and mental health: A meta-analysis of twenty-six studies. *The Counseling Psychologist*, *10*, 105–112.

Baucom, D. H., & Danker-Brown, P. (1984). Sex role identity and sex stereotyped tasks in the development of learned helplessness in women. *Journal of Personality and Social Psychology*, *46*, 422–430.

Baum, C., Kennedy, D. L., Knapp, D. E., Juergens, J. P., & Faich, G. A. (1988). Prescription drug use in 1984 and changes over time. *Medical Care*, *26*, 105–114.

Beck, A. T. (1967). *Depression: Clinical, experimental and theoretical aspects.* Philadelphia: University of Pennsylvania Press.

Beck, A. T., & Emery, G. (1985). *Anxiety disorders and phobias: A cognitive perspective.* New York: Basic Books.

Beck, A. T., & Greenberg, R. L. (1974a). Cognitive therapy with depressed women. In V. Franks & V. Burtle (Eds.), *Women in therapy: New psychotherapies for a changing society.* New York: Brunner Mazel.

Beck, A. T., & Greenberg, R. L. (1974b). *Coping with depression.* New York: Institute for Rational Living.

Beck, A. T., Rush, A. J., Shaw, B. F., & Emery, G. (1979). *Cognitive therapy of depression.* New York: Guilford.

Beck, A. T., Steer, R. A., & McElroy (1982). Self-reported precedence of depression in alcoholism. *Drug and Alcohol Dependence*, *10*(2/3), 185–190.

Beck, A. T., Ward, C. H., Mendelsohn, M., Mock, J., & Erbaugh, J. (1961). An inventory for measuring depression. *Archives of General Psychiatry*, *4*, 561–571.

Becker, R. E., Heimberg, R. G., & Bellack, A. S. (1987). *Social skills training treatment for depression.* New York, Pergamon Press.

Bell, C. C., & Mehta, H. (1980). The diagnosis of black patients with manic depressive illness. *Journal of the National Medical Association*, *72*, 141–145.

Bell, J. S. (1981). Psychological problems among patients attending an infertility clinic. *Journal of Psychosomatic Research*, *25*, 1–3.

Bellack, A. S., Hersen, M., & Himmelhoch, J. (1981). Social skills training for depression: A treatment manual. *JSAS: Catalog of Selected Documents in Psychology*, *11*, 36.

Belle, D. (Ed.). (1982a). *Lives in stress: Women and depression.* Beverly Hills, CA: Sage.

Belle, D. (1982b). Social ties and social support. In D. Belle (Ed.), *Lives in stress: Women and depression.* Beverly Hills, CA: Sage.

Belle, D. (1988). *The Women's Mental Health Research Agenda: Poverty* (National Institute of Mental Health Occasional Paper Series). Rockville, MD: National Institute of Mental Health.

Belle, D. (1990). Poverty and women's mental health. *American Psychologist*, *45*, 385–389.

Belle, D., Dill, D., Longfellow, C., & Makosky, V. (1988, August). *Poverty and depression.* Paper presented at the annual meeting of the American Psychological Association, Atlanta.

Belle, D., & Longfellow, C. (1984, August). *Turning to others: Children's use of confidants.* Paper presented at the annual meeting of the American Psychological Association, Toronto.

Belsey, E. M., Greer, H. S., Lai, S., Lewis, S. C., & Beard, R. W. (1977). Predictive factors in emotional response to abortion: King's termination study—IV. *Social Science and Medicine, 11,* 71–82.

Belsky, J., Lang, M., & Huston, T. (1986). Sex typing and division of labor as determinants of marital change across the transition to parenthood. *Journal of Personality and Social Psychology, 50,* 517–522.

Bemporad, J. R. (1985). Long-term analytic treatment of depression. In E. E. Beck & W. R. Leber (Eds.), *Handbook of depression: Treatment, assessment, and research.* Homewood, IL: Dorsey Press.

Bepko, C., & Krestan, J. A. (1985). *The responsibility trap.* New York: Free Press.

Berger, R. M., & Kelly, J. J. (1986). Working with homosexuals of the older population. *The Journal of Contemporary Social Work, 67,* 203–210.

Bernard, J. (1971). *Women and the public interest.* Chicago: Aldine.

Berry, J. M., Storandt, M., & Coyne, A. (1984). Age and sex differences in somatic complaints associated with depression. *Journal of Gerontology, 39,* 465–467.

Biederman, J., Rivinus, T. M., Herzog, D. H., Harmtz, J. S., Shanley, K., & Yunis, E. J. (1984). High frequency of HLA-HW16 in patients with anorexia nervosa. *American Journal of Psychiatry, 14,* 1109–1110.

Billings, A. G., Cronkite, R. C., & Moos, R. H. (1983). Social-environmental factors in unipolar depression: Comparisons of depressed patients and nondepressed controls. *Journal of Abnormal Psychology, 92* 119–133.

Billings, A. G., & Moos, R. H. (1985). Psychosocial processes of remission in unipolar depression: Comparing depressed patients with matched community controls. *Journal of Consulting and Clinical Psychology, 53,* 314–325.

Blachly, P. H., Osterud, H. T., & Josslin, R. (1963). Suicide in professional groups. *New England Journal of Medicine, 268,* 1278–1282.

Black, D. W., Winokur, G., Bell, S., Nasrallah, A., & Hulbert, J. (1988). Complicated mania: Comorbidity and immediate outcome in the treatment of mania. *Archives of General Psychiatry, 45,* 232–236.

Blazer, D., Swartz, M., Woodbury, M., Manton, K. G., Huges, D., & George, L. K. (1988). Depressive symptoms and depressive diagnoses in a community population. *Archives of General Psychiatry, 45,* 1087–1084.

Blechman, E. A. (1980). Behavior therapies. In A. Broadsky & R. Hare-Mustin (Eds.), *Women and psychotherapy.* New York: Guilford Press.

Blechman, E. A. (1981). Competence, depression, and behavior modification with women. In M. Hersen, R. M. Eisler, & P. M. Miller (Eds.), *Progress in behavior modification* (pp. 227–263). New York: Academic Press.

Blechman, E. A. (1985). *Solving child behavior problems at home and at school.* Champlain, IL: Research Press.

Block, J., & Gjerde, P. F. (in press). Depressive symptomatology in late adolescence: A longitudinal perspective on personality antecedents. In J. E. Rolf, A. Masten, D. Cicchetti, K. Neuchterlein, & S. Weintraub (Eds.), *Risk and protective factors in the development of psychopathology.* New York: Cambridge University Press.

Bluestone, H., & Purdy, B. (1977). Psychiatry services: Two Puerto Rican patients in the Bronx. In Padilla & Padilla (Eds.), *Transcultural psychiatry: An Hispanic perspective.* Los Angeles: Spanish Speaking Research Center.

Blumenthal, S. J. (1988). A guide to risk factors assessment and treatment of suicidal patients. *Medical Clinics of North America, 72*(4).

Blumstein, P., & Schwartz, P. (1983). *American couples.* New York: William Morrow.

Bograd, M. (1989). Power, gender, and the family. Feminist perspectives on family systems theory. In M. A. Dutton-Doyglass & L. E. A. Walker (Eds.), *Feminist psychotherapies: Interaction of therapeutic and feminist systems.* Norwood, NJ: Ablex.

Bornstein, P. E., Clayton, P. J., Halikas, J. A., Maurice, W. L., & Robins, E. (1973). The depression of widowhood after thirteen months. *British Journal of Psychiatry, 122,* 561–566.

Bottinger, L. E., Furhoff, A. K., & Holmberg, L. (1979). Fatal reactions to drugs: A 10 year material from the Swedish Adverse Drug Reaction Committee. *Acta Medica Scandinavica, 205*, 451–456.

Boyd, J. H., & Weissman, M. M. (1981). Epidemiology of affective disorders: A re-examination and future directions. *Archives of General Psychiatry, 38*, 1039–1046.

Bradford, J., & Ryan, C. (1988). *National lesbian health care survey: Final report.* Washington, DC: National Lesbian and Gay Health Foundation.

Bratfos, D., & Haug, J. (1966). Puerperal mental disorders in manic-depressive females. *Acta Psychiatrica Scandinavica, 42*, 285–294.

Brewer, J. C. (1977). Incidence of post-abortion psychosis: A prospective study. *British Medical Journal, 1*, 476.

Brewin, C. R. (1985). Depression and causal attribution: What is their relation? *Psychological Bulletin, 98*, 297–309.

Brockington, I. F., & Kumar, R. (1982). *Motherhood and illness.* New York: Grune & Stratton.

Brody, C. M. (1984). *Women therapists working with women: New theory and process of feminist therapy.* New York: Springer.

Brody, C. M. (1987). *Women's therapy groups: Paradigms of feminist treatment.* New York: Springer.

Brody, E., & Schoonover, C. (1986). Patterns of parent-care when adult daughters work and when they do not. *The Gerontologist, 26*, 372–382.

Brooks-Gunn, J., & Warren, M. P. (1989). Biological and social contributions to negative affect in young adolescent girls. *Child Development, 60*, 40–55.

Broverman, I. K., Broverman, D., Clarkson, F. E., Rosencrantz, P., & Vogel, S. (1970). Sex role stereotypes and clinical judgments of mental health. *Journal of Consulting and Clinical Psychology, 34*, 1–7.

Brown, C., Ni Bhrolchain, M. N., & Harris, T. O. (1975). Social class and psychiatric disturbance among women in an urban population. *Sociology, 9*, 225–254.

Brown, G. W., Bifulco, A., Harris, T., & Bridge, L. (1986). Life stress, chronic subclinical symptoms and vulnerability to clinical depression. *Journal of Affective Disorders, 11*, 1–19.

Brown, G. W., & Harris, T. O. (1978). *Social origins of depression: A study of psychiatric disorder in women.* New York: Free Press.

Brown, G. W., & Prudo, R. (1981). Psychiatric disorder in a rural and urban population: 1. Aetiology of depression. *Psychological Medicine, 11*, 601–616.

Brown, L. S. (1982). Choosing a therapist. In G. Hongladarom, R. McCorkle, & N. Fugate-Woods (Eds.), *The complete book of women's health.* New York: Prentice-Hall.

Brown, L. S. (1984). Finding new language: Beyond analytic verbal shorthand in feminist therapy. *Women and Therapy, 3*, 73–80.

Brown, L. S. (1986). Gender-role analysis: A neglected component of psychological assessment. *Psychotherapy, 23*, 243–248.

Brown, L. S. (1987). From alienation to connection: Feminist therapy with post traumatic stress disorder. *Women and Therapy, 5*, 13–26.

Brown, L. S. (1989). Feminist therapy with lesbians and gay men. In M. A. Dutton-Douglas & L. E. A. Walker (Eds.), *Feminist psychotherapies: Integration of therapeutic and feminist systems.* Norwood, NJ: Ablex.

Brown, L. S. (1990). Taking account of gender in the clinical assessment interview. *Professional Psychology: Research and Practice, 21*, 12–17.

Bryer, J. B., Nelson, B. A., Miller, J. B., & Krol, P. A. (1987). Childhood sexual and physical abuse as factors in adult psychiatric illness. *American Journal of Psychiatry, 114*, 1426–1430.

Bucholz, K. K., & Dinwiddie, S. H. (1989). Influence of nondepressive psychiatric symptoms on whether patients tell a doctor about depression. *American Journal of Psychiatry, 146*(5), 640–644.

Buesching, D. P., Glasser, M. L., & Frate, D. A. (1986). Progression of depression in the prenatal and postpartum periods. *Women's Health, 11*, 61–78.

Buhrich, N., & Loke, C. (1988). Homosexuality, suicide, and parasuicide in Australia. *Journal of Homosexuality, 15*, 113–129.

Bungay, G. T., Vessey, M. P., & McPherson, C. K. (1980). Study of symptoms in middle life with specific reference to the menopause. *British Medical Journal, 281*, 181–183.

Burns, D. (1980). *The feeling good handbook: Using the new mood therapy in everyday life.* New York: William Morrow.

Cabaj, R. P. (1988). Homosexuality and neurosis: Considerations for psychotherapy. *Journal of Homosexuality, 15*, 13–23.

Cafferata, G. L., Kasper, J., & Bernstein, A. (1983). Family roles, structure, and stressors in relation to sex differences in obtaining psychotropic drugs. *Journal of Health and Social Behavior*, *24*, 132–143.

Caldwell, M. A., & Peplau, L. A. (1982). Sex differences in same-sex friendship. *Sex Roles*, *8*, 721–732.

Campbell, A., Converse, P., & Rodgers, W. (1976). *The quality of American life: Perceptions, evaluations, and satisfactions*. New York: Russell Sage.

Campbell, E. A., Cope, S. J., & Teasdale, J. D. (1983). Social factors and affective disorder: An investigation of Brown and Harris' model. *British Journal of Psychiatry*, *138*, 548–553.

Canino, G., Rubio-Stipec, M., Shrout, P., Bravo, M., Stolberg, R., & Bird, H. (1987). Sex differences and depression in Puerto Rico. *Psychology of Women Quarterly*, *11*, 443–459.

Carkhuff, R. R., & Pierce, R. (1967). Differential effects of therapist race and social class upon patient depth of self-exploration in the initial clinical interview. *Journal of Clinical and Consulting Psychology*, *31*, 632–634.

Carlson, G. A., & Miller, D. C. (1981). Suicide, affective disorder, and women physicians. *American Journal of Psychiatry*, *138*, 1330–1335.

Carmen, E., Reiker, P. B., & Mills, T. (1984). Victims of violence and psychiatric illness. *American Journal of Psychiatry*, *141*(3), 378–382.

Cartwright, R. D. (1988). *Sex differences in depression as revealed by the biological markers of sleep*. Paper presented at Women and Depression Task Force meeting of the American Psychological Association.

Cartwright, R. D. (1989, August). *Sleep and dreams in depressed men and women undergoing divorce*. Paper presented at the meeting of the American Psychological Association, New Orleans, LA.

Caste, C., Blodgett, J., & Rubinow, D. (1978). *Cross cultural differences in presenting problems: Implications for service delivery and treatment modality*. Unpublished manuscript, Yale University School of Medicine, Department of Psychiatry, New Haven, CT.

Castello, C. (1982). Social factors associated with depression: A retrospective community study. *Psychological Medicine*, *12*, 329–339.

Chiles, J. A., Strosahl, K. D., Ping, Z. Y., Michael, M. C., et al. (1989). Depression, hopelessness, and suicidal behavior in Chinese and American psychiatric patients. *American Journal of Psychiatry*, *146*, 339–344.

Chodorow, N. (1974). Family structure and feminine personality. In M. Rosaldo & L. Lampere (Eds.), *Women, culture, and society*. Stanford, CA: Stanford University Press.

Chodorow, N. (1978). *The reproduction of mothering*. Berkeley, CA: University of California Press.

Chollet, D. (1987). *Uninsured in the U.S.: The non-elderly population without health insurance*. Washington, DC: Employee Benefit Research Institute.

Citizens' Commission on Human Rights. (1990). *Prozac: A dangerous drug which is falsely promoted as being virtually harmless*. Los Angeles: Author.

Clare, A. W. (1979). The treatment of premenstrual symptoms. *British Journal of Psychiatry*, *135*, 576–579.

Clark, V. A., Aneshensel, C. S., Frerichs, R. R., & Morgan, T. M. (1981). Analysis of effects of sex and age on response to items on the CES-D Scale. *Psychiatry Research*, *5*, 171–181.

Clayton, P. J., Marten, S., Davis, M. A., & Wochnik, E. (1980). Mood disorder in women professionals. *Journal of Affective Disorders*, *2*, 37–46.

Climent, C. E., Ervin, F. R., Rollins, A., Pletchnik, R., & Batinelli, C. J. (1977). Epidemiological studies of female prisoners. *Journal of Nervous and Mental Disease*, *164*, 25–29.

Cloninger, C. R., Christiansen, K. O., Reich, T., & Gottesman, I. (1978). Implications of sex differences in the prevalence of antisocial personality, alcoholism, and criminality for familial transmission. *Archives of General Psychiatry*, *35*, 941–951.

Cobb, S. (1976). Social support as a moderator of life stress. *Psychosomatic Medicine*, *38*(5), 314–330.

Cohen, L., & Roth, S. (1984). *Journal of Human Stress*, *10*(3), 140–145.

Cohler, B., & Leiberman, M. (1980). Social relations and mental health: Middle-aged and older men and women from three European ethnic groups. *Research on Aging*, *2*, 445–469.

Coleman, J. S. (1961). *The adolescent society: The social life of the teenager and its impact on education*. New York: Free Press.

Colliver, J. D., & Malin, H. (1986). State and national trends in alcohol related morbidity: 1975–1982. *Alcohol and Health Research World*, *10*, 60–64.

Comas-Diaz, L. (1981). Effects of cognitive and behavioral group treatment in the depressive symptomology of Puerto Rican women. *Journal of Consulting and Clinical Psychology*, *49*, 627–632.

Comas-Diaz, L. (1986). Puerto Rican alcoholic women: Treatment considerations. *Alcoholism Treatment Quarterly, 3,* 47–57.

Comas-Diaz, L. (1987). Feminist therapy with Puerto Rican women. *Psychology of Women Quarterly, 11,* 461–474.

Comas-Diaz, L. (1988). Feminist therapy with Hispanic/Latina women: Myth or reality? *Women and Therapy, 6,* 39–61.

Comas-Diaz, L., & Duncan, J. W. (1985). The cultural context: A factor in assertiveness training with mainland Puerto Rican women. *Psychology of Women Quarterly, 9.*

Connolly, K. J., Edelmann, R. J., & Cooke, I. D. (1987). Distress and marital problems associated with infertility. *Journal of Reproductive and Infant Psychology, 5,* 49–57.

Conrad, C. D., & Hamilton, J. A. (1986). Recurrent premenstrual decline in serum lithium concentration: Clinical correlates and treatment implications. *Journal of the American Academy of Child Psychiatry, 26,* 852–853.

Conte, H. R., Plutchik, R., Wild, C. V., & Karasu, T. B. (1986). Combined psychotherapy and pharmacotherapy for depression. A systematic analysis of the evidence. *Archives of General Psychiatry, 43,* 471–479.

Cooperstock, R. (1981). A review of women's psychotropic drug use. In E. Howell, & M. Bayes (Eds.), *Women and mental health* (pp. 131–140). New York: Basic Books.

Cooperstock, R., & Sims, M. (1971). Mood modifying drugs prescribed in a Canadian city: Hidden problems. *American Journal of Public Health, 65.*

Costello, C. G. (1982). Social factors associated with depression: A retrospective community study. *Psychological Medicine, 12,* 329–339.

Covi, L., Lipman, R. S., Derogatis, L. R., Smith, J. E., & Patterson, J. H. (1974). Drugs and group psychotherapy in neurotic depression. *American Journal of Psychiatry, 131,* 191–198.

Cowan, C. P., Cowan, P. A., Heming, G., Garrett, E., Coysh, W. S., Curtis-Boles, H., & Boles, A. J., III. (1985). Transitions to parenthood: His, hers, and theirs. *Journal of Family Issues, 6,* 451–481.

Coyne, J. C. (1976). Depression and the response of others. *Journal of Abnormal Psychology, 85,* 186–193.

Craig, A., & Pitts, F. (1968). Suicide by physicians. *Diseases of the Nervous System, 29,* 763–772.

Craig, P. E. (1953). Premenstrual tension and the menopause. *Medical Times, 81.*

Craig, T. J., & Van Natta, P. A. (1979). Influence of demographic characteristics on two measures of depressive symptoms. *Archives of General Psychiatry, 36,* 149–154.

Crook, T., & Raskin, A. (1975). Association of childhood parental loss with attempted suicide and depression. *Journal of Consulting and Clinical Psychology, 43*(2).

Cunningham, J. D., & Anthill, J. K. (1984). Changes in masculinity and femininity across the family life cycle: A re-examination. *Developmental Psychology, 20,* 1135–1141.

Dalton, K. (1964). *The premenstrual syndrome.* London: Heineman Medical.

Dalton, K. (1977). *The premenstrual syndrome and progesterone therapy.* Chicago: William Heineman.

Daniluk, J. C., Leader, A., & Taylor, P. J. (1985). Infertility: Clinical and psychological aspects. *Psychiatric Annals, 14,* 461–467.

Dannello, M. A. (1986). FDA's perspective on women and drugs. In B. A. Ray & M. C. Braude (Eds.), *Women and drugs: A new era for research* (Monograph 65). Rockville, MD: National Institute on Drug Abuse Research.

David, H. P., Rasmussen, N., & Holst, E. (1981). Postpartum and postabortion psychotic reactions. *Family Planning Perspectives, 13*(2), 88–93.

Davidson, J., & Pelton, S. (1986). Forms of atypical depression and their response to antidepressant drugs. *Psychiatry Research, 17,* 87–95.

Davidson-Muskihn, M., & Golden, C. (1989). Lao Depression Inventory. *Journal of Personality Assessment, 53,* 161–168.

Davis, M. (1985). Premenstrual syndrome. In *Report of the Public Health Service Task Force on Women's Health* (Vol. 2). Washington, DC: U.S. Government Printing Office.

De Rubis, R. J., Hollon, S. D., Evans, M. D., & Bemis, K. M. (1982). Can psychotherapies for depression be discriminated? A systematic investigation of cognitive therapy and interpersonal therapy. *Journal of Consulting and Clinical Psychology, 50,* 744–756.

Deykin, E. Y., Klerman, G. L., & Wells, V. E. (1986). The prevalence of depressive symptoms in college students. *Social Psychiatry, 22*(1):20–28.

Diamond, D. L., & Wilsnack, S. C. (1978). Alcohol abuse among lesbians: A descriptive study. *Journal of Homosexuality, 4*, 123–142.

Doane, B. K., & Quigley, B. G. (1981). Psychiatric aspects of therapeutic abortion. *Canadian Medical Association, 125*, 427.

Dohrenwend, B. S. (1973). Social status and stressful life events. *Journal of Personality and Social Psychology, 28*, 225–235.

Dohrenwend, B. S. (1976). *Anticipation and control of stressful life events: An explanatory analysis.* Paper presented to the annual meeting of the Eastern Psychological Association, New York.

Domincq, C., Naranjo, C. A., Rulz, I., & Busto, U. (1980). Sex-related variations in the frequency and characteristics of adverse drug reactions. *International Journal of Clinical Pharmacology, Therapy and Toxicology, 18*, 362–366.

Donnelson, E. (1977). Becoming a single woman. In E. Donnelson & J. E. Gullahorn (Eds.), *Women: A psychological perspective.* New York: John Wiley & Sons.

Dornbusch, S. M., Carlsmith, J. M., Duncan, P. D., Gross, R. T., Martin, J. A., Ritter, P. L., & Siegel-Gorelick, B. (1984). Sexual masturbation, social class, and the desire to be thin among adolescent females. *Developmental and Behavioral Pediatrics, 5*, 308–314.

Dorpat, T., Jackson, J., & Ripley, H. (1965). Broken homes and attempted and completed suicide. *Archives of General Psychiatry, 39*, 1205–1212.

Doyne, E. J., Chambless, D. L., & Beutler, L. E. (1983). Aerobic exercise as a treatment for depression in women. *Behavior Therapy, 14*, 434–440.

Dunner, F. J., Patrick, R., & Fieve, R. R. (1977). Rapid cycling manic depressive patients. *Comprehensive Psychiatry, 18*.

Dutton-Douglas, M. A., & Walker, L. E. A. (Eds.). (1989). *Feminist psychotherapies: Interaction of therapeutic and feminist systems.* Norwood, NJ: Ablex.

Dychtwald, K., & Flower, J. (1989). *Age wave: The challenges and opportunities of an aging America.* Los Angeles: Jeremy P. Tarcher.

Eaves, G., & Rush, A. J. (1984). Cognitive patterns in symptomatic and remitted unipolar major depression. *Journal of Abnormal Psychology, 93*, 31–40.

Eckenrode, J., & Gore, S. (1981). Stressful events and social support: The significance of context. In B. Gottlieb (Ed.), *Social networks and social support.* Beverly Hills, CA: Sage.

Eckert, E. D., Goldberg, S. C., Halni, K. A., Casper, R. C., & Davis, J. M. (1982). Depression in anorexia nervosa. *Psychological Medicine, 12*, 115–122.

Egeland, J. A., & Hostetter, A. M. (1983). Amish Study: I. Affective disorders among the Amish. 1976–1980. *American Journal of Psychiatry, 140*, 56–61.

Ehlers, C. L., Frank, E., & Kupfer, D. J. (1988). Social zeitgebers and biological rhythms: A unified approach to understanding the etiology of depression. *Archives of General Psychology, 45*, 948–952.

Eichenbaum, L., & Orbach, S. (1983). *Understanding women: A feminist psychoanalytic perspective.* New York: Basic Books.

Eichler, A., & Parron, D. L. (1987). *NIMH Women's Mental Health: Agenda for Research.* Maryland: National Institute of Mental Health.

Elkin, I., Parloff, M. B., Hadley, S. W., & Autry, J. H. (1985). NIMH Treatment of Depression Collaborative Research Program. *Archives of General Psychiatry, 42*, 305–316.

Elkin, I., Shea, T., Watkins, J. T., Imber, S. D., Stosky, S. M., Collins, J. F., Glass, D. R., Pilkonis, P. A., Leber, W. R., Docherty, J. P., Fiester, S. J., & Perloff, M. B. (1989). National Institute of Mental Health Treatment of Depression Collaborative Research Program: General effectiveness of treatments. *Archives of General Psychiatry, 46*, 971–982.

Ellis, E. M., Atkeson, B. M., & Calhoun, K. S. (1981). An assessment of long-term reaction to rape. *Journal of Abnormal Psychology, 90*, 263–266.

Ellis, E. M., Atkeson, B. M., & Calhoun, K. S. (1982). An examination of differences between multiple- and single-incident victims of sexual assault. *Journal of Abnormal Psychology, 91*, 221–224.

Emery, G. (1982). *Own your own life.* New York: New American Library.

Emery, G. (1988). *Getting undepressed.* New York: Touchstone.

Emery, G., & Campbell, J. (1987). *Rapid release from emotional distress.* New York: Fawcett Book Group.

Endicott, J., Halbreich, U., Schact, S., & Nee, J. (1981). Premenstrual changes and affective disorders. *Psychosomatic Medicine, 43*, 519–530.

Ensel, W. M. (1982). The role of age and the relationship of gender and marital status to depression. *Journal of Nervous and Mental Disease, 170*, 536–543.

Etaugh, C., & Brown, B. (1975). Perceiving the cause of success and failure of male and female performances. *Developmental Psychology, 11*(1).

Ettorre, E. M. (1986). Social lesbians and social lesbianism. In E. M. Ettorre (Ed.), *Lesbians, women, and society.* London: Routledge & Kegan Paul.

Evans, G., & Farberow, N. L. (1988). *The Encyclopedia of Suicide.* New York: Facts on File.

Ewing, J. A., & Rouse, B. A. (1973). Therapeutic abortion and a prior psychiatric history. *American Journal of Psychiatry, 130*, 37–40.

Feldman, S. S., Birigen, Z. C., & Nash, S. C. (1981). Fluctuations of sex-related self-attributions as a function of stage of family life cycle. *Developmental Psychology, 17*, 24–35.

Feminist Therapy Institute. (1987). *Feminist therapy ethical code.* Denver: Author.

Fidel, L. S. (1981). Sex differentials in psychotrophic drug use. *Professional Psychologist 12*, 156–162.

Fidel, L. S. (1982). Gender and drug use and abuse. In I. Al-Issa (Ed.), *Gender and psychopathology.* New York: Academic Press.

Fiffield, L. (1975). *On my way to nowhere: Alienated, isolated, drunk.* Unpublished report, Gay Community Services Center, Los Angeles, CA.

Fingerer, M. (1973). Psychological sequelae of abortion: Anxiety and depression. *Journal of Community Psychology, 1*, 221–225.

Finkelhor, D. (1979). *Sexually victimized children.* New York: Free Press.

Finkelhor, D. (1987). The sexual abuse of children: Current research reviewed. *Psychiatric Annals, 17*, 233–241.

Finkelhor, D., & Yilo, K. (1985). *License to rape.* New York: Holt, Rinehart, and Winston.

Firth, H., McKeown, P., McIntee, J., & Britton, P. (1987). Professional depression, "burnout" and personality in longstay nursing. *International Journal of Nursing Students, 24*, 227–237.

Firth, J., & Brewin, C. R. (1982). Attributions and recovery from depression: A preliminary study using cross-lagged correlation analysis. *British Journal of Clinical Psychology, 21*, 229–330.

Fisher, C. (1982). *To dwell among friends: Personal networks in town and city.* Chicago: University of Chicago Press.

Flett, G. L., Vredenburg, K., & Pliner, P. (1985). Sex roles and depression: A preliminary investigation of the direction of causality. *Journal of Research in Personality, 19*, 429–435.

Fodor, I. G. (1989). Cognitive behavior therapy: Evaluation of theory and practice for addressing women's issues. In M. A. Dutton-Douglas & L. E. A. Walker (Eds.), *Feminist psychotherapies: Integration of therapeutic and feminist systems.* Norwood, NJ: Ablex.

Folkins, C. H., & Sime, W. E. (1981). Physical fitness training and mental health. *American Psychologist, 36*, 373–389.

Follingstad, D. R., Robinson, E. A., & Pugh, M. (1977). Effects of consciousness raising groups on measures of self-esteem and social desirability. *Journal of Counseling Psychology, 24*, 223–230.

Foorman, S., & Lloyd, C. (1986). The relationship between social support and psychiatric symptomology in medical students. *Journal of Nervous and Mental Disease, 174*, 229–239.

Formanek, R., & Gurian, A. (Eds.). (1987). *Women and depression: A lifespan perspective.* New York: Springer.

Frank, J. D. (1974). *Persuasion and healing.* New York: Schocken.

Freeman, E. W. (1977). Influence of personality attributes on abortion experiences. *American Journal of Orthopsychiatry, 47*, 503–513.

Freeman, E. W. (1978). Abortion: Subjective attitudes and feelings. *Family Planning Perspectives, 10*, 150–155.

Freeman, S. J., O'Neil, M. K., & Lance, W. J. (1985). Sex differences in depression in university students. *Social Psychiatry, 20*(4), 186–190.

Freeman, T. (1951). Pregnancy as a precipitant of mental illness in men. *British Journal of Medical Psychology, 24*, 49–54.

Friedman, A. S. (1975). Interaction of drug therapy with marital therapy in depressive patients. *Archives of General Psychiatry, 32*, 619–637.

Friend, R. A. (1987). The individual and social psychology of aging: Clinical implications for lesbians and gay men. *Journal of Homosexuality, 14*, 307–331.

Fuchs, C. Z., & Rehm, L. P. (1977). A self-control behavior therapy program for depression. *Journal of Consulting and Clinical Psychology, 45,* 206–215.

Gallant, S. J., & Hamilton, J. A. (1988). On a premenstrual psychiatric diagnosis: What's in a name? *Professional Psychology: Research and Practice, 19,* 271–278.

Ganley, A. (1989). Feminist therapy with male clients. In M. A. Dutton-Douglas & L. E. A. Walker (Eds.), *Feminist psychotherapies: Interaction of therapeutic and feminist systems.* Norwood, NJ: Ablex.

Gartrell, N. (1981). The lesbian as a "single" woman. *American Journal of Psychotherapy, 35,* 502–509.

Garza-Guerrero, A. C. (1974). Culture shock: Its mourning and vicissitudes of identity. *Journal of the American Psychoanalytic Association, 22,* 408–429.

Gelinas, D. J. (1983). The persisting negative effects of incest. *Psychiatry, 46,* 312–332.

Gershon, E. S. (1983). The genetics of affective disorders. In L. Grinspoon (Ed.), *Psychiatric update* (Vol. 2, pp. 434–457). Washington, DC: American Psychiatric Press.

Gershon, E. S., Berrettini, W., Nurnberger, J., & Goldin, L. R. (1987). Genetics of affective illness. In H. Y. Meltzer (Ed.), *Psychopharmacology: The third generation of progress.* New York: Raven Press.

Gibaldi (1984). *Biopharmaceutics and clinical pharmacokinetics* (3rd. ed.). Philadelphia: Lea and Febiger.

Gidycz, C. A., & Koss, M. P. (1989). The impact of adolescent sexual victimization: Standardized measures of anxiety, depression, and behavioral deviancy. *Violence and Victims, 4,* 139–149.

Gilbert, L. A. (1980). Feminist therapy. In A. Brodsky & R. Hare-Mustin (Eds.), *Women in psychotherapy.* New York: Guilford Press.

Gilbert, L. A. (1985). *Men in dual-career families: Current realities and future prospects.* Hillsdale, NJ: Erlbaum.

Gilligan, C. (1977). In a different voice: Women's conceptions of the self and of morality. *Harvard Educational Review, 47,* 481–517.

Gilligan, C. (1982). *In a different voice: Psychological theory and women's development.* Cambridge, MA: Harvard University Press.

Gilligan, C., Lyons, N., & Hammer, T. J. (Eds.). (1989). *Making connections: The relational worlds of adolescent girls at Emma Willard School.* Troy, NY: Emma Willard School.

Girgus, J. S. (1989, August). *Why do sex differences in depression emerge during adolescence?* Paper presented at the annual convention of the American Psychological Association, New Orleans.

Glaus, K. O. (1989). Alcoholism, chemical dependency and the lesbian client. *Women and Therapy, 8,* 131–144.

Glenn, N. D., & Weaver, C. N. (1979). Attitudes toward premarital, extramarital, and homosexual relations in the U.S. in the 1970s. *The Journal of Sex Research, 15,* 108–118.

Gold, P. W., Goodwin, F. K., & Chrousos, G. P. (1988a). Clinical and biochemical manifestations of depression, part one: Relation to the neurobiology of stress. *New England Journal of Medicine, 319,* 348–353.

Gold, P. W., Goodwin, F. K., & Chrousos, G. P. (1988b). Clinical and biochemical manifestations of depression, part two: Relation to the neurobiology of stress. *New England Journal of Medicine, 319,* 413–420.

Golding, J. M. (1988). Gender differences in depressive symptoms: Statistical considerations. *Psychology of Women Quarterly, 12,* 61–74.

Goldman, N., & Ravid, R. (1980). Community surveys: Sex differences in mental illness. In M. Guttentag, S. Salasin, & D. Belle (Eds.), *The mental health of women.* New York: Academic Press.

Goldstein, M. B. (1980). Interpersonal support and coping among first-year dental students. *Journal of Dental Education, 44,* 202–205.

Gonzales, L. R., Lewinsohn, P. M., & Clarke, G. N. (1985). Longitudinal follow-up of unipolar depression: An investigation of predictors of relapse. *Journal of Clifton and Consulting Psychology, 53,* 461–469.

Goodwin, D. W. (1982). Alcohol and affective disorders: The basic questions. In J. Solomon (Ed.), *Alcoholism and clinical psychiatry.* New York: Plenum.

Goodwin, F. K., & Jamison, K. R. (1990). *Manic depressive illness.* New York: Oxford University Press.

Gove, W. R. (1972). The relationship between sex roles, marital status, and mental illness. *Social Forces, 51,* 34–44.

Gove, W. R., & Geerken, M. R. (1977). The effect of children and employment on the mental health of married men and women. *Social Forces, 56,* 66–76.

Gove, W. R. G., Hughes, M., & Styles, C. G. (1983). Does marriage have positive effects on the psychological well-being of the individual? *Journal of Health and Social Behavior, 24,* 122–131.

Gove, W. R., & Tudor, J. F. (1973). Adult sex roles and mental illness. *American Journal of Sociology, 78,* 812–835.

Grahn, J. (1986). Strange country this: Lesbianism and North American Indian tribes. *Journal of Homosexuality, 12,* 43–57.

Greenberg, J. S. (1976). The effects of a homophile organization of the self-esteem and alienation of its members. *Journal of Homosexuality, 1,* 313–317.

Greenblatt, D. J., Abernethy, D. R., Locniskar, A., Ochs, H. R., Harmatz, J. S., & Shader, R. I. (1985). Age, sex, and nitrazepam kinetics: Relation to antipyrine disposition. *Clinical Pharmacology and Therapeutics, 38,* 697–703.

Griffin, M. L., Weiss, R. D., Mirin, S. M., & Lange, U. (1989). A comparison of male and female cocaine abusers. *Archives of General Psychiatry, 46,* 122–126.

Gurman, A. S., & Klein, M. S. (1980). Marital and family conflicts. In A. Brodsky & R. Hare-Mustin (Eds.), *Women in psychotherapy.* New York: Guilford Press.

Gurman, A. S., & Kniskern, D. P. (1978). Research on marital and family therapy: Progress, perspective, and prospect. In S. L. Garfield & E. E. Bergin (Eds.), *Handbook of psychotherapy and behavior change.* New York: Wiley.

Gurman, A. S., & Kniskern, D. P. (1981). Family therapy outcome research: Knowns and unknowns. In A. S. Gurman & D. P. Kniskern (Eds.), *Handbook on family therapy.* New York: Brunner/Mazel.

Haas, G. L., Clarkin, J. F., & Glick, I. D. (1985). Marital and family treatment of depression. In E. E. Beckham & W. R. Leber (Eds.), *Handbook of depression: Treatment, assessment, and research.* Homewood, IL: Dorsey Press.

Hagnell, O., Lanke, J., Rorsman, B., & Ojesjo, L. (1982). Are we entering an age of melancholy? Depressive illnesses in prospective epidemiological study over 25 years: The Lundby Study, Sweden. *Psychological Medicine, 12,* 279–289.

Hale, W. D., & Cochran, C. D. (1983). Sex differences in patterns of self-reported psychopathology in the married elderly. *Journal of Clinical Psychology, 39,* 647–650.

Hall, M. (1981). Lesbian families: Cultural and clinical issues. In E. Howell & M. Bayes (Eds.), *Women and mental health.* New York: Basic Books.

Hall, M. (1986). The lesbian corporate experience. *Journal of Homosexuality, 12,* 59–75.

Hall, D. T., & Gordon, F. E. (1972). Career choices of married women: Effects on conflict role behavior and satisfaction. *Journal of Applied Psychology, 58,* 42–48.

Hallstrom, T., & Persson, G. (1984). The relationship of social setting to major depression. *Acta Psychiatrica Scandinavica, 70,* 327–336.

Hamilton, E. W., & Abramson, L. Y. (1983). Cognitive patterns and major depressive disorder: A longitudinal study in a hospital setting. *Journal of Abnormal Psychology, 92,* 173–184.

Hamilton, J. A. (1984). Psychobiology in context: Reproductive-related events in men's and women's lives (review of *Motherhood and mental illness*). *Contemporary Psychiatry, 3,* 12–16.

Hamilton, J. A. (1986). An overview of the clinical rationale for advancing gender-related psychopharmacology and drug abuse research. In B. A. Ray & M. C. Braude (Eds.), *Women and drugs: A new era for research* (National Institute on Drug Abuse Research Monograph 65, pp. 14–20). Rockville, MD: National Institute on Drug Abuse.

Hamilton, J. A. (1986). Working with adolescent girls: New findings and clinical application (excerpts from a workshop sponsored by The American Healthcare Institute).

Hamilton, J. A. (Ed.). (1988). *Risk factors for depression in women and diagnostic subtypes* (Report from the Committee on Etiology and Diagnosis, Task Force on Women and Depression). Washington, DC: American Psychological Association.

Hamilton, J. A. (1989). Emotional consequences of victimization and discrimination in "special populations" of women. In B. Perry (Ed.), *Women's disorders.* Philadelphia: W. B. Saunders.

Hamilton, J. A., Alagna, S. W., King, L. S., & Lloyd, C. (1987). The emotional consequences of gender-based abuse in the workplace: New counseling programs for sex discrimination. *Women and Therapy, 6(1/2):*155–182.

Hamilton, J. A., Alagna, S. W., Parry, B., Herz, E. K., Blumenthal, S., & Conrad, C. (1985). An update on premenstrual depression: Evaluation and treatment. In J. H. Gold (Ed.), *The psychiatric implications of menstruation* (pp. 2–19). Washington, DC: American Psychiatric Press.

Hamilton, J.A., & Conrad, C. D. (1987). Toward a developmental psychopharmacology: The physiological basis of age, gender, and hormonal effects on drug responsivity. In J. D. Noshpitz, J. D. Call, R. L. Cohen, et al. (Eds.), *Basic handbook of child psychiatry: Vol. 5. Advances and new directions* (pp. 66–87). New York: Basic Books.

Hamilton, J. A., & Gallant, S. A. (in press). Problematic aspects of diagnosing premenstrual phase dysphoria: Recommendations for psychological research and practice. *Professional Psychology*.

Hamilton, J. A., & Jensvold, M. (1989). Complicated depressions and antidepressants in women. *Psychiatric Times*. (Note: This was an invited CE article submitted in July 1989.)

Hamilton, J. A., Lloyd, C., Alagna, S. W., Phillips, K., & Pinkel, S. (1984). Gender, depressive subtypes, and gender-age effects on antidepressant response: Hormonal hypotheses. *Psychopharmacology Bulletin, 20*, 475–480.

Hamilton, J. A., Parry, B. L., & Blumenthal, S. J. (1988a). The menstrual cycle in context: I. Affective syndromes associated with reproductive hormonal changes. *Journal of Clinical Psychiatry, 49*, 474–480.

Hamilton, J. A., Parry, B. L., & Blumenthal, S. L. (1988b). The menstrual cycle in context: II. Human gonadal steroid hormone variability. *Journal of Clinical Psychiatry, 49*, 480–484.

Hammen, C., Gordon, D., Burge, D., Adrian, C., Jaenicke, C., & Hiroto, D. (1987). Maternal affective disorders, illness, and stress: Risk for children's psychopathology. *American Journal of Psychiatry, 144*, 736–741.

Hammen, C. L., & Padesky, C. A. (1977). Sex differences in the expression of depressive responses on the Beck Depression Inventory. *Journal of Abnormal Psychology, 86*, 609–614.

Hammond, N. (1989). Lesbian victims of relationship violence. *Women and Therapy, 8*, 89–105.

Harrison, M. (1985). *Self-help for premenstrual syndrome*. New York: Random House.

Hatsukami, D., Eckert, E., Mitchell, J. E., & Pyle, R. (1984). Affective disorder and substance abuse in women with bulimia. *Psychological Medicine, 14*, 701–704.

Haug, M. R., & Folmar, S. J. (1986). Longevity, gender, and life quality. *Journal of Health and Social Behavior, 27*, 332–345.

Haug, M. R., Ford, A. B., & Sheafor, M. (Eds.). (1985). *The physical and mental health of aged women*. New York: Springer.

Hayman, P. M., & Cope, C. S. (1980). Effects of assertion training on depression. *Journal of Clinical Psychology, 36*, 534–543.

Healy, D., & Williams, J. M. G. (1988). Dysrhythmia, dysphoria, and depression: The interaction of learned helplessness and circadian dysrhythmia in the pathogenesis of depression. *Psychological Bulletin, 103*, 163–178.

Heath, D. E. (1983). Alcohol use among North American Indians: A cross-cultural survey patterns and problems. In R. G. Smart & F. B. Glaser (Eds.). *Research advances in alcohol and drug problems* (pp. 343–396). New York: Plenum Press.

Heins, M. (1985). Update: Women in medicine. *Journal of the American Medical Association, 40*, 43–50.

Henderson, S., Byrne, D. G., Duncan-Jones, P., Adcock, S., Scott, R., & Steele, G. P. (1978). Social bonds in the epidemiology of neurosis: A preliminary communication. *British Journal of Psychiatry, 132*, 463–466.

Henderson, S., Duncan-Jones, P., Byrne, D. G., Scott, R., & Adcock, S. (1978, October). *Social bonds, adversity and neurosis*. Paper presented at the triennial meeting of the Western Psychological Association, St. Louis, MO.

Herman, M. F. (1983). Depression and women: Theories and research. *Journal of the American Academy of Psychoanalysis, 11*, 493–512.

Hernandez, M. (1986, September). *Depression among Mexican Women: A transgenerational perspective*. Paper presented at the biannual meeting of the National Coalition of Hispanic Health and Human Services Organization, New York.

Hersen, M., Bellack, A. S., Himmelhoch, J., & Thase, M. E. (1984). Effects of social skills training and amitriptyline and psychotherapy in unipolar depressed women. *Behavior Therapy, 15*, 21–40.

Hesselbrock, V. M., Hesselbrock, M. N., & Workman-Daniels, K. L. (1986). Effect of major depressions and antisocial personality on alcoholism: Course and motivational patterns. *Journal of Studies on Alcoholism, 47*, 201–212.

Hilberman, E. (1980). The "Wife-Beater's Wife" reconsidered. *American Journal of Psychiatry, 137*, 1336–1347.

Hilberman, E., & Munson, K. (1977–1978). Sixty battered women. *Victimology: An International Journal*, *2*, 460–470.

Himmelfarb, S. (1984). Age and sex differences in the mental health of older persons. *Journal of Consulting and Clinical Psychology*, *52*, 844–856.

Hirschfeld, R. M. A. (1986). Personality and bipolar disorder. In H. Hippius et al. (Eds.), *New results in depression research* (pp. 45–52). Berlin: Springer-Verlag.

Hirschfeld, R. M. A. (1987). State and personality in depressed and panic patients. *American Journal of Psychiatry*, *144*, 181–187.

Hirschfeld, R. M. A. (1987). The epidemiology, classification and clinical course of depression. In S. M. Channabasavanna & S. A. Shah (Eds.), *Affective Disorders: Recent research and related developments*. Proceedings of an Indo-U.S. Symposium at the National Institute of Mental Health & Neuro Sciences, Bangalore-560-029, India.

Hirschfeld, R. M. A., & Cross, C. K. (1982). Epidemiology of affective disorders: Psychosocial risk factors. *Archives of General Psychiatry*, *39*, 35–46.

Hirschfeld, R. M. A., & Klerman, G. L. (Eds.). (1984). Sex-related differences in depression: A reappraisal. *Journal of Affective Disorders*, *7*, 177–243.

Hirschfeld, R. M. A., Klerman, G. L., Clayton, P. J., & Keller, M. B. (1983). Personality and depression: Empirical findings. *Archives of General Psychiatry*, *40*, 993–998.

Hirschfeld, R. M. A., Klerman, G. L., Clayton, P. J., Keller, M. T., & Andreasen, N. C. (1984). Personality and gender-related differences in depression. *Journal of Affective Disorders*, *7*, 211–221.

Hirschfeld, R. M. A., Klerman, G. L., Clayton, P. J., Keller, M. B., McDonald-Scott, P., & Larkin, B. H. (1983). Assessing personality: Effects of the depressive state on trait measurement. *American Journal of Psychiatry*, *140*, 695–699.

Hoberman, H., & Lewinsohn, P. (1985). The behavioral treatment of depression. In E. E. Beckman & W. R. Leber (Eds.), *Handbook of depression: Treatment, assessment, and research*. Homewood, IL: Dorsey Press.

Holden, C. (1986). Youth suicide: New research focuses on a growing social problem. *Science*, *233*, 839–841.

Holinger, P. C., & Offer, D. (1981). Perspectives on suicide in adolescence. *Research in Community Mental Health*, *2*, 139–157.

Hollister, L. E. (1978). Tricyclic antidepressants. *New England Journal of Medicine*, *299*, 1106–1109.

Holubowycz, O. T. (1987). Predictors of alcohol dependence in a sample of women. *Australian Alcohol and Drug Review*, *5*(3), 225–228.

Holzer, C., Shea, B., Swanson, J., Leaf, P., Myers, J., George, L., Weissman, M., & Bednarsky, P. (1986). The increased risk for specific psychiatric disorders among persons of low socioeconomic status. *American Journal of Social Psychiatry*, *6*(4), 259–271.

Hopkins, J. H. (1969). The lesbian personality. *British Journal of Psychiatry*, *115*, 1433–1436.

Horowitz, A. V., & White, H. R. (1987). Gender role orientations and styles of pathology among adolescents. *Journal of Health and Social Behavior*, *28*, 158–170.

Horowitz, M. J., Marmar, C., Weiss, D. S., DeWitt, K. N., & Rosenbaum, R. (1984). Brief psychotherapy of bereavement reactions. *Archives of General Psychiatry*, *41*, 438–448.

Hsu, L. K. G. (1980). Outcome of anorexia nervosa: A review of the literature (1954 to 1978). *Archives of General Psychiatry*, *37*, 1041–1046.

Hurwitz, N. (1969). Predisposing factors in adverse reactions to drugs. *British Medical Journal*, *1*, 536–539.

Hyde, J. S. (1985). *Half the human experience* (3rd ed.). Lexington, MA: D. C. Health & Co.

Institute for Research on Women's Health. (1988). *Information packet: Sexual harassment and employment discrimination*. Washington, DC: Author.

Jack, D. (1987). Silencing the self: The power of social imperitives in female depression. In R. Formanek & A. Gurian (Eds.), *Women and depression: A lifespan perspective* (pp. 161–181). New York: Springer.

Jacobson, A., & Richardson, B. C. (1987). Assault experiences of 100 psychiatric inpatients: Evidence of the need for routine inquiry. *American Journal of Psychiatry*, *144*, 908–913.

Jacobsen, F. M., & Rosenthal, N. E. (1985). Seasonal affective disorder and the use of light for depression in women. *Behavior Therapy*, *14*, 434–440.

Jacobsen, F. M., Wehr, T. A., Sack, D. A., James, S. P., & Rosenthal, N. E. (1987). Seasonal affective disorder: A review of the syndrome and its public health implications. *American Journal of Public Health, 77,* 57–60.

James, S. P., Wehr, T. A., Sack, D. A., Parry, B. L., & Rosenthal, N. E. (1985). Treatment of seasonal affective disorder with evening light. *British Journal of Psychiatry, 147,* 424–428.

Jamison, K. R. (1988). Suicide prevention in depressed women. *Journal of Clinical Psychology, 49*(9) (Suppl.): 42–45.

Jarvik, L. F., Mintz, J., Steuer, J., & Garner, R. (1982). Treating geriatric patients: A 26-week interim analysis. *Journal of the American Geriatrics Society, 30,* 713–717.

Jarvik, L. F., & Small, G. (1988). *Parent care: A commonsense guide for adult children.* New York: Crown.

Jehu, D. (1989). Mood disturbances among women clients sexually abused in childhood: Prevalence, etiology, treatment. *Journal of Interpersonal Violence, 4,* 164–184.

Jensvold, M. F. (1989). *Gender issues in pharmacological treatment of depression.* Paper prepared for the National Task Force on Women and Depression, American Psychological Association.

Jensvold, M. F., Reed, K., & Jarrett, D. B. (in press). Recurrent late luteal phase dysphoric disorder successfully treated with variable antidepressant dosage: A case report.

Johnson, M. (1976). An approach to feminist therapy. *Psychotherapy: Theory, Research and Practice, 30,* 713–717.

Jones, B. E., & Gray, B. A. (1984). Similarities and differences in Black men and women in psychotherapy. *Journal of the National Medical Association, 76,* 21–27.

Josef, N. C. et al. (May, 1986). *Suicide attempts by school-age adolescents.* Paper presented at the annual meeting of the New Research, American Psychiatric Association, Washington, D.C. (NR 57, abstract).

Kandel, D. B., & Davies, M. (1982). Epidemiology of depressive mood in adolescents: An empirical study. *Archives of General Psychiatry, 39,* 1205–1212.

Kandel, D. B., Davies, M., & Ravels, V. (1985). The stressfulness of daily social roles for women: Marital, occupational and household roles. *Journal of Health and Social Behavior, 26,* 64–78.

Kandel, D. B., & Lesser, G. S. (1982). *Youth in two worlds: U.S. and Denmark.* San Francisco: Jossey-Bass.

Kaplan, A. G. (1984). Female or male psychotherapists for women: New formulations (work in progress, Stone Developmental Services and Studies). Wellesley, MA: Wellesley College.

Kaplan, A. G. (1986). The "self-in-relation": Implications for depression in women. *Psychotherapy: Theory, Research, and Practice, 23,* 235–242.

Kaplan, A. G., & Yasinsky, L. (1980). Psychodynamic perspectives. In A. Brodsky & R. Hare-Mustin (Eds.), *Women and psychotherapy.* New York: Guilford Press.

Kaplan, G., Roberts, R., Camacho, T., & Coyne, J. (1987). Psychosocial predictors of depression: Prospective evidence from the Human Population Laboratory Studies. *American Journal of Epidemiology, 125,* 206–220.

Keisler, E. R. (1955). Peer group ratings of high school pupils with high and low marks. *Journal of the American Academy of Child Psychiatry, 143,* 9.

Keller, M. B., Klerman, G. L., Lavori, P. W., Coryell, W., Endicott, J., & Taylor, J. (1984). Long-term outcome of episodes of major depression. *Journal of the American Medical Association, 252,* 788–792.

Keller, M. B., Lavori, P. W., Endicott, J., Corywell, W., & Klerman, G. L. (1983). Double-depression: Two year follow-up. *American Journal of Psychiatry, 140,* 6.

Kendall, D. A., Stancel, G. M., & Enna, S. J. (1982). The influence of sex hormones on antidepressant-induced alterations in neurotransmitter receptor binding. *Journal of Neuroscience, 2,* 354–360.

Kendall, R. R. (1983). Alcohol and suicide. *Substance and Alcohol Actions/Misuse, 4,* 121–127.

Kessler, R. C. (1979). A strategy for studying differential vulnerability to the psychological consequences of stress. *Journal of Health and Social Behavior, 20,* 100–108.

Kessler, R. C., & McLeod, J. D. (1984). Sex differences in vulnerability to undesirable life events. *American Sociological Review, 49,* 620–631.

Kessler, R. C., McLeod, J. D., & Wethington, E. (1984). The cost of caring: A perspective on the relationship between sex and psychological distress. In I. G. Sarason & B. R. Sarason (Eds.), *Social support: Theory, research, and applications* (pp. 491–506). The Hague, the Netherlands: Martinus Nijhof.

Kessler, R. C., & McRae, J. A. (1982). The effect of wives' employment on the mental health of married men and women. *American Sociological Review, 47,* 216–227.

Kessler, R. C., & Neighbors, H. W. (1986). A new perspective on the relationships among race, social class, and psychological distress. *Journal of Health and Social Behavior, 27,* 107–115.

Kikopulos, A., Reginaldi, P., Laddomada, G. F., & et al. (1980). Course of the manic depressive cycle and changes caused by treatments. *Pharmacopsychiatry, 13*, 1560–1567.

Kinsey, J. D., Fredrickson, R. B., Fleck, J., & Karis, W. (1984). Posttraumatic stress disorder among survivors of Cambodian concentration camps. *American Journal of Psychiatry, 141*, 1276–1281.

Kirsh, B. (1974). Consciousness raising groups as therapy for women. In A. Broadsky & R. Hare-Mustin (Eds.), *Women and psychotherapy.* New York: Guilford Press.

Klein, D. F., Gittelman, R., Quitkin, F., & Rifkin, A. (Eds.). (1980). *Diagnosis and drug treatment of psychiatric disorders in adults and children* (2nd ed.). Baltimore: Williams & Wilkins.

Kleinman, A. (1980). *Patients and healers in the context of culture.* Berkeley: University of California Press.

Klerman, G. L. (1986, June). *The treatments of depressive conditions.* Background paper presented for Scientific Advisory Committee, National Institute of Mental Health, Project D/ART (Depression: Awareness, Recognition, and Treatment).

Klerman, G. L. (1987). The treatment of depressive conditions. In *Perspectives on depressive disorders: A review of recent research.* Rockville, MD: U.S. Department of Health and Human Services.

Klerman, G. L., Di Mascio, A., Weissman, M. M., Prusoff, B. A., & Paykel, E. S. (1974). Treatment of depression by drugs and psychotherapy. *American Journal of Psychiatry, 131*, 186–191.

Klerman, G. L., & Hirschfeld, R. M. A. (1988). Personality as a vulnerability factor: With special attention to clinical depression. In Henderson & Burrows (Eds.), *Handbook of social psychiatry* (pp. 41–53). New York: Elsevier.

Klerman, G. L., Lavori, P. W., Rice, J., Reich, T., Endicott, J., Andreasen, N. C., Keller, M. B., & Hirschfeld, R. M. A. (1985). Birth cohort trends in rates of major depressive disorder among relatives of patients with affective disorder. *Archives of General Psychiatry, 42*, 689–695.

Klerman, G. L., & Weissman, M. (1980). Depression among women: Their nature and causes. In M. Guttentag, S. Salasin, & D. Belle (Eds.), *The mental health of women* (pp. 57–92). New York: Academic Press.

Klerman, G. L., & Weissman, M. M. (1985a). Depressions among women. In J. H. Williams (Ed.), *Psychology of women: Selected readings.* New York: W.W. Norton.

Klerman, G. L., & Weissman, M. M. (1985b). Gender and depression. *Trends in NeuroSciences, 8*, 416–420.

Klerman, G. L., & Weissman, M. M. (1987). Interpersonal psychotherapy and drugs in the treatment of depression. *Pharmacopsychiatry, 20*, 3–7.

Klerman, G. L., Weissman, M. M., Rounsaville, B. J., & Chevron, E. (1984). *Interpersonal psychotherapy of depression.* New York: Basic Books.

Koeske, R. D. (1981). Theoretical and conceptual complexities in the design and analysis of menstrual cycle research. In P. Komenich, M. McSweeney, J. A. Noack & S. N. Elders (Eds.), *The menstrual cycle* (Vol. 2, pp. 54–70). New York: Springer.

Kolb, L. C. (1988). A critical survey of hypotheses regarding posttraumatic stress disorders in light of recent research findings. *Journal of Traumatic Stress, 1*, 291–304.

Kon, I. S., & Losenkov, V. A. (1978). Friendship in adolescence: Values and behavior. *Journal of Marriage and the Family, 40*, 143–155.

Koop, E. C. (1987, September). *Keynote address.* Presented at the Surgeon General's Northwest Conference on Interpersonal Violence, Seattle, WA.

Koss, M. P. (1988). Women's mental health research agenda: Violence against women. *Women's mental health occasional paper series.* Rockville, MD: National Institute of Mental Health.

Koss, M. P. (1990). The women's mental health research agenda: Violence against women. *American Psychologist, 45*, 374–380.

Kourany, R. F. C. (1987). Suicide among homosexual adolescents. *Journal of Homosexuality, 13*, 111–117.

Kovacs, M., Rush, A. J., Beck, A. T., & Hollon, S. D. (1981). Depressed outpatients treated with cognitive therapy and pharmacotherapy: A one year follow up. *Archives of General Psychiatry, 38*, 33–39.

Kravetz, D. (1976). Consciousness raising groups and group psychotherapy: Alternative mental health resources for women. *Psychotherapy: Theory, Research and Practice, 13*, 66–71.

Krenzelok, E. P., & Anderson, G. M. (1983). Patient profile of fatal tricyclic antidepressant overdoses. *Veterinary and Human Toxicology, 25*, 47–50.

Kroft, C., & Leichner, P. (1987). Sex role conflicts in alcoholic women. *International Journal of Addictions, 22*, 685–693.

Kukopulos, A., Reginals, P., Laddomada, G. F., Floris, G., Serra, G., Tondo, L. (1980). Course of the manic-depressive cycle and changes caused by treatment. *Pharmacopsychiatry, 13*, 156–167.

Kurdek, L. A. (1987). Perceived social support in gays and lesbians in cohabiting relationships. *Journal of Personality and Social Psychology, 54,* 504–509.

Kurdek, L. A. (1988). Perceived social support in gays and lesbians in cohabiting relationships. *Journal of Personality and Social Psychology, 54,* 504–509.

Kurdek, L. A., & Schmidtt, J. P. (1987). Perceived emotional support from family and friends in members of homosexual, married, and heterosexual cohabiting couples. *Journal of Homosexuality, 14,* 57–68.

Kwentus, J. A., Hart, R. P., Peck, E. T., & Kornstein, S. (1985). Psychiatric complications of closed-head trauma. *Psychosomatics, 26,* 8–14.

LaFromboise, T., & Ozer, E. (in press). Changing and diverse roles of women in American Indian culture. In P. Reid & L. Comas-Diaz (Eds.), Sex roles and ethnic minority communities [Special Issue]. *Sex Roles.*

Laner, M. R., & Laner, R. H. (1980). Sexual preference or personal style? Why lesbians are disliked. *Journal of Homosexuality, 5,* 339–356.

LaPointe, K. A., & Rimm, D. C. (1980). Cognitive, assertive and insight oriented group therapies in the treatment of reactive depression in women. *Psychotherapy: Theory, Research and Practice, 17,* 312–320.

Lavie, P., Kremerman, S., & Wiel, M. (1982). Sleep disorders and safety at work in industry workers. *Accident Analysis and Prevention, 14,* 311–314.

Leavy, R. L. (1983). Social support and psychological disorder: A review. *Journal of Community Psychology, 11,* 3–21.

Leavy, R. L., & Adams, E. M. (1986). Feminism as a correlate of self-esteem, self-acceptance, and social support among lesbians. *Psychology of Women Quarterly, 10,* 321–326.

Leger, R. G. (1987). Lesbianism among women prisoners: Participants and nonparticipants. *Criminal Justice and Behavior, 14,* 448–467.

Lemkau, J. P., & Landau, C. (1986). The "selfless syndrome": Assessment and treatment considerations. *Psychotherapy: Theory, Research and Practice, 23,* 227–233.

Lerman, H. (1987). *A mote in Freud's eye: From psychoanalysis to the psychology of women.* New York: Springer.

Lerner, H. G. (1987). Female depression: Self sacrifice and self betrayal in relationships. In R. Formanek & A. Guiran (Eds.), *Women and depression: A lifespan perspective.* New York: Springer.

Lerner, R. M., & Karabenick, S. A. (1974). Physical attractiveness, body attitudes, and self-concept in late adolescents. *Journal of Youth and Adolescence, 3,* 307–316.

LeUnes, A. D., Nation, J. R., & Turley, N. M. (1980). Male-female performance in learned helplessness. *Journal of Psychology, 104,* 225–258.

Levitt, E. E., & Klassen, A. D. (1974). Public attitudes toward homosexuality. *Journal of Homosexuality, 1,* 29–43.

Lewinsohn, P. M., Fenn, D. S., Stanton, A. K., & Franklin, J. (1986). Relation of age at onset to duration of episode in unipolar depression. *Psychology and Aging, 1,* 63–68.

Lewinsohn, P. M., Sullivan, J. M., & Grosscup, J. J. (1979). Reinforcement and depression. In R. A. Dupue (Ed.), *The psychology of depressive disorders: Implications for the effect of stress.* New York: Academic Press.

Li, F. P. (1969). Suicide among chemists. *Archives of Environmental Health, 19,* 518–520.

Link, B., & Dohrenwend, B. (1980). Formulation of hypotheses about the true prevalence of demoralization in the U. S. In B. P. Dohrenwend, M. Schwartz-Gould, R. Neugebauer, & R. Wunsch-Hitzig (Eds.), *Mental Illness.* New York: Praeger.

Lloyd, C. (1983). Sex differences in medical students requesting psychiatric intervention. *Journal of Nervous and Mental Disease, 171,* 535–545.

Lloyd, C. (1988). *Depression in professional women.* Unpublished manuscript.

Lloyd, C. (in press). Psychiatric symptoms in dental students. *The Journal of Nervous and Mental Disease.*

Lloyd, C., & Gartrell, N. K. (1981). Sex differences in medical student mental health. *American Journal of Psychiatry, 25,* 1346–1351.

Lloyd, C., & Gartrell, N. K. (1984). Psychiatric symptoms in medical students. *Comprehensive Psychiatry, 25,* 552–565.

Lobel, B. & Hirschfeld, R. M. (1985). *Depression: What we know.* (DHHS Publication No. ADM 85-1318) Washington, DC: U. S. Department of Health and Human Services.

Loewenstein, S. (1984). *Fathers and mothers in midlife.* Presentation to the Family Track Seminar of the Boston University Department of Psychology, Boston.

Logue, C. M., & Moos, R. H. (1985). Perimenstrual symptoms: Prevalence and risk factors. *Psychosomatic Medicine, 48*, 388–414.

Loo, C. (1988, August). *Sociocultural barriers to the achievement of Asian American women.* Paper presented at the annual meeting of the American Psychological Association, Atlanta.

Loo, C., & Ong, P. (1982). Slaying demons with a sewing needle: Feminist issues for Chinatown's women. *Berkeley Journal of Sociology, 17*, 77–88.

Lopez, S. (1990). Patient variable biases in clinical judgment: A conceptual overview and some methodological considerations. *Psychological Bulletin.*

Loring, M., & Powell, B. (1988). Gender, race, and DSM-III: A study of the objectivity of psychiatric diagnostic behavior. *Journal of Health and Social Behavior, 29*, 1–22.

Lott, J. T. (1990). A portrait of Asian and Pacific American women. In S. E. Rix (Ed.), *The American women, 1990–91: A status report* (pp. 258–264). New York: W. W. Norton.

Lowenthal, M. J., & Haven, C. (1968). Interaction and adaptation: Intimacy as a critical variable. *American Sociological Review, 33*, 20–30.

Luborsky, L. (1984). *Principles of psychoanalytic psychotherapy: A manual for supportive-expressive treatment.* New York: Basic Books.

Luepnitz, D. (1988). *The family interpreted.* New York: Norton.

Maeder, T. (1989). Wounded healers. *Atlantic, 263*(1).

Makosky, V. P. (1982). Sources of stress: Events or conditions? In D. Belle (Ed.), *Lives in stress: Women and depression* (pp. 35–53). Beverly Hills: Sage.

Major, B., Mueller, P., & Hildebrandt, K. (1985). Attributions, expectations and coping with abortion. *Journal of Personality and Social Psychology, 48*, 585–599.

Mann, J. (1973)). *Time-limited psychotherapy.* Cambridge, MA: Harvard University Press.

Manson, S., Shore, J. H., & Bloom, J. (1985). The depressive experience in American Indian communities: A challenge for psychiatric theory and diagnosis. In A. Kleinman & B. Good (Eds.), *Culture and depression* (pp. 331–368). Berkeley: University of California Press.

Maracek, J. (1986). Legal and ethical issues in counseling pregnant adolescents. In G. B. Melton (Ed.), *Adolescent abortion: Psychological and legal issues* (pp. 96–115). Lincoln, NE: University of Nebraska Press.

Maracek, J., Kravetz, D., & Finn, S. A. (1979). A comparison of women who enter feminist therapy and women who enter traditional therapy. *Journal of Consulting and Clinical Psychology, 47*, 734–742.

Marsella, A. J. (1977). Depressive experience and disorder across cultures. In H. Triandis & J. Draguns (Eds.), *Handbook of cross-cultural psychology: Vol. 5. Culture and psychopathology* (pp. 30–72). Boston: Allyn & Bacon.

Mausner, J. D., & Steppacher, R. C. (1973). Suicide in professionals: A study of male and female psychologists. *American Journal of Epidemiology, 98*, 436–445.

May, P. (1987). Suicide and self destruction among American Indian youths. *American Indian and Alaska Native Mental Health Research, 1*(1), 52–69.

Mays, V. M., & Comas-Dias, L. (1989). Feminist therapy with ethnic minority populations: A closer look at Blacks and Hispanics. In M. A. Dutton-Douglas & L. E. A. Walker (Eds.), *Feminist psychotherapies: Integration of therapeutic and feminist systems.* New York: Springer.

Mazon, M. D. (1984). Emotional reactions to infertility. In M. D. Mazor & H. F. Simmons (Eds.), *Infertility: Medical, emotional, and social considerations* (pp. 23–55). New York: Human Sciences Press.

Mazon, M. D., & Simons, H. F. (Eds.). (1984). *Infertility: Medical, emotional and social considerations.* New York: Human Sciences Press, Inc.

Mazor, A. (1987). The development of the individuation process from a social-cognitive perspective. *Journal of Adolescence, 11*(1), 29–47.

McAdoo, H. (1980). Black mothers and the extended family support network. In L. Rogers-Rose (Ed.), *The black woman.* Beverly Hills, CA: Sage.

McBride, A. B. (1987). *The secret of a good life with your teenager.* New York: Times Books.

McCarthy, M. (1989). *Greater depression in women and a greater concern for thinness: is there a relationship?* Unpublished manuscript.

McDonald-Scott, P., & Larkin, B. H. (1983). Assessing personality: Effects of the depressive state on trait measurement. *American Journal of Psychiatry, 140*, 695–699.

McGrath, E. (1988, August). *Women and depression: Etiology and treatment issues.* (Public Lecture Series).

Presented at the annual meeting of the American Psychological Association, Atlanta.

McGrath, E. (1990, September). Prozac: The not so wonderful wonder drug of the 90s. *Psychology Today*.

McHenry, M. C., Hamdorf, K. G., Walthers, C. M., & Murray, C. I. (1985). Family and job influences on role satisfaction of employed rural mothers. *Psychology of Women Quarterly, 9*, 242–257.

McKinlay, J. B., McKinlay, S. M., & Brambilla, D. J. (1987a). Health status and utilization behavior associated with menopause. *American Journal of Epidemiology, 125*, 110–121.

McKinlay, J. B., McKinlay, S. M., & Brambilla, D. J. (1987b). The relative contributions of endocrine changes and social circumstances to depression in mid-aged women. *Journal of Health and Social Behavior, 28*, 345–363.

McKnew, D. H., Cytrm, L. A., & Yahraes, H. (1985). *Why Isn't Johnny Crying? Coping with depression in children*. New York: W. W. Norton.

McLean, P. D., & Hakstian, A. R. (1979). Clinical depression: Comparative efficacy of outpatient treatments. *Journal of Consulting and Clinical Psychology, 47*, 818–838.

McMillian, M. J., & Pihl, R. O. (1987). Premenstrual depression: A distinct entity. *Journal of Abnormal Psychology, 96*, 149–154.

Merikangas, K. R., Weissman, M. M., & Pauls, D. L. (1985). Genetic factors in the sex ratio of major depression. *Psychological Medicine, 15*, 63–69.

Metalsky, G. I., Abramson, L. Y., Seligman, M. E. P., Semmel, A., & Peterson, C. (1982). Attributional styles and life events in the classroom: Vulnerability and invulnerability to depressive mood reactions. *Journal of Personality and Social Psychology, 43*, 612–617.

Midlarsky, E. (1989). Feminist therapies with the elderly. In M. A. Dutton-Douglas & L. E. A. Walker (Eds.), *Feminist psychotherapies: Integration of therapeutic and feminist systems*. Norwood, NJ: Ablex.

Miller, D. (1987). *Helping the strong: An exploration of the needs of families headed by women*. Silver Spring, MD: National Association of Social Workers.

Miller, J. B. (1986). *Toward a new psychology of women*. Boston: Beacon.

Miller, P. M., & Ingham, J. C. (1976). Friends, confidants, and symptoms. *Social Psychiatry, 11*, 51–58.

Mollica, R. F., & Lavelle, J. (1988). Southeast Asian refugees. In L. Comas-Diaz & E. E. Griffin (Eds.), *Clinical guidelines in cross cultural mental health* (pp. 262–304). New York: Wiley.

Mollica, R. F., Wyshack, G., Coelho, R., & Lavelle, J. (1985). *The Southeast Asian psychiatry patient: A treatment outcome study*. Washington, DC: U. S. Office of Refugee Resettlement.

Mollica, R. F., Wyshak, G., de Marneffe, D., Khuon, F., & Lavelle, J. (1987). Indochinese versions of the Hopkins Symptom Checklist 25: A screening instrument for the psychiatric care of refugees. *American Journal of Psychiatry, 144*, 497–500.

Mollica, R. F., Wyshack, G., & Lavelle, J. (1987). The psychosocial impact of war trauma and torture on the Southeast Asian refugee. *American Journal of Psychiatry, 144*, 1567–1572.

Morales, E. S., & Graves, M. A. (1983). *Substance abuse: Patterns and barriers to treatment for gay men and lesbians in San Francisco*. San Francisco: Department of Public Health.

Morgan, R. (1984). *Sisterhood is global*. Garden City, NY: Anchor Books.

Morton, J. H. (1950). Premenstrual tension. *American Journal of Obstetrics and Gynecology, 60*, 343.

Moseley, D. T., Follingstad, D. R., Harley, H., & Heckel, R. V. (1981). *Journal of Clinical Psychology, 37*, 276.

Moss, S. R. (1986). Women in prison: A case of pervasive neglect. *Women and Therapy, 5*, 177–185.

Mostow, E., & Newberry, P. (1975). Work role and depression in women: A comparison of workers and housewives in treatment. *American Journal of Orthopsychiatry, 45*, 538–548.

Mueller, C. W. (1984). The effects of mood and type and timing of influence on the perception of crowding. *Journal of Psychology, 116*(2):155–158.

Murphy, D. L., Lipper, S., Pickar, D., Jimerson, D., Cohen, R. M., Garrick, N. A., Alterman, I. S., & Campbell, I. C. (1981). Selective inhibition of monoamine oxidase type A: Clinical antidepressant effects & metabolic changes in man. In M. B. H. Youdim & E. S. Paykel (Eds.), *Monoamine oxidase inhibitors— The State of the Art* (pp. 189–205). New York: Wiley.

Murphy, G. E., Simons, A. D., Wetzel, R. D., & Lustman, P. J. (1984). Cognitive therapy and pharmacotherapy. *Archives of General Psychiatry, 41*, 33–41.

Murphy, G. E., Woodruff, R. A., Herjanic, M., & Super, G. (1974). Variability of the clinical course of primary affective disorder. *Archives of General Psychiatry, 30*, 757–761.

Murphy, S. M. (1984). Monoamine oxidase-inhibiting antidepressants: A clinical update. *Psychiatric Clinics of North America, 7*(3), 549–562.

Murphy, S. M., Kilpatrick, D. G., Amick-Mcmullan, A., Veronen, L., Paduhovich, J., Best, C. L., Villenponteauz, L. A., & Saunders, B. E. (1988). Current psychological functioning of child sexual assault survivors. *Journal of Interpersonal Violence, 3*, 55–79.

Murphy, W. D., Coleman, E., Hoon, E., & Scott, C. (1980). Sexual dysfunction & treatment in alcoholic women. *Sexuality and Disability, 3*,(X), 240–255.

Nadelson, C., & Notman, M. T. (1972). The woman physician. *Journal of Medical Education, 47*, 176–183.

Nadelson, C., Notman, M. T., & Ellis, E. A. (1983). Psychosomatic aspects of obstetrics and gynecology [Special issue]. *Psychosomatics, 24*(10).

National Center for Health Statistics. (1989). Supplements to the monthly vital statistics report. *Vital Health Statistics, 24*(1).

National Coalition for Women's Mental Health. (1985). *Women and psychotherapy: A consumer handbook.*

National Council on Alcoholism. (1987). *A federal response to a hidden epidemic: Alcohol and other drug problems among women.* Washington, DC: Author.

National Health Care Campaign and Citizen Action. (1987). *Insuring the uninsured: Options for state action.* Washington, DC: Author.

National Institute of Mental Health. (1987). *National lesbian health care survey.* Washington, DC: U. S. Department of Health and Human Services.

National Institute of Mental Health. (1988). *Sex differences in depressive disorders: A review of recent research* (DHHS Publication, D/ART). Rockville, MD: NIMH.

Neugarten, B. L., & Kraines, R. J. (1965). Menopausal symptoms in women of various ages. *Psychosomatic Medicine, 27*, 266–273.

Newmann, J. P. (1984). Sex differences in symptoms of depression: Clinical disorder or normal distress? *Journal of Health and Social Behavior, 25*, 136–160.

Newmann, J. P. (1986). Gender, life strains, and depression. *Journal of Health and Social Behavior, 27*, 161–178.

Newmann, J. P. (1987a, August). *Gender differences in self-disclosure tendencies: Their nature and impact on vulnerability to depression.* Unpublished manuscript, University of Wisconsin, School of Social Work, Madison, WI.

Newmann, J. P. (1987). Gender differences in vulnerability to depression. *Social Service Review, 61*, 447–468.

Newmann, J. P. (1988). *Aging and depression: A review and critique of the empirical literature.* Unpublished manuscript, University of Wisconsin, Madison.

New York Public Interest Group. (1981). *Study on sexual harassment.* Albany, NY: Author.

Noble, K. D. (1987). The dilemma of the gifted woman. *Psychology of Woman Quarterly, 11*, 367–378.

Nolen-Hoeksema, S. (1987). Sex differences in unipolar depression: Evidence and theory. *Psychological Bulletin, 101*, 259–282.

Nolen-Hoeksema, S. (1990). *Sex differences in depression.* Stanford, CA: Stanford University Press.

Nolen-Hoeksema, S., Girgus, J. S., & Seligman, M. E. P. (1986). Learned helplessness in children: A longitudinal study of depression, achievement, and explanatory style. *Journal of Personality and Social Psychology, 51*, 435–442.

Noll, K. M., Davis, J. M., & De Leon-Jones, F. (1985). Medication and somatic therapies in the treatment of depression. In E. E. Beckman & W. R. Leber (Eds.), *Handbook of depression: Treatment, assessment, and research.* Homewood, IL: Dorsey Press.

Notman, M. (1986, November). *Depression in women: Psychoanalytic concepts.* Paper presented at the Women and Depression conference, Boston.

Ochberg, F. (Ed.). (1988). *Post-traumatic therapy and victims of violence.* New York: Brunner/Mazel.

O'Connell, R. A., & Mayo, J. A. (1988). The role of social factors in affective disorders: A review. *Hospital and Community Psychiatry, 39*(8), 842–851.

Olarte, S. W., & Lenz, R. (1984). Learning to do psychoanalytic therapy with inner city population. *Journal of the American Academy of Psychoanalysis, 12*, 89–99.

Oppenheim, G. (1984). A case of rapid mood cycling with estrogen: Implications for therapy, *Journal of Clinical Psychiatry, 45*, 34.

Ossip-Klein, D. J., Doyne, E. J., Bowman, E. D., Osborn, K. M., et al. (1989). Effects of running or weight lifting on self-concept in clinically depressed women. *Journal of Consulting and Clinical Psychology, 57*, 158–161.

Padfield, M. (1976). The comparative effects of two counseling approaches on the intensity of depression among rural women of low socioeconomic status. *Journal of Consulting Psychology, 23*, 209–214.

Parry, B. L. (1989). Reproductive factors affecting the course of affective illness in women. *Psychiatric Clinics of North America, 12*, 207–220.

Parry, B. L., Rosenthal, N. E., Tamarkin, L., & Wehr, T. A. (1987). Treatment of a patient with seasonal premenstrual syndrome. *American Journal of Psychiatry, 144*(6), 762–766.

Paul, S. M., Extein, I., Calil, H. M., Potter, W. Z., Chodoff, P., & Goodwin, F. K. (1981). Use of the ECT with treatment-resistant depressed patients at the National Institute of Mental Health. *American Journal of Psychiatry, 138*, 486–489.

Paulson, J. D., Harman, B. S., Salerno, R. L., & Asman, P. (1988). An investigation of the relationship between emotional maladjustment and infertility. *Fertility and Sterility, 49*, 258–262.

Paykel, E. S. (1989). Treatment of depression: The relevance of research for clinical practice. *British Journal of Psychiatry, 155*, 754–766.

Peplau, L. A., Cochran, S., Rook, K., & Padesky, C. (1978). Loving women: Attachment and autonomy in lesbian relationships. *Journal of Social Issues, 34*, 2–27.

Perlin, L. I. (1975). Sex roles and depression. In N. Datan & L. Ginsberg (Eds.), *Life-span developmental psychology: Normative life crises* (pp. 191–207). New York: Academic Press.

Perlin, L., & Johnson, J. (1977). Marital status, life-strains and depression. *American Sociological Review, 42*, 704–715.

Perlin, L., & Lieberman, M. (1979). Social sources of emotional distress. In R. G. Simmons (Ed.), *Research in community and mental health*. Greenwich, CT: JAI Press.

Perris, C. (1966). A study of bipolar (manic-depressive) and unipolar recurrent depressive psychosis. *Acta Psychiatrica Scandinavica* (Suppl. 194), 1–89.

Peterson, C., Luborsky, L., & Seligman, M. E. P. (1983). Attributions and depressive mood shifts: Case study using the symptom-content method. *Journal of Abnormal Psychology, 92*, 96–103.

Peterson, C., & Seligman, M. E. P. (1984). Causal explanations as a risk factor for depression: Theory and evidence. *Psychological Review, 91*, 347–374.

Pezel, S., & Riddle, M. (1981). Suicide's psychosocial and cognitive aspects. *Adolescent Psychiatry, 9*, 399–410.

Pitts, F. N., Schuller, A. B., Rich, C. L., & Pitts, A. F. (1979). Suicide amongst U. S. women physicians, 1967–1972. *American Journal of Psychiatry, 136*, 694–696.

Post, R. D. (1982). Dependency conflicts in high achieving women: Toward an integration. *Psychotherapy: Theory, Research, and Practice, 19*, 82–87.

Post, R. D. (1987, August). *Self sabotage among successful women.* Paper presented at the annual meeting of the American Psychological Association, New York.

Powell, E. H. (1958). Occupation, status and suicide: Toward a redefinition of anomie. *American Sociological Review, 23*, 131–139.

Preskorn, S. H., & Mas, D. S. (1985). Plasma levels of amitriptyline: Effects of age and sex. *Journal of Clinical Psychiatry, 46*, 276–277.

Preskorn, S. H. (1989). Treatment of tricyclic-resistant depression: The role of tricyclic antidepressant plasma level monitoring. In I. L. Extein (Ed.), *Treatment of tricyclic-resistant depression* (pp. 1–25). Washington, DC: American Psychiatric Press.

Public Health Service Task Force on Women's Health Issues. (1985). *Women's Health: Report of the Public Health Service Task Force on Women's Health Issues* (DHHS Pub. No (PHS)85-50206). Washington, DC: U. S. Government Printing Office.

Puglisi, J. T. (1983). Self-perceived age changes in sex role self concept. *International Journal of Aging and Human Development, 16*, 183–191.

Quesada, G. M., Spears, W., & Ramos, P. (1978). Interracial depressive epidemiology in the Southwest. *Journal of Health and Social Behavior, 19*(1), 77–85.

Quitkin, F. M., Rabkin, J. D., Markowitz, J. M., Stewart, J. W., McGrath, P. J, & Harrison. W. (1987). Use of pattern analysis to identify true drug response. *Archives of General Psychiatry, 44*, 259–264.

Quitkin, F. M., Stewart, J. W., McGrath, J., & Liebowitz, M. R. (1988). Phenelzine vs. imipramine in the treatment of probable atypical depression: Defining syndrome boundaries of selective MAOI responders. *American Journal of Psychiatry, 145*, 306–311.

Rabkin, J. G., & Klein, D. F. (1987). The clinical measurement of depressive disorders. In A. J. Marsella,

R. M. Hirshfeld, & M. M. Katz (Eds.), *The measurement of depression: Clinical, biological, psychological, and psychosocial perspectives*. New York: Guilford Press.

Radloff, L. S. (1975). Sex differences in depression: The effects of occupation and marital status. *Sex Roles*, *1*, 249–265.

Radloff, L. S. (1977). The CES-D scale: A self-report depression scale for research in the general population. *Applied Psychological Measurement*, *1*, 385–401.

Radloff, L. S., & Rae, D. S. (1981). Components of the sex difference in depression. In R. G. Simmons (Ed.), *Research in community and mental health* (pp. 76–95). Greenwich, CT: JAI Press.

Rawlings, E. I., & Graham, D. L. R. (1989). Feminist therapy with divorced, single, female patients. In M. A. Dutton-Douglas & L. E. A. Walker (Eds.), *Feminist psychotherapies: Integration of therapeutic and feminist systems*. Norwood, NJ: Ablex.

Refugee Women Development Project. (1985). *Alert: Pirate attacks on refugee women in the Gulf of Thailand*. Washington, DC: Author.

Rehm, L. P. (1989, April). *Psychotherapies for depression*. Paper presented at the meeting of the Boulder Symposium on Clinical Psychology: Depression, Boulder, CO.

Rehm, L. P., Fuchs, C. Z., Roth, D. M., Kornblith, S. J., & Romano, J. M. (1979). A comparison of self control and social skills treatment of depression. *Behavior Therapy*, *10*, 429–442.

Reiker, P. P., & Carmen, E. H. (1986). The victim-to-patient process: The disconfirmation and transformation of abuse. *American Journal of Orthopsychiatry*, *56*, 360–370.

Riessman, C. K. (1987). When gender is not enough: Women interviewing women. *Gender and Society*, *1*(2), 172–207.

Rippere, V., & Williams, R. (1985). *Wounded healers: Mental health worker's experiences of depression*. New York: Wiley.

Rivinus, T. M., Biederman J., Herzog, D. B., Kemper, K., Harper, G. P., Harmatz, J. S., & Houseworth, S. (1984). Anorexia nervosa and affective disorders: A controlled family history study. *American Journal of Psychiatry*, *141*, 1414–1418.

Roberts, R. E., & O'Keefe, S. J. (1981). Sex differences in depression reexamined. *Journal of Health and Social Behavior*, *22*, 394–399.

Robins, D. R., Alessi, N. E., Yanchyshyn, G. W., & Colfer, M. (1982). Preliminary report on the dexamethasone suppression test in adolescents. *American Journal of Psychiatry*, *139*, 942–943.

Robins, E., Murphy, C. E., Wilkinson, R. H., Gassner, S., & Kayes, J. (1959). Some clinical considerations in the prevention of suicide based on a study of 134 successful suicides. *American Journal of Public Health*, *49*, 888–899.

Roizen, J. (1982). *Estimating alcohol involvement in serious events* (Department of Health and Human Services Publication no. (ADM) 82-1190, WDC, 179–219). Washington, DC: U.S. Government Printing Office.

Root, M. P., & Fallon, P. (1986). The incidence of victimization experiences in a bulimic sample. *Journal of Interpersonal Violence*, *3*, 161–173.

Rosenberg, S. E. (1985). Brief dynamic therapy for depression. In E. E. Beckham & W. R. Leber (Eds.), *Handbook of depression: Treatment, assessment, and research*. Homewood, IL: Dorsey Press.

Rosencrantz, P. S., Delorey, C., & Broverman, I. K. (1985, August). *One-half a generation later: Sex-role stereotypes revisited*. Paper presented at the annual meeting of the American Psychological Association, Los Angeles.

Rosenthal, H. G. (1986). The learned helplessness syndrome: Specific strategies for crisis intervention with the suicidal sufferer—Emotional first aid. *American Journal of Crisis Intervention*, *3*(2), 5–8.

Rosenthal, N. E., Sack, D. A., Carpenter, C. J., Parry, B. L., Mendelson, W. B., Wehr, T. A. (1985). Antidepressant effects of light in seasonal affective disorder. *American Journal of Psychiatry*, *142*, 163–170.

Rosenthal, N. E., Sack, D. A., Gillin, J. C., Lewy, A. J., Goodwin, F. K., Mueller, P. S., Newsome, D. A., & Wehr, T. A. (1984). Seasonal affective disorder: A description of the syndrome and preliminary findings with light therapy. *Archives of General Psychiatry*, *41*, 72–80.

Rosenthal, N. E., Sack, D. A., James, S. P., Parry, B. L., Mendelson, W. B., Tamarkin, L., & Wehr, T. A. (1984). Seasonal affective disorder and phototherapy. *Annals of the New York Academy of Sciences*, *453*, 260.

Rosewater, L. B. (1985). Feminist interpretation of traditional testing. In L. B. Rosewater and L. E. A.

Walker (Eds.), *Handbook of feminist therapy: Women's issues in psychotherapy* (pp. 266–273). New York, Springer.

Rosewater, L. B. (1989). Feminist therapies with women. In M. A. Dutton-Douglas & L. E. A. Walker (Eds.), *Feminist psychotherapies: Interaction of therapeutic and feminist systems*. Norwood, NJ: Ablex.

Ross, C. E., & Huber, J. (1985). Hardship and depression. *Journal of Health and Social Behavior, 26*, 312–327.

Ross, C. E., & Mirowsky, J. (1988). Child care and emotional adjustment to wives' employment. *Journal of Health and Social Behavior, 29*, 127–138.

Rose, C. E., Mirowsky, J., & Huber, J. (1983). Dividing work, sharing work, and in-between: Marriage patterns and depression. *American Sociological Review, 48*, 809–823.

Ross, M. W., Paulsen, J. A., & Stalstrom, O. W. (1988). Homosexuality and mental health: A cross-cultural review. *Journal of Homosexuality, 15*, 131–152.

Roth, D., Bielski, R., Jones, M., Parker, W., & Osborne, G. (1982). A comparison of self-control therapy and combined self-control therapy and antidepressant medication in the treatment of depressive behavior. *Behavior Therapy, 13*, 133–144.

Roth, S., & Leibowitz, L. (1988). The experiences of sexual trauma. *Journal of Traumatic Stress, 1*, 79–108.

Rothblum, E. D. (1983). Sex-role stereotypes and depression in women. In V. Franks & E. D. Rothblum (Eds.), *The stereotyping of women: Its effects on mental health*. New York: Springer.

Rothblum, E. D. (1990). Depression among lesbians: An invisible and unresearched phenomenon. *Journal of Gay and Lesbian Psychotherapy, 1*(3), 67–87.

Rounsaville, B. S., Klerman, G. L., Weissman, M. M., & Chevron, E. S. (1985). Short-term interpersonal psychotherapy for depression. In E. E. Beckham & W. R. Leber (Eds.), *Handbook of depression: Treatment, assessment, and research*. Homewood, IL: Dorsey Press.

Roy, A. (1985). Suicide in doctors. *Psychiatric Clinics of North America, 8*, 377–387.

Rubinow, D. R., & Schmidt, J. (1989). Models for the development and expression of symptoms in premenstrual syndrome. *Psychiatric Clinics of North America, 12*, 53–68.

Rudorfer, M. V., & Potter, W. Z. (1989). The new generation of antidepressants. In I. L. Extein (Ed.). *Treatment of tricyclic-resistant depression*. Washington, DC: American Psychiatric Press.

Rush, F. (1980). *The best-kept secret: The sexual abuse of children*. New York: McGraw-Hill.

Russell, D. E. H. (1984). *Sexual exploitation*. Beverly Hills, CA: Sage Library of Social Research.

Russell, D. E. H. (1986). *The secret trauma: Incest in the lives of girls and women*. New York: Basic Books.

Russell, D. E. H. (1988). Language and psychotherapy. In L. Comas-Diaz & E. H. Griffin (Eds.), *Clinical guidelines in cross-cultural mental health*. New York: Wiley.

Russo, N. F. (1984). Women in the mental health delivery system: Implications for research and public policy. In L. E. Walker (Ed.), *Women and mental health policy*. Beverly Hills: Sage.

Russo, N. F. (Ed.). (1985). *A women's mental health agenda*. Washington, DC: American Psychological Association.

Russo, N. F. (1986). Adolescent abortion: The epidemiological context. In G. B. Melton (Ed.), *Adolescent abortion: Psychological and legal issues* (pp. 40–73). Lincoln, NE: University of Nebraska Press.

Russo, N. F. (1987). Position Paper. In A. E. Eichler & D. L. Parron (Eds). *Women's mental health: Agenda for research*. Rockville, MD: National Institute of Mental Health.

Russo, N. F. (1988, August). *Methodological issues in depression research*. Presented at the annual meeting of the American Psychological Association, Atlanta.

Russo, N. F., Amaro, H., & Winter, M. (1987). The use of inpatient mental health services by Hispanic women. *Psychology of Women Quarterly, 11*, 427–442.

Russo, N. F., & Olmedo, E. L. (1983). Women's utilization of outpatient psychiatric services: Some emerging priorities for rehabilitation psychologists. *Rehabilitation Psychology, 28*, 141–155.

Russo, N. F., & Sobel, S. B. (1981). Sex differences in the utilization of mental health facilities. *Professional Psychology, 12*, 7–19.

Rutter, M. (1986). The developmental psychopathology of depression: Issues and perspectives. In M. Rutter & C. E. Izard (Eds.), *Depression in young people* (pp. 3–32). New York: Guilford Press.

Sacco, W. P., & Beck, A. T. (1985). Cognitive theory of depression. In E. E. Beckham & W. R. Leber (Eds.), *Handbook of depression: Treatment, assessment, and research*. Homewood, IL: Dorsey Press.

Saghir, M. T., & Robins, E. (1973). *Male and female homosexuality: A comprehensive investigation.* Baltimore, MD: Williams and Wilkins.

Saghir, M. T., Robins, E., Walbrann, B., & Gentry, K. A. (1970). Psychiatric disorders and disability in the female homosexual. *American Journal of Psychiatry, 127,* 147–154.

Salgado de Snyder, V. N. (1987). Factors associated with acculturative stress and depressive symptomology among married Mexican immigrant women. *Psychology of Women Quarterly, 11,* 475–488.

Salt, P., Nadelson, C., & Notman, M. (1984, August). *Depression and anxiety among medical students.* Paper presented at meeting of the American Psychological Association, Los Angeles.

Sandmaier, M. (1980). *The invisible alcoholics: Women and alcohol abuse in America.* New York: McGraw Hill.

Saunders, J. M., & Valente, S. M. (1987). Suicide risk among gay men and lesbians: A review. *Death Studies, 11,* 1–23.

Schatzberg, A. F., & Cole, J. O. (1986). Antidepressants. In *Manual of clinical pharmacology* (pp. 3–65). Washington, DC: American Psychiatric Press.

Schatzberg, A. F., Dessain, E., O'Neil, P., et al. (1987). Recent studies on selective serotonergic antidepressants: Trazodone, fluoxetine, and fluvoxamine. *Journal of Clinical Psychopharmacology, 7*(6, Suppl.), 446–495.

Schmitt, J. P., & Kurdek, L. A. (1987). Personality correlates of positive identity and relationship involvement in gay men. *Journal of Homosexuality, 13,* 101–109.

Schrut, A. (1968). Some typical patterns in the behavior and background of adolescent girls who attempt suicide. *American Journal of Psychiatry, 125,* 107–112.

Schwartz, R. A. (1986). Abortion on request: The psychiatric implications. In J. D. Butler & D. F. Walbert (Eds.), *Abortion, medicine and the law* (pp. 323–337). New York: Facts on File.

Scovern, A. W., & Kilman, P. R. (1980). Status of electro convulsive therapy: Review of the outcome literature. *Psychological Bulletin, 87,* 206–303.

Seligman, M. E. P. (1975). *Helplessness: On depression, development and death.* San Francisco: W. H. Freeman.

Sesan, R. (1988). Sex bias and sex-role stereotyping in psychotherapy with women: Survey results. *Psychotherapy: Theory, Research, Practice, Training, 25,* 107–116.

Shaffer, D. (1974). Suicide in childhood and early adolescence. *Journal of Child Psychology and Psychiatry, 15,* 275–291.

Shaffer, D. (1985). Depression and suicide in children and adolescents. In M. Rutter & L. Hersov (Eds.), *Child and adolescent psychiatry: Modern approaches* (2nd ed.). Oxford: Blackwell Scientific Publications.

Shea, M. T., Glass, D. R., Pilkonis, P. A., McKain, T. L., et al. (1987). Frequency and implications of personality disorders in a sample of depressed outpatients. *Journal of Personality Disorders, 1,* 27–42.

Shore, J. H., & Manson, S. M. (1981). Cross-cultural studies of depression among American Indians. *White Cloud Journal, 2*(2), 5–12.

Shore, J. H., Manson, S. M., Bloom, J. D., Keepers, G., & Neligh, G. (1987). A pilot study of depression among American Indian patients with research diagnostic criteria. *American Indian and Alaska Native Mental Health Research, 1*(2), 4–15.

Shusterman, L. R. (1979). Predicting the psychological consequences of abortion. *Social Science and Medicine, 13A,* 683–689.

Simmons, J. L. (1966). Public stereotypes of deviants. *Social Problems, 13,* 223–232.

Simons, R., & Miller, M. (July–August, 1987). Adolescent Depression: Assessing the impact of negative cognitions and socioenvironmental problems. *Social Work, 32*(4), 326–330.

Skegg, D. C., Doll, R., & Perry, J. (1977). Use of medicines in general practice. *British Medical Journal, 1,* 1561–1563.

Smith, E. M. J. (1973). A follow-up study of women who request abortion. *American Journal of Orthopsychiatry, 43,* 574–585.

Smith, E. M. J. (1985). Counseling Black women. In P. Pedersen (Ed.), *Handbook of cross-cultural counseling and therapy.*

Smith, I., Adkins, S., & Walton, J. (1988, January). Pharmaceuticals: Therapeutic Review. *Shearson, Lehman, Hutton International Research Publication.* New York.

Smith, J. (1988). Psychopathology, homosexuality, and homophobia. *Journal of Homosexuality, 15,* 59–73.

Smith, M. L., & Glass, G. V. (1977). Meta-analysis of psychotherapy outcome studies. *American Psychologist, 32,* 752–760.

Smith, T. M. (1982). *Specific approaches and techniques in the treatment of gay male alcohol abusers.* San Francisco: Alcoholism Evaluation and Treatment Center.

Snipp, C. M. (1990). A portrait of American Indian women and their labor force experiences. In S. E. Rix (Ed.), *The American woman, 1990–91: A status report* (pp. 265–272). New York: W. W. Norton.

Snodgrass, S. E. (1985). Women's intuition: The effect of subordinate role on interpersonal sensitivity. *Journal of Personality and Social Psychology, 49,* 146–155.

Solomon, B. C., Ostrov, E., Offer, D., Howard, K. I., & Schwartz, S. S. (1983). *Suicide among women physicians: A cohort study.* Chicago, IL: Michael Reese Hospital.

Sophie, J. (1987). Internalized homophobia and lesbian identity. *Journal of Homosexuality, 14,* 53–65.

Sorenson, S. B., & Golding, J. M. (1990). Depressive sequelae of recent criminal victimization. *Journal of Traumatic Stress, 3,*(3), 337–350.

Speckhard, A. (1987). *Post abortion counseling: A manual for Christian counselors.* Falls Church, VA: PACE.

Spence, J. T., Helmreich, R., & Stapp, J. (1975). Ratings of self and peers on sex-role attributes and their relation to self-esteem and conceptions of masculinity and feminity. *Journal of Personality and Social Psychology, 32,* 29–39.

Spendlove, D. C., West, D. W., & Stanish, W. M. (1984). Risk factors and the prevalence of depression in Mormon women. *Social Science and Medicine, 18,* 491–495.

Spitzer, R. L., Williams, J. B. W., Gibbon, M., & First, M. (1990). *Structured Clinical Intervention for DSM-III-R (SCID): User's guide.* Washington, DC: American Psychiatric Press.

Stack, C. (1974). *All our kin: Strategies for survival in a Black community.* New York: Harper & Row.

Steele, R. E. (1978). Relationship of race, sex, social class, and social mobility to depression in normal adults. *Journal of Social Psychology, 104,* 34–47.

Steinbrueck, S. M., Maxwell, S. E., & Howard, G. S. (1983). A meta-analysis of psychotherapy and drug therapy in the treatment of unipolar depression with adults. *Journal of Consulting and Clinical Psychology, 51,* 856–863.

Steinmann, A. (1974). Cultural values, female role expectancies and therapeutic goals: Research and interpretation. In V. Franks & V. Burtle (Eds.), *Women in therapy.* New York: Brunner/Mazel.

Steinmetz, S. L., Lewinsohn, P. M., & Antonuccio, D. G. (1983). Prediction of individual outcome in a group intervention for depression. *Journal of Consulting and Clinical Psychology, 51,* 331–337.

Steinmetz, S. L., Strauss, M. A., & Gelles, R. J. (1980). *Behind closed doors: Violence in the American family.* Garden City, NY: Anchor/Doubleday.

Steppacher, R. C., & Mausner, J. D. (1974). Suicide in male and female physicians. *Journal of American Medical Association, 2238,* 323–328.

Stern, S. L., Dixon, K. N., Nemzer, E., Lake, M. D., Sansone, R. A., Smelter, D. J., Lantz, S., & Schrier, S. S. (1984). Affective disorder in the families of women with normal weight bulimia. *American Journal of Psychiatry, 141,*1224–1227.

Strickland, B. R. (1988). Sex-related differences in health and illness. *Psychology of Women Quarterly, 12,* 381–399.

Strickland, B. R. (1989, April). *Gender differences in depression.* Paper presented at the meeting of the Boulder Symposium on Clinical Psychology: Depression (as part of the Milton E. Lipetz Memorial Lecture Series), Boulder, CO.

Stroebe, M. S., & Stroebe, W. (1983). Who suffers more? Sex differences in health risks of the widowed. *Psychological Bulletin, 93,* 279–301.

Strumphauzer, J. S., & Davis, L. C. (1983). Training Mexican American mental health personnel in behavior therapy. *Journal of Behavior Therapy and Experimental Psychiatry, 14,* 215–217.

Strupp, H. (1982). *Time limited dynamic psychotherapy.* New York: Basic Books.

Strupp, H. H., & Binder, J. L. (1984). *Psychotherapy in a new key: A guide to time-limited dynamic psychotherapy.* New York: Basic Books.

Surrey, J. L. (1987). Relationship and empowerment (work in progress No. 30). Wellesley, MA: Stone Center for Developmental Services and Studies.

Surtees, P. G. (1980). Social support, residual adversity, and depressive outcome. *Social Psychiatry, 15,* 71–80.

Swallow, S. R., & Kulper, N. A. (1988). Social comparison and negative self-evaluations. An application to depression. *Clinical Psychology Review, 8*, 55–76.

Sweeney, P. D., Anderson, K., & Bailey, S. (1986). Attributional style in depression: A meta-analytic review. *Journal of Personality and Social Psychology, 50*, 974–991.

Taffel, S. M. (1987). Characteristics of American Indian and Alaska Native births: United States, 1984. *NCHS Monthly Vital Statistics Report, 36*(3)(Suppl.).

Teasdale, J. D., & Fennell, M. J. V. (1982). Immediate effects on depression of cognitive therapy interventions. *Cognitive Therapy and Research, 6*, 343–352.

Tennant, C. (1985). Female vulnerability to depression. *Psychological Medicine, 15*, 733–737.

Theodore, A., Berger, A. G., & Palmer, C. E. (1956). A follow-up study of tuberculosis in student nurses: II. Mortality from all causes in the first decade after entering training. *Journal of Clinical Diseases, 4*, 111–130.

Thoits, P. A. (1986). Multiple identities: Examining gender and marital status differences in distress. *American Sociological Review, 51*, 259–272.

Thomas, D. A., & Reznioff, M. (1984). Sex role orientation, personality structure, and adjustment in women. *Journal of Personality Assessment, 48*, 28–36.

Thompson, N. L., McCandless, B. R., & Strickland, B. R. (1971). Personal adjustment of male and female homosexuals and heterosexuals. *Journal of Abnormal Psychology, 78*, 237–240.

Torres-Matrullo, C. (1976). Acculturation and psychopathology among Puerto Rican women in mainland United States. *American Journal of Orthopsychiatry, 46*, 710–719.

Towne, R. D., & Afterman, J. (1955). Psychosis in males related to parenthood. *Bulletin of the Menninger Clinic, 19*.

Trautman, E. C. (1961). The suicidal fit. *Archives of General Psychiatry, 5*, 76–83.

Trunnell, E. P., Turner, C. W., & Keye, W. K. (1988). A comparison of the psychological and hormonal factors in women with and without premenstrual syndrome. *Journal of Abnormal Psychology, 4*, 429–436.

Tsai, M., Feldman-Summers, S., & Edgar, M. (1979). Childhood molestation: Variables related to differential impact of psychosexual functioning in adult women. *Journal of Abnormal Psychology, 88*, 407–417.

Turner, R. J., & Noh, S. (1988). Physical disability and depression: A longitudinal analysis. *Journal of Health and Social Behavior, 29*, 23–37.

U. S. Census Bureau. (1987). *Money, income and poverty status in the U. S. 1987: Advanced report from March 1988 current population survey* (Current Population Report Series P60 No. 16).

U. S. Department of Health and Human Services. (1980). *Public Health Reports Supplement.* Washington, DC: U. S. Government Printing Office.

U. S. Department of Health and Human Services. (1985). *National Institute of Mental Health research highlights 1984* (Stock No. 461-357-20328). Washington, DC: U. S. Government Printing Office.

U. S. Department of Health and Human Services. (1988). *Indian Health Service: Chart Series Book.* Washington, DC: U. S. Government Printing Office.

U. S. Department of Health and Human Services. (1985). *Report of the Secretary's Task Force on Black and Minority Health,* Washington, DC: U. S. Government Printing Office.

van der Kolk, B. A. (1988). The trauma spectrum: The interaction of biological and social events in the genesis of the trauma response. *Journal of Traumatic Stress, 1*, 273–290.

van der Kolk, B. A., Greenberg, M., Boyd, H., & Krystal, J. (1985). Inescapable shock, neurotransmitters, and addiction to trauma: Toward a psychobiology of post traumatic stress. *Biological Psychiatry, 20*, 314–325.

van der Kolk, B. A., Herman, J. L., & Perry, C. (1987, October). *Traumatic antecedents of borderline personality disorder.* Paper presented at the fourth annual meeting of the Society for Traumatic Stress Studies, Baltimore, MD.

Vanfossen, B. (1981). Sex differences in the mental health effects of spouse support and equity. *Journal of Health and Social Behavior, 22*, 130–143.

Veroff, J., Douvan, E., & Kulka, R. (1981). *The Inner American: A self-portrait from 1957 to 1976.* New York: Basic Books.

Vitaliano, P. P., Maiuro, R. D., Russo, J., Mitchell, E. S., Carr, J. E., & Van Critters, R. L. (in press). A biopsychosocial model of medical student distress. *Journal of Behavioral Medicine.*

Walker, L. E. A. (1979). *The battered woman.* New York: Harper & Row.

Walker, L. E. A. (1984). *The battered woman syndrome.* New York: Springer.

Walrath J., Li, F. P., Hoar, S. K., Mead, M. W., & Fraumeni, J. F., Jr. (1985). Causes of death among female chemists. *American Journal of Public Health, 75*, 883–885.

Warren, L. W., & McEachren, L. (1983). Psychosocial correlates of depressive symptomology in adult women. *Journal of Abnormal Psychology, 92*, 151–160.

Warren, R. (1975). *The woek rose and problem coping: Sex differentials in the use of helping systems in urban communities.* Paper presented at the annual meeting of the American Sociological Association, San Francisco.

Wehr, T. A., Sack, D. A., Rosenthal, N. E., & Cowdry, R. W. (1988). Rapid cycling affective disorder: Contributing factors and treatment responses in 51 patients. *American Journal of Psychiatry, 145*, 179–184.

Weiner, A. E., Marten, S., Wochnik, E., Davis, M. A., Fishman, R., & Clayton, P. J. (1979). Psychiatric disorders among professional women. *Archives of General Psychiatry, 35*, 169–173.

Weissman, M. M. (1987). Advances in psychiatric epidemiology: Rates and risks for major depression. *American Journal of Public Health, 77*, 445–451.

Weissman, M. M., John, K., Merikangas, J., Prusoff, B., Wickramaratne, P., Gammon, G., Angold, A., & Warner, V. (1986). Depressed parents and their children: General health, social and psychiatric problems. *American Journal of Diseases of Children, 140*, 801–805.

Weissman, M. M., Kasi, S., & Klerman, G. L. (1976). Follow-up of depressed women after maintenance treatment. *American Journal of Psychiatry, 133*, 757–760.

Weissman, M. M., & Klerman, G. L. (1977). Gender and depression. *Trends in Neurosciences, 8*, 416–420.

Weissman, M. M., & Klerman, G. L. (1985). Sex differences in the epidemology of depression. *Archives of General Psychiatry, 34*, 98–111.

Weissman, M. M., Klerman, G. L., Prusoff, B. A., Sholomskas, D., & Padkan, N. (1981). Depressed outpatients: Results one year after treatment with drugs and/or interpersonal psychotherapy. *Archives of General Psychiatry, 36*, 51–55.

Weissman, M. M., Leaf, P. J., Bruce, M. L., & Florio, L. (1988). The epidemiology of dysthymia in five communities: Rates, risks, comorbidity, and treatment. *American Journal of Psychiatry, 145*, 815–819.

Weissman, M. M., Leaf, P. J., Holzer, C. E., Myers, J. K., & Tischler, G. L. (1984). The epidemiology of depression: An update on sex differences in rates. *Journal of Affective Disorders, 7*, 179–188.

Weissman, M. M., & Meyers, J. K. (1978). Affective disorders in a United States community: The use of research diagnostic criteria in an epidemological survey. *Archives of General Psychiatry, 35*, 104–131.

Weissman, M. M., Meyers, J., Thompson, W., et al. (1986). Depressive symptoms as a risk factor for mortality and for major depression. In L. Erlenmayer-Kimling & N. Miller (Eds.), *Life span research on the predictors of psychopathology* (pp. 251–260). Hillsdale, NJ: Erlbaum.

Weissman, M. M., Prusoff, B. A., Di Mascio, A., Neu, C., Goklaney, M., & Klerman, G. L. (1979). The efficacy of drugs and psychotherapy in the treatment of acute depressive episodes. *American Journal of Psychiatry, 136*, 555–558.

Weissman, M. M., Scolomskas, D., Pottenger, M., Prusoff, B. A., & Locke, B. Z. (1977). Assessing depressive symptoms in five psychiatric populations: A validation study. *American Journal of Epidemiology, 106*, 203–214.

Wethington, X., McLeod, X. & Kessler, R. (1987). The importance of life events for explaining sex differences in psychological distress. In R. Barnett, L. Biener, & G. Baruch (Eds.), *Gender and stress*. New York: Free Press.

Wexler, B. E., Mason, J. W., & Giller, E. L. (1989). Possible subtypes of affective disorder suggested by differences in cerebral laterality and testosterone. *Archives of General Psychiatry, 46*, 429–433.

Wheeler, L., Reis, H., & Nezlek, J. (1983). Loneliness, social interaction, and sex roles. *Journal of Personality and Social Psychology 45*, 943–953.

Whiffen, V. E. (1988). Vulnerability to postpartum depression: A prospective multivariate study. *Journal of Abnormal Psychology, 97*, 467–474.

Whiteley, B. E., Jr. (1985). Sex role orientation and psychological well-being: Two meta-analyses. *Sex Roles, 12*, 207–225.

Whitley, R. (1983). Sex role orientation and self esteem: A critical meta-analytic review. *Journal of Personality and Social Psychology, 44*, 765–778.

Williams, J. B., & Spitzer, R. L. (1983). The issue of sex bias in DSM-III. *American Psychologist, 38*, 793–798.

Wilmoth, G., & Adelstein, D. (1988, August). *Psychological sequelae of abortion and public policy.* Paper presented at the annual meeting of the American Psychological Association, Atlanta.

Wilsnack, R. W., Klassen, A. D., & Wilsnack, S. C. (1986). Retrospective analysis of lifetime changes in women's drinking behavior. *Advances in Alcohol and Substance Abuse, 5*(3), 9–28.

Wilsnack, S. C. (1984). Drinking, sexuality, and sexual dysfunction in women. *Alcohol problems in women,* 33.

Wilsnack, S. C. & Beckman, L. J. (1984). *Alcohol Problems in Women: Antecedents, Consequences and Intervention.* New York: Guilford Press.

Wilson, M. A., & Roy, E. J. (1986). Pharmacokinetics of imipramine are affected by age and sex in rats. *Life Sciences, 38,* 711–718.

Wilson, P. H. (1982). Combined pharmacological and behavioral treatment of depression. *Behavior Research and Therapy, 20,* 173–184.

Winokur, A., March, V., & Mendels, J. (1980). Primary affective disorder in relatives of patients with anorexia nervosa. *American Journal of Psychiatry, 137,* 695–698.

Winokur, G., & Tanna, V. L. (1969). Possible role of X-linked dominant factor in manic-depressive disease. *Diseases of the Nervous System, 30,* 89–93.

Winokur, G., Zimmerman, M., & Cadoret, R. (1988). Cause the Bible tells me so. *Archives of General Psychiatry, 45,* 683–684.

Wolfe, J. L., & Fodor, I. (1977). Modifying assertive behavior in women: A comparison of three approaches. *Behavior Therapy, 8,* 567–574.

World Health Organization. (1977). *Manual of the international statistical classification of diseases, injuries, and causes of death* (9th rev.). Geneva: Author.

World Health Organization Scientific Group. (1981). *Report of research on the menopause.* Geneva: World Health Organization.

Yalom, I. D. (1975). *The theory and practice of group psychotherapy.* New York: Basic Books.

Yogev, S. (1981). Do professional women have egalitarian marital relationships? *Journal of Marriage and the Family, 43,* 865–871.

Young, M., & Willmott, P. (1957). *Family and kinship in East London.* London: Routledge and Kegan Paul.

Young, R. C. (1986). Plasma nor-chlorpro-mazine concentrations: Effects of age, race, and sex. *Therapeutic Drug Monitoring, 8,* 23–26.

Youniss, J., & Smollar, J. (1985). *Adolescent relations with mothers, fathers, and friends.* Chicago: University of Chicago Press.

Zeiss, A. M., Lewinsohn, P. M., & Munoz, R. F. (1979). Nonspecific improvement effects in depression using interpersonal skills training, pleasant activity schedules, or cognitive training. *Journal of Consulting and Clinical Psychology, 47,* 427–439.

Zetin, M., Sklansky, G. J., & Cranier, M. (1984). Sex differences in inpatients with major depression. *Journal of Clinical Psychiatry, 45,* 257–259.

Zoccoillio, M., Murphy, G. E., & Wetzel, R. D. (1986). Depression among medical students. *Journal of Affective Disorders, 11,* 91–96.

Books of Interest

The following is a list of current books on or related to depression. Only books published in 1989 or 1990 are included.

Brown, L. S., & Root, M. P. P. (1990). *Diversity and complexity in feminist therapy*. New York: Haworth Press.

    Presents excellent background information on feminist therapy and multicultural perspectives on women.

Burns, D. D. (1989). *The feeling good handbook: Using the new mood therapy in everyday life*. New York: William Morrow.

    Provides practical applications and exercises for cognitive behavioral therapy.

Goodwin, F. K., & Jamison, D. R. (1990). *Manic-depressive illness*. New York: Oxford University Press.

    This book provides the most comprehensive summary currently available on the research and treatment issues involved with manic depression.

Klerman, G. L. (Ed.). (1990). *Suicide and depression among adolescents and young adults*. Washington, DC: American Psychiatric Press.

    Excellent overview of the suicide and depression issues for this age range. While the book is not specifically geared to women, there is a helpful chapter by Myrna Weissman on female adolescents.

Nolen-Hoeksema, S. (1990). *Sex differences in depression*. Stanford, CA: Stanford University Press.

    An in-depth review of psychological, biological, and social theories of why women are more prone to depression than men. One of the most comprehensive books currently available on this subject.

Riessman, C. (1990). *Divorce talk: Women and men make sense of personal relationships*. New Brunswick, NJ: Rutgers University Press.

    Contains some interesting information on the subject of divorce and related depression.

Spitzer, R. L., Williams, J. B., Gibbin, M., & First, M. B. (1990). *Structured clinical interview for DSM-III-R*. Washington, DC: American Psychiatric Press.

    The user's guide is helpful in assessing the different kinds of depression and differentiating depression from other disorders.